Real Rights in the Virtual World

Real Rights in the Virtual World

Human Rights in the Age of Artificial Intelligence and Virtual Reality

Edited by

Riku Neuvonen

Professor of Public Law, Faculty of Management and Business, Tampere University, Finland

Jukka Viljanen

Professor of Public Law, Faculty of Management and Business, Tampere University, Finland

Edward Elgar PUBLISHING

Cheltenham, UK • Northampton, MA, USA

Published by

Edward Elgar Publishing Limited
The Lypiatts
15 Lansdown Road
Cheltenham
Glos GL50 2JA
UK

Edward Elgar Publishing, Inc.
William Pratt House
9 Dewey Court
Northampton
Massachusetts 01060
USA

Authorised representative in the EU for GPSR queries only: Easy Access System Europe – Mustamäe tee 50, 10621 Tallinn, Estonia, gpsr.requests@easproject.com

A catalogue record for this book is available from the British Library

Library of Congress Control Number: 2026932097

This book is available electronically in the Elgaronline
Law subject collection
https://doi.org/10.4337/9781035338856

MIX
Paper | Supporting responsible forestry
FSC® C013604

ISBN 978 1 0353 3884 9 (cased)
ISBN 978 1 0353 3885 6 (eBook)
ISBN 978 1 0494 0328 1 (ePub)

Printed and bound by CPI Group (UK) Ltd, Croydon, CR0 4YY

Contents

List of contributors

Toni Ahlqvist is a Professor and Research Director of Futures Research at the Finland Futures Research Centre, Turku School of Economics, University of Turku. His research focuses on futures studies, strategic foresight, spatial planning, and spatial political economy. He has led numerous research projects that have covered, e.g., the construction and use of futures knowledge in organisations and regions, societal antagonisms of emerging technologies, future generations in law-making, and futures of various industrial domains, such as the game industry, maritime logistics, pharmaceutical industry and forest industry. He has published in such scientific journals as *Technological Forecasting & Social Change*; *Futures*; *International Journal of Urban & Regional Research*; *Antipode*; *New Political Economy*; *Geopolitics*; *Geografiska Annaler A*; *Space & Polity*; *Technology Analysis & Strategic Management*; *European Planning Studies*; *Foresight*; *Journal of Futures Studies*; *Fennia and Science & Public Policy*.

Juan Diego Arregui Acosta is an Ecuadorian qualified lawyer and a graduate of the Erasmus Mundus Master in Law, Data and Articifial Intelligence (EMILDAI). Juan Diego is a former legal trainee at the Law and Tech Research Cluster of Dublin City University (DCU), Ireland.

Edoardo Celeste is an Associate Professor of Law, Technology and Innovation at the School of Law and Government of Dublin City University (DCU), Ireland. He is the Programme Chair of the Erasmus Mundus Master in Law, Data and Artificial Intelligence (EMILDAI), the Deputy Director of the Dublin European Law Institute, and the coordinator of the DCU Law and Tech Research Cluster.

Wian Erlank (Hons.BA (Classical lit) LLB LLM (International Trade Law) LLD (Stellenbosch)) works as Professor of Law at North-West University, South Africa, where he currently teaches space law and cyber law. He is an Advocate of the High Court of South Africa, a Fellow of the European Law Institute and a Member of the International Institute of Space Law. He serves as Editor-in-Chief of the *Potchefstroom Electronic Law Journal (PER/PELJ)* as well as on the editorial board of *Lex ad Coelum*. Additionally, he serves as a member of the NWU Artificial Intelligence Steering Committee and is currently supervising various M and D students writing on AI-related topics.

Victor Henriquez Diaz is a PhD candidate in Law at the School of Law and Government of Dublin City University (DCU), Ireland. He is the Deputy Coordinator of the DCU Law and Tech Research Cluster, where he acts as the Editor of the *Comparative Digital Law Blog* and the Co-producer of the DCU Digital Law Perspectives podcast.

Philippe Jougleux is a Professor at the Law School of European University Cyprus. He holds a Master's Degree in Media Law from France, which he completed with distinction, and was awarded a merit scholarship to pursue doctoral studies. During his PhD, he served as a teaching and research assistant at Aix-Marseille III University. He earned his doctorate in 2002, with a dissertation on 'The Protection of Information in the Age of New Technologies'. Following his doctoral studies, he moved to Greece and successfully passed the Thessaloniki Bar examination. In 2010, he relocated to Cyprus and joined European University Cyprus, where he teaches Cypriot civil law, EU copyright law, and EU internet law. Professor Jougleux has authored numerous scholarly articles in both Greek and English, focusing primarily on legal issues related to emerging technologies, including online copyright, data protection, cybercrime, and AI law. He has published several books on the Cypriot law of obligations and EU internet law, co-edited academic volumes, and co-organised international legal conferences. He is a Fellow of the Higher Education Academy (HEA) and regularly contributes to EU-funded research programmes. He serves as the Chief Editor of the legal journal *ENTHA* and is a founding member of the Cypriot branch of ALAI, the national association for the promotion of intellectual property law.

Mikkel Knudsen is a Project Specialist at the Finland Futures Research Centre, University of Turku, and Doctoral Researcher in Political Science at Åbo Akademi University. His primary research interests include technology foresight, industrial transitions, anticipatory governance, and policy foresight. He is currently engaged as WP leader in the Horizon Europe Project (2023–26) on R&I Foresight, The Eye of Europe, and as a project researcher in multiple other national and international foresight projects, funded by, e.g., Academy of Finland, Business Finland, the European Commission, and the European Union Drugs Agency. He has regularly been involved in international foresight training for public officials and skilled professional audiences, during 2024–25, e.g., in Slovakia, Denmark, Estonia, and Belgium. He is a reviewer in journals such as *Futures*; *Futures & Foresight Science*; *Comparative European Politics*; *Political Behavior*; and *American Sociological Review*. He is a Danish national.

Maarit Koponen is Professor of Translation Studies at the University of Eastern Finland where she leads the research group Translation and Multilingual Communication in Digital Society (TraDiSoc). Her research focuses on theoretical and practical aspects of translation technology, particularly the use of machine translation both in professional translation workflows and in non-professional settings. She has published various articles on the use and usability of machine translation and other translation technologies, the impact of technology on professional translators and the use of translation technology for information purposes.

Joanna Kulesza is Assistant Professor of International Law and Director of the Lodz Cyber Hub at the University of Lodz, Poland, and also serves as Professor at Vilnius University. Her research focuses on the application of international law in cyberspace. She has served on the Scientific Committee of the European Union Agency for Fundamental Rights (2018–23) and is a liaison to the Governmental Advisory Committee of ICANN. From 2019 to 2021, she was Co-Chair of the Advisory Board of the Global Forum on Cyber Expertise (GFCE). She contributed to the Oxford Process on International Law Protections in Cyberspace and co-authored several of its key declarations. Her publications include *International Internet Law* (Routledge, 2012) and *Due Diligence in International Law* (Brill, 2016). She has delivered invited lectures at leading institutions including Stanford, Oxford, LMU Munich, and the Hebrew University of Jerusalem.

Anu Mutanen works as Associate Professor of Public Law (Faculty of Management and Business, Tampere University, Finland). She holds an LLD (University of Helsinki) and Title of Docent in Constitutional Law (University of Turku). Mutanen has written several publications in the field of European public law, focusing on constitutional law. She regularly acts as an expert in the Constitutional Law Committee of the Finnish Parliament. She has previously worked as Senior Specialist in Law Drafting at the Ministry of Justice of Finland.

Riku Neuvonen is Professor of Public Law at Tampere University, Finland. He also holds a position as Associate Professor of Media Law at the University of Helsinki. Neuvonen has published ten books and over 100 articles on media law and constitutional law.

Antonio Pareja-Lora was awarded a PhD in Computer Science and Artificial Intelligence from the Universidad Politécnica de Madrid (UPM) in 2012. He is an Assistant Professor (Profesor Ayudante Doctor) at the Departamento de Filología Moderna (Modern Philology Department) of the Universidad de Alcalá (UAH). His research interests focus on (1) natural language processing; (2) the linguistic and/or ontological annotation and the ontological representation of linguistic phenomena, data categories and relations; (3) linguistic linked data; (4) computer engineering applied to terminology and translation; (5) technology-enhanced language learning (TELL: CALL, MALL, LMOOCs, etc.). He collaborated in several European and national projects with the Ontology Engineering Group (OEG) of Universidad Politécnica de Madrid (UPM) for more than eight years. More recently, he has been collaborating with and become a member of FITISPos (Formación e Investigación en Traducción e Interpretación en los Servicios Públicos, UAH), ATLAS (Applying Technologies to LAnguageS, from UNED) and the DMEG (Data Mining Engineering Group, from Universidad de Guadalajara, Mexico) research groups. Dr Pareja-Lora is an expert of the ISO/TC 37 Committee (standardisation of terminology, language resources and linguistic annotations), and a former Convenor of UNE/CTN 191 (Terminology). He is also one of the officers of the Special Interest Group for Annotation of the Association for Computational Linguistics (ACL SIGANN).

Siina Raskulla PhD is a Senior Lecturer of Public Law at Tampere University, Finland. She has published works on legal personhood, legal relations, legal argumentation, and the relationship between law and sustainability in social, economic, and environmental contexts.

Bart van der Sloot is Associate Professor at the Tilburg Institute for Law, Technology, and Society of the University of Tilburg, Netherlands. He specialises in questions revolving around law and technology, artificial intelligence and human rights.

Rui Sousa-Silva is Assistant Professor at the Faculty of Arts and Humanities and researcher at the Centre for Linguistics of the University of Porto. He holds a PhD in Forensic Linguistics from Aston University, Birmingham, UK. His primary research areas are forensic authorship analysis, plagiarism detection and analysis of cybercriminal communications. He is co-editor of the international bilingual journal *Language and Law / Linguagem e Direito* and of *The Routledge Handbook of Forensic Linguistics.*

Amos Taylor is a project researcher at the Finland Futures Research Centre, University of Turku. His work explores crisis, resilience, future generations, and the role of foresight in navigating high uncertainty. His focus is on participatory and creative approaches to futures; he works and publishes on current projects spanning creative ecosystems, foresight for sustainability, and the future of work. Amos holds master's degrees in Futures Studies and Media Culture, grounded in a background in design. Originally from Britain, he has lived in Finland for over 25 years. He also teaches widely on strategic foresight, futures methods, and media culture.

Eneken Tikk is a researcher at the Tallinn University of Technology, Estonia and Tampere University, Finland. Her research focuses on digital technologies, data and cybersecurity in various contexts of law, policy and strategy. Eneken also teaches data law and digital regulation strategies at the University of Tartu.

Jean Du Toit is an Associate Professor in the Department of Politics and Philosophy at the University of Fort Hare, South Africa. He completed his Doctorate in Philosophy in 2018, after concluding his postgraduate studies in Biochemistry. He has studied at both North-West University in South Africa and Ghent University in Belgium. His research focuses on the question of technological politics, and tracing the existential and social implications of embodiment in digital technologies. He conducts research in the fields of Phenomenology, Philosophy of Technology, Critical Theory, Existentialism, and Posthumanism.

Jukka Viljanen is Professor of Public Law at the Tampere University, Finland. He is an expert before the Constitutional Law Committee of the Finnish Parliament. He was a Member of the Finnish Human Rights Delegation (2020–24). His recent research projects have been on youth participation in law drafting (ALL-YOUTH) and on monitoring and implementing Council of Europe Human Rights Treaties (EVOLUTIVE). He was also a member of the Core Group in the Global Digital Human Rights Network. Professor Viljanen has published extensively on the doctrines of the European Court of Human Rights (ECtHR) and has been a Third-Party Intervener before the ECtHR.

1. Introduction to real rights in virtual worlds

Riku Neuvonen and Jukka Viljanen

1. TOWARDS VIRTUALITY AND BEYOND

We live in a world where many things happen digitally. Ones and zeros determine everyday actions and the course of life. The current digital world is two-dimensional. We see, hear and influence it using tools that are clearly part of the physical world. In the current digital world, we see things on screens. During this millennium, screens have become smaller, and in addition to computer monitors, virtual worlds can now be viewed on the screens of tablets and smartphones. Hardware and devices delivering augmented reality experiences are already on the market, as are virtual reality glasses. Headsets of different types are already commonplace.

A *real* virtual world is one that we experience like the physical world. In this book, we imagine the potential of such worlds and we examine these from the perspective of law and related disciplines. The current digital world has led us to questions about the applicability of rights. In theory, the regulation of the physical world also applies to the digital world. In practice, this is not always the case, as problems associated with the protection of privacy but also disinformation, online hate and others have emerged. In this context, we can talk about digital human rights, digital rights and digital constitutionalism.

The problems we face in the digital world are related to access, access to information, and privacy. The virtual world has the same problems, but virtuality as an all-encompassing experience also creates new challenges. In the age of platforms, algorithms have played a key role in displaying content and users are now shown what they or advertisers think they want to see. Various forms of artificial intelligence are also involved. These opportunities and problems of the platform era will also transfer to the virtual worlds of the future. This is especially the case when the advocates of virtual worlds, such as the metaverse, want them to be worlds where users spend a significant portion of their time. These questions will be approached and explored from several different starting points.

This book is about considering, imagining and reflecting on virtual worlds. In this introduction, we will establish a picture of what virtual worlds can be, largely based on entertainment, films, books, television series, and games. This basis is logical since these forms of entertainment have been creating and experimenting with virtual worlds for decades. After establishing this picture, we will provide an overview of the research that deals with rights in virtual worlds before introducing the authors of the chapters and how each will approach this challenging theme from different perspectives.

2. BRIEF HISTORY OF VIRTUAL WORLDS IN FICTION AND REALITY

Virtual worlds have been part of science fiction for decades. The classic sci-fi series Star Trek introduced the holodeck, which is a complete and comprehensive 3D simulation.[1] These environments require special rooms and equipment to create holograms and realistic experiences. Some visions show how entire civilisations can abandon face-to-face interaction in favour of virtual encounters, or present the possibility to create and destroy virtual worlds. The idea of replacing or adding something to our expressions of reality using virtual elements is old. Humans are dreamers and making imaginary visions real has tempted us for thousands of years.

In the age of modern computers, these visions of a virtual reality are approaching an unprecedented realness – not in the sense of a new reality but as virtual places and interactions. Science fiction writer William Gibson introduced the concept of cyberspace in his novel *Neuromancer* in 1984.[2] Cyberspace is an abstract graphic representation of data, which soon became synonymous with the internet and other forms of new electronic worlds.

In addition to Gibson, tech geeks and nerds have been influenced by Neal Stephenson's book *Snow Crash* in the 1990s,[3] which presented the concept of the metaverse. Along with the expansion of the internet through the world wide web and the improvement of the 3D capabilities of computers, it became possible to create functional and credible virtual worlds. The film The Matrix and its sequels presented virtual visions to the general public, where the action

[1] Star Trek: The Original Series, 1966–1969 and Star Trek: The Next Generation, 1987–1994. Paramount. Star Trek also includes films and other series, but these two series form a clear framework.

[2] William Gibson, *Neuromancer*, Ace Books 1984.

[3] Neal Stephenson, *Snow Crash*, Bantam Spectra 1992.

took place in a 3D simulation of reality.[4] Many of the readers of Gibson and Stephenson went on to become the developers and leaders of major technology companies in the 2010s. Largely due to science fiction, *A Declaration of the Independence of Cyberspace*[5] has been issued, and Facebook changed its name to Meta, and for a while, it seemed that the visions presented in science fiction were being realised. Therefore, we should not underestimate the impact of popular culture on developments in society, especially in the technology industry.

In the gaming industry, virtual worlds have been commonplace for decades. Among current popular games, for example, Roblox allows users to create their own worlds, and there are significant business opportunities in this as a result of advertising.[6] Fortnite[7] and Minecraft are two of the most popular games and cultural events of the past decade,[8] and these can also be considered virtual worlds. Among virtual worlds intended for socialising, Habbo Hotel[9] and Second Life[10] realised many features of the metaverse. Along with online multiplayer games, real money was used in these virtual living rooms. What these visions of the metaverse have in common is that users can create money, the experience is virtual, and with some mechanisms they can also generate money.

Software developer and venture capitalist Matthew Ball has been at the centre of these developments and has been writing his views on the metaverse since 2018. His book *The Metaverse* was published in 2021 at the height of the hype.[11] In his analysis, the metaverse is broader than the apps and games we have seen before. The metaverse connects numerous virtual worlds, but completely in a manner prescribed by large companies. While the original development of the internet was based on public money and research, the metaverse is a project driven entirely by corporations. The first to achieve a breakthrough in functional technology wins.

---

4 The Matrix films 1999–2021, Village Roadshow Pictures and Warner Bros. Entertainment.

5 John Perry Barlow, *A Declaration of the Independence of Cyberspace*, 1996, https://commonplace.knowledgefutures.org/pub/gkcowtdg/release/1, accessed on 4 February 2026.

6 *Roblox*, Roblox Corporation 2006.

7 *Fortnite*, Epic Games 2017.

8 *Minecraft*, Mojang Studios 2011.

9 *Habbo Hotel*, Sulake 2000.

10 *Second Life*, Linden Lab 2003.

11 Matthew Ball, *The Metaverse and How It Will Revoluzionate Everything*, Liveright 2022.

Virtual reality understood as the metaverse and 3-dimensional digital space is something different compared to the current internet. Despite the power of video, audio and game technology, the internet is still based on a user interface that requires a monitor and controls. Therefore, we are still living in the age of a two-dimensional internet. A true virtual environment adds another layer of experience with the feeling of really being a part of the virtual world. The best examples involve immersive technologies that create virtual worlds that look, sound and feel like real worlds. In addition, virtual elements can be added to the real world via augmented reality. This leads us to a mixed reality where virtual reality imitates the real world and the real world consists of virtual elements.

The focus of this volume is specifically on how to manage human rights in such environments. We have demonstrated that human rights have developed slowly and to some extent in the digital context. It is fair to say that even in the early 2020s, human rights are still not fully protected on the internet. Some may argue that freedom of speech is the most fundamental right in the digital world and one that has developed and progressed, but fake news, harassment and cybercrime are still harmful to freedom of speech. From that perspective, there is a need for the internet (and especially platforms) to be regulated more, whether by companies or states.

It is clear that the transition from a 2D digital environment to a 3D environment creates even more challenges for human rights. A good example is that one of the first policies established by Meta in their 'Metaverse' is a safety distance of two (virtual) metres. This is to protect the integrity of avatars from harassment. We have to remember that in the virtual world harassment is not only targeted at avatars but real people in the real world could feel everything depending on the technology. That creates unique issues because the metaverse is not just a program or an application but more of a place.

Therefore, access to the digital environment is more important as is the availability of information and services. In the virtual space, physical integrity must be understood in a different way. Freedom of speech takes on a new meaning when avatars can gather in virtual spaces. Solutions to these issues could involve creating international treaties, all-powerful regulations led by EU- or US-based corporate approaches, where businesses create the rules and how to enforce them. Another option would be that the virtual future is entirely Chinese.

3. THE METAVERSE AND VIRTUAL WORLDS IN LEGAL RESEARCH

Research in this field tends to follow the hype and current affairs after a slight delay. In the case of the metaverse, the hype had already died before it became a buzzword in research. The next big trend was artificial intelligence, which is now impossible to follow in research and literature. The purpose of this book is to focus on rights in virtual reality, so in connection with previous research, we emphasise research related to rights and law.

A central work in the field is Matthew Ball's *The Metaverse*, in which Ball, who has written extensively on the subject, summarises the development up to the moment of hype in the early 2020s.[12] Previous to that, such popular virtual worlds as those in games like Second Life had been discussed to some extent.[13] The internet has always been a place where activities that move between what is permitted and what is prohibited are present. The unauthorised distribution of copyrighted material, child pornography, and cybercrime have been three activities that have been regulated internationally since the early days of the internet. Crime has also been no stranger to virtual worlds, with virtual property being stolen in multiplayer games and virtual worlds.[14]

Virtuality is the next step after web 2.0, which can be called the era of platforms. This era has been characterised by the growing power of big technology giants and especially the importance of social media companies. From a rights perspective, this has generally been linked to the debate on the normative regulation of the internet.[15] One consequence has been digital rights and digital constitutionalism.[16] At the same time, the legal debate focused on web 2.0 has been accompanied by industrial virtual reality. Various simulators and virtual realities have revolutionised a range of fields, from pilot training to industrial

---

[12] Ibid., see also Fatih Sinan Esen, Hasan Tinmaz and Madhusudan Singh (eds), *Metaverse: Technologies, Opportunities and Threats*, Studies in Big Data 133, Springer Singapore 2023.

[13] Andreas M. Kaplan and Michael Haenlein, 'The Fairyland of Second Life: Virtual Social Worlds and How to use Them' (2009) 52 *Business Horizon* 563, 565–66.

[14] Audrey Guinchard, 'Crime in Virtual Worlds: The Limits of Criminal Law' (2010) 24(2) *International Review of Law, Computers & Technology* 175; Susan W. Brenner, 'Fantasy Crime: The Role of Criminal Law in Virtual Worlds' (2020) 11(1) *Vanderbilt Journal of Entertainment and Technology Law* 19.

[15] Matthias C. Kettemann, *The Normative Order of the Internet: A Theory of Rule and Regulation Online*, Oxford University Press 2020.

[16] A few key examples are: Oreste Pollicino, *Judicial Protection of Fundamental Rights on the Internet: a Road Towards Digital Constitutionalism?*, Bloomsbury Publishing Plc 2021; Giovanni De Gregorio, *Digital Constitutionalism in Europe: Reframing Rights and Powers in the Algorithmic Society*, Cambridge University Press 2022; Edoardo Celeste, *Digital Constitutionalism: The Role of Internet Bills of Rights*, Taylor & Francis Group 2023.

work and especially the military.[17] In this book, we will not focus on industrial virtual reality, but on other applications.

Virtual reality and the metaverse have not remained a sideline in legal studies. The research handbook edited by Larry A. DiMatteo and Michel Cannarsa is a good basis for research on the subject.[18] Their volume shows the diversity and speculative basis of the subject. From the perspective of this book, the research handbook was published after this book had already been written. On the other hand, the perspective of this book is more focused on private law and technology law, such as the question of the status of non-fungible tokens.

Developments in the relationship between the metaverse and regulation have been described in the book *Regulating the Metaverse* by Ignas Kalpokas and Julija Kalpokiene.[19] Their book brings many aspects under critical examination, which the authors of this book have deepened and updated.

In addition to virtual reality, there has also been talk of augmented reality. Augmented reality involves virtual elements added to the experience of the real world. One of the authors in this volume, Bart van der Sloot, has in his book called this development 'a synthetic society'.[20] The book focuses on generative AI, examining its impacts and regulation from the perspectives of humanoid robots, deepfakes, augmented reality and virtual reality.

Virtual reality and its development, known as the metaverse, have been a part of technology research and legal science. As the hype has subsided, the focus of research has shifted to studying artificial intelligence, leaving virtual reality as a brief interim stage between the privacy boom and the AI boom.

PART I: VIRTUAL REALITY AND HUMAN RIGHTS

In the first chapter of *Real Rights in Virtual World*, we present the history of virtual worlds, the development between the internet and human rights, and create an overview of the key research (state-of-the-art) on the topic. We demonstrate how the internet has transformed and has become increasingly virtual. Virtual systems are an integral part of work and entertainment in technologically developed societies. Virtual projects like the metaverse and artificial

---

[17] Xinyi Tu and Bruna de Castro e Silva, 'Are We Ready for the Metaverse? Implications, Legal Landscape, and Recommendations for Responsible Development (2025) 4 *Digital Society*.

[18] Larry A. DiMatteo and Michael Cannarsa (eds), *Research Handbook on the Metaverse and Law,* Edward Elgar Publishing 2024.

[19] Ignas Kalpokas and Julija Kalpokiene, *Regulating the Metaverse: A Critical Assessment*, Routledge 2023.

[20] Bart van der Sloot, *Regulating the Synthetic Society: Generative AI, Legal Questions and Societal Challenges*, Hart Publishing 2024.

intelligence are changing this into a three-dimensional landscape where people engage with different forms of artificial intelligence in their work.

In their chapter, Juan Diego Arregui Acosta, Edoardo Celeste and Victor Henriquez Diaz discuss 'Digital constitutionalism in AI-populated metaverses'. The authors apply digital constitutionalism as a theoretical lens to identify emerging constitutional reactions. The first section analyses the effect of AI metaverses on fundamental rights, mapping the opportunities and risks of virtual worlds. A 'health check' of existing constitutional frameworks allows the authors to identify areas of stress in relation to four fundamental rights: the right to data protection; to privacy; freedom of expression' and the right to property. They also examine the reactions of the constitutional ecosystem to technological developments. The third section focuses on how effectively these emerging norms will interact in global virtual worlds.

Philippe Jougleux in his chapter discusses issues related to intellectual property. One of the key questions relates to how trademark laws and patents can be adapted to the virtual world. There is also further discussion on the question of territoriality in the virtual world. When intellectual property is considered under the principle of territoriality, the legislation around jurisdiction in the metaverse is still developing.

In their chapter, Maarit Koponen, Rui Sousa-Silva and Antonio Pareja-Lora discuss 'Language rights in the metaverse: the implications of translingual metaverse communication'. This includes an interesting discussion of possible adverse effects related to translingual metaverse communication. According to the authors, a common language in the metaverse would jeopardise diversity and the inclusion of languages, cultures, identities and people(s). Translation is essential, in collaboration with artificial intelligence, for the development and success of interaction and communication in the metaverse. It is especially important that language models reach a sufficient level of quality. They also include liability issues in their discussion, especially the question of who will be responsible for translation errors or hallucinations (i.e., falsehoods presented as truth).

In his chapter, Riku Neuvonen deals with the difficult question of the dichotomy of public and private spaces and how this kind of prevailing doctrine in the traditional freedom of speech context can be analogically used in the context of the metaverse. If access is restricted or access costs too much, it shuts many groups out from the political and societal sphere. Availability supports access and dialogue, ensuring that different contents are available to those who have access as material for public discourse. One of the key arguments presented here is that there is clearly a need for public virtual spaces.

PART II: LEGAL SUBJECTS IN VIRTUAL WORLDS

In their chapter, Wian Erlank and Jean Du Toit discuss 'The experience of virtual worlds – believability, immersion and embodiment'. The experience of virtual worlds is examined via the concept of embodiment. This concept is also important in considering legal consequences. They claim that the more immersive the environment and the more users feel embodied within it, the stronger the argument for recognising embodiment in terms of its legal ramifications since embodied characteristics shape the individual's (altered) experience of space and time, bodily integrity and avatars, and informs contemporary understandings of the virtual object in terms of property law. One of the messages is that we need to take the more immersive environments and the spillover effects from the virtual world into the real world seriously.

Siina Raskulla in her chapter discusses legal relations between humans and software-generated characters in the metaverse. She looks at avatars, electronic representations controlled by computer users, but also the more recent emergence of software-generated characters or daemons potentially indistinguishable from human-controlled avatars. Raskulla argues that the concept of relational personhood provides a theoretical basis for granting legal personhood to non-human and non-sentient entities based on social relations and moral agency. She concludes by discussing the possible benefits and risks of granting daemons legal personhood.

In his chapter, Bart van der Sloot discusses 'Generative AI's impact on autonomy, truth and equality: three regulatory quagmires for the proto- and the metaverse. Generative AI powers different technological applications, including deepfakes, augmented reality and virtual reality. There are three themes that are discussed – autonomy, truth, and equality. In the part on autonomy and the rule of law, the author points out that the power of tech companies will increase the power of generative AI. This strengthens the trend towards the privatisation, datafication, and commercialisation of society and public life. In the part on democracy and truth, the author warns that companies are not accountable and there is no democratic control over them. In addition, the harmful use of AI against political adversaries has become common. In relation to equality, the question is posed of whether leaving the friction out of people's lives is causing more problems because it is through friction that people develop. Finally, the chapter discusses different solutions and the pros and cons of different measures.

PART III: VIRTUAL WORLD AND FUTURE TRENDS

The third part of the book focuses on the virtual world and future trends. Joanna Kulesza and Eneken Tikk in their chapter discuss the rules for virtual worlds. The authors recognise that there is no consensus on many issues related to metaverses; instead, they intend to bridge the different professional communities and settings striving towards greater legal certainty and clarity about assets and activities online. The authors present the lessons learned from existing legal frameworks and the need to review and restate established norms. One of the main findings relates to the differences between how industry and member states approach norms. It is evident that the wide margin left to national authorities can result in extensive restrictions on human rights and privacy. One of the key contributions of this chapter introduces the role of the European Union in advancing a legal framework that could be applied in global discourse as a benchmark, especially the EU focus on safe, secure and privacy-protective digital technologies, products and services. Describing the overall digital landscape, the authors suggest that the different stakeholders should collaborate to ensure that the future of virtual worlds is aligned with human rights, security and sustainability.

In her chapter, Anu Mutanen contributes to the discussion on future generations, the digital world and human rights. She applies the concept of virtual human rights as an extension of the existing human rights regime. In the realisation of human rights within virtual realities, Mutanen claims the need for innovative tools. She points out that the key challenge is to maximise the benefits of digitalisation while mitigating emerging risks as digitalisation evolves. The changes in human life brought about by virtual environments should be reflected in the human rights regime. The answer, according to Mutanen, relies on the concept of virtual human rights. The extension of the current human rights framework is illustrated by the continuum of realities, future generations and human rights. It acknowledges the interconnectedness of human generations (past, present and future), human rights (real and virtual), and different realities (physical, augmented and fully virtual).

In their chapter, Toni Ahlqvist, Mikkel Knudsen and Amos Taylor discuss different alternative futures related to the metaverse. They approach the topic through three lenses: (1) a relational lens; (2) a lens of contradictions or dialectics; and (3) a lens of future folds. The metaverse is multiple. Their chapter reveals the tensions that are part of the metaverse. The primary contradiction is the materiality and immateriality of the metaverse. Through an in-depth exploration of the philosophy of the metaverse as an alternative reality, they adapt the concept of future folds developed by Gilles Deleuze. The folds exist simultaneously as a parallel bent strata of the metaverse that metamorphoses and evolves continuously. The authors introduce five different folds as archetypes to analyse the future of the metaverse.

PART I

VIRTUAL REALITY AND HUMAN RIGHTS

2. Real rights in virtual worlds

Riku Neuvonen and Jukka Viljanen

1. REAL RIGHTS CONQUERING VIRTUAL WORLDS

In recent decades, the internet has transformed many of the ways we work so they have become increasingly virtual. Virtual systems are an integral part of work and entertainment in technologically developed societies. Until recently, the internet has been text-based and two-dimensional, where people have been responsible for the content. Virtual projects like the metaverse and artificial intelligence are changing this into a three-dimensional landscape where people engage with different forms of artificial intelligence in their work.

The traditional administration of justice by nation states and transnational actors, such as the UN and the EU, has been limited to certain geographical areas. In principle, the internet is borderless and its functions differ significantly from the regulatory objects of law in the modern nation state.[1] In the UN system, human rights are global and universal in nature. In regional human rights systems, especially in Europe, the implementation and observance of human rights are monitored effectively. In nation states, the fundamental rights of the constitution and national legislation are binding norms. The collision of the internet and regulation has resulted in problems for supervision and the implementation of justice. The internet and virtual worlds are not an area free of norms, rights and rules.[2]

This chapter presents a brief history of virtual worlds and what importance human rights have had in the development of the internet. First, we show how human rights have become part of the internet landscape. The United Nations Special Rapporteur has considered the internet as vital for freedom of

[1] However, modern state law can adapt; see Kaarlo Tuori, *Properties of Law: Modern Law and After* (Cambridge University Press 2021).

[2] See Matthias C Kettemann, *The Normative Order of the Internet: A Theory of Rule and Regulation Online* (Oxford University Press 2020).

expression.[3] Later, the European Court of Human Rights (ECtHR) has stated that access to the internet is a human right.[4] Second, we establish the context for virtual worlds as part of the internet and technology. Many concepts and images of virtuality are based on fiction – movies, books and comics. These concepts and images have had a significant impact on how tech-companies have developed virtual worlds and how we discuss virtual reality. Finally, we take a look at state-of-the-art research on human rights and the internet. In recent decades there have been many initiatives exploring communication rights, digital rights, epistemic rights and digital constitutionalism. All these ideas are shaping how we are seeing and implementing real rights in virtual worlds.

2. HUMAN RIGHTS IN THE INTERNET

2.1 Access to the Internet as a Right

The development of the internet was influenced by science, military research and a culture of freedom.[5] Even the concept of cyberspace refers more to cyber-libertarianism and the idea of an unregulated and borderless internet. However, networks were developed originally to decentralise important information systems both in the case of (nuclear) war and for academic research. The internet is a network of networks, and was possible only after the creation of the TCP/IP protocol between 1974 and 1982.

Currently, the internet is divided into three levels: the physical/transport layer (infrastructure, cables, satellites), the logical/protocol layer (TCP/IP and related standards) and the application layer (the HTTP protocol, WWW and platforms). Virtual reality belongs to the application layer; it is not some new physical infrastructure or protocol, but new applications built on the other layers. There is control at every layer – we need a device and software to access the internet, a connection that functions in the logical layer and finally, the possibility to use applications. The internet is a technical structure; its virtual space is only accessible with the right equipment (plus electricity and skills).

The internet was originally divided into MILNET (military) and ARPANET (research), which means that it was not originally used for commercial or other

---

3 Frank La Rue, 'Report of the Special Rapporteur on the promotion and protection of the right to freedom of opinion and expression' (UN Doc. A/ HRC/17/ 27 of 26 April 2011).

4 See Marta Maroni, *The Right to Access the Internet: A Critical Analysis of the Constitutionalisation of the Internet* (Unigrafia 2022).

5 Manuel Castells, *The Rise of the Network Society* (Wiley-Blackwell 2010), 58.

purposes. However, different layers were handed to commercial operators in the 1990s.[6] Similarly, computers were developed for smaller home uses and different network technologies then emerged. Finally, the invention of the World Wide Web by Berners-Lee made accessible interference and hypertext protocols possible.

Initially, the internet was mainly for tech enthusiasts, universities and some businesses, but it experienced a breakthrough in the early 2000s. The debate on the internet in the 1990s mostly focused on the issue of whether it should be regulated, and this focused on copyright issues as well as on, for example, child pornography. Other activities were regulated and monitored nationally, which caused several problems due to the borderless nature of the internet in the technological sense.

At the infrastructure level, servers, cables and devices exist in the physical reality and norms associated with physical location apply. Organisations and companies established and registered for operation in one of the legal systems are responsible for the functions of the logical level and the application level. As legal entities, all entities responsible for internet services and operations are subject to the jurisdiction of a state. The biggest problems involve the supervision and enforcement of legal norms in cross-border cases and the lack of effective supervision at the global level. From the viewpoint of the law, the internet has never been borderless or lawless.

The internet has evolved into a significant information channel and is now part of everyday life. Access to the internet has become an increasingly important issue in order to obtain and spread information, as well as to take care of, for example, bank issues or deal with business and everyday life. The extensive use of the internet and some other networks raises the question of access. While functioning as a fully fledged citizen, a consumer or individual in modern society requires access to the internet; to what extent must this be legally protected?

The first landmark ruling is *Reno v. American Civil Liberties Union* in 1997 by the Supreme Court of the United States.[7] In this case, the Supreme Court ruled that two provisions of the Communication Decency Act[8] described the unconstitutional criminalisation of the spread of obscene material through the internet. The internet was a new medium of mass communication, and therefore protected by the First Amendment. In Europe, the French Conseil Constitutionnel ruled that access to the internet is a fundamental right.[9]

---

[6] Janet Abbate, *Inventing the Internet* (MIT Press 1999).

[7] *Reno v. American Civil Liberties Union* [1997] 521 U.S. [844].

[8] Communications Decency Act of 1996 47 U.S.C. [223].

[9] LOI 2009-669 12 Juin 2009.

The UN Special Rapporteur on the Promotion and Protection of the Right to Freedom of Expression Frank La Rue focused his report of 2011 on access to the internet.[10] However, he stated that access to the internet was not yet a human right. Still, access to the internet was essential to enjoy freedom of speech. Therefore, he suggests that states have a positive obligation to promote access to the internet as part of the right to free speech. Later, the Human Rights Council adopted the view in its resolution that people should have the same rights online and offline and an open internet is a driving force of development.

In Europe, the ECtHR remarks in the landmark case of *Yıldırım v. Turkey* that the right to access the internet is similar to the right to access information, and therefore part of freedom of speech. States should guarantee the right to unhindered internet access as a constitutional right. In *Kalda v. Estonia*,[11] the Strasbourg Court stated that the Council of Europe and international instruments have recognised both the public-service value of the internet and its importance for human rights.

Access to the internet is considered a human right in Europe according to the Council of Europe and the ECtHR. In addition, there have been different national solutions. For example, in Greece and Portugal, the constitution protects access to the internet. Likewise, the practice of the ECtHR and the views of various UN bodies support access as a right. On a practical level, for example, in Finland, internet access can be financed through social security. Article 5 of the Greek Constitution states that all persons are entitled to participate in the information society as part of the right to information. Similarly, Article 35 of the Portuguese Constitution is literally titled *Use of Information Technology*, and gives every citizen the right to access all computerised data. In addition, everyone shall be guaranteed free access to public-use computer networks. Furthermore, several declarations or other legal instruments, for example, the Declaration of Internet Rights in Italy, describe access to the internet as a right.

In the regulation of the internet, utopian ideas have influenced the regulatory solutions of states and transnational actors, such as the EU. However, this traditionally tough regulation of the internet has always been framed by a discussion about human rights. In the system of international law, human rights are universal and indivisible, meaning they belong to all people. The special status of freedom of speech has been especially important in terms of the power of social media platforms.

10 Frank La Rue, n 3.
11 *Kalda v. Estonia*, 19.1.2016, § 52.

The central documents in the UN system are the Universal Declaration of Human Rights and the Covenants on civil and political rights, as well as economic, social and cultural rights that reinforce them. In 2016, the UN Human Rights Council issued a resolution according to which the same human rights apply in information networks as in the outside world. The resolution particularly emphasises the importance of freedom of speech and the availability of various contents. The starting point of the 2003 UN summit on the information society was a human-centred, inclusive and development-oriented information society, which is built on the basis of sustainable development and a good life in compliance with the UN Charter and the UN Declaration of Human Rights.

The GGE (Group of Governmental Experts, Inter-Governmental Expert Group) set up to investigate information and telecommunications issues stated in its report that the UN Charter is also applicable to activities in information networks in order to secure peace and stability and to achieve an open, safe, peaceful and accessible environment. Some states tried to deny the importance of international law and, to that extent, the UN agreements on information networks. This interpretation was confirmed in a new report in 2015, when the views of the previous report were considered to form an accepted consensus. After these interpretations, Article 17 on the protection of privacy and Article 19 on freedom of expression of the Covenant on Civil and Political Rights have been considered to be the central human rights norms of the UN system concerning the internet.

The GGE prepared the so-called Tallinn Manual in 2012, which was then updated in 2015. According to it, in the regulation of cyberspace, the task of nation states is to respect the human rights secured in the agreements, but also to protect them in the online environment. With regard to the UN human rights treaty system, it is therefore clear that the treaty system applies in the same way in information networks as outside them. In the Council of Europe's human rights system, the question of the applicability of the agreement in the information network environment has not even been raised: the agreement is considered to protect rights online without a separate mention. The starting point of the EU Charter of Fundamental Rights is the applicability of rights in all EU activities and the scope of EU law, so a separate mention is not necessary. Likewise, the fundamental rights systems of individual nation states are considered to be valid in the online environment as well.

The Internet Rights and Principles Coalition, created in 2009 at the meeting of the Internet Governance Forum (IGF) based on the guidelines of the information society summits, has maintained and updated the Charter of Human Rights and Principles for the Internet. According to the charter, the following human rights and principles must be taken into account in the development of the internet.

1. UNIVERSALITY AND EQUALITY: All humans are born free and equal in dignity and rights, which must be respected, protected and fulfilled in the online environment.
2. RIGHTS AND SOCIAL JUSTICE: The internet is a space for the promotion, protection and fulfilment of human rights and the advancement of social justice. Everyone has the duty to respect the human rights of all others in the online environment.
3. ACCESSIBILITY: Everyone has an equal right to access and use a secure and open internet.
4. EXPRESSION AND ASSOCIATION: Everyone has the right to seek, receive and impart information freely on the internet without censorship or other interference. Everyone also has the right to associate freely through and on the internet, for social, political, cultural or other purposes.
5. PRIVACY AND DATA PROTECTION: Everyone has the right to privacy online. This includes freedom from surveillance, the right to use encryption, and the right to online anonymity. Everyone also has the right to data protection, including control over personal data collection, retention, processing, disposal and disclosure.
6. LIFE, LIBERTY AND SECURITY: The rights to life, liberty, and security must be respected, protected and fulfilled online. These rights must not be infringed upon, or used to infringe other rights, in the online environment.
7. DIVERSITY: Cultural and linguistic diversity on the internet must be promoted, and technical and policy innovation should be encouraged to facilitate plurality of expression.
8. NETWORK EQUALITY: Everyone shall have universal and open access to the internet's content, free from discriminatory prioritisation, filtering or traffic control on commercial, political or other grounds.
9. STANDARDS AND REGULATION: The internet's architecture, communication systems, and document and data formats shall be based on open standards that ensure complete interoperability, inclusion and equal opportunity for all.
10. GOVERNANCE: Human rights and social justice must form the legal and normative foundations upon which the internet operates and is governed. This should happen in a transparent and multilateral manner, based on principles of openness, inclusive participation and accountability.

In December 2022, the EU reached an agreement on the European Declaration on Digital Rights and Principles. From the viewpoint of human rights, the Declaration states that technology should unite people and approaches should be human-centred. In particular, the Declaration emphasises access to digital technologies and products and protection of personal data, as well as the right to privacy. Through the Declaration, the EU commits to safeguarding all human rights in the digital environment.

The status of such declarations of principles, programmes and the like forms a practical guide – it is a matter of soft regulation. Their importance depends very much on the extent to which states and organisations capable of stricter regulation, such as the EU, take these principles into account in their concrete actions. Similarly, companies in the internet industry can follow the principles and implement them; for example, in self-regulation or co-regulation. So far, the principles have been most important in the discussion of digital rights. With the help of such declarations, summits and various organisations provide institutional support for a certain kind of development, and the participants of the meetings and the members of the organisations also commit themselves politically to these principles and declarations to some extent. Therefore, such declarations and principles are signs of a common will.

2.2 The Expanding Boundaries of Human Rights on the Internet

Supranational human rights and nationally protected fundamental rights, as well as criminal law, are all limited by the boundaries of jurisdictions. Constitutional law and criminal law extend to the boundaries of the state, and human rights to the boundaries of Member States. However, in some cases, the ECtHR has developed doctrines relating to extraterritoriality; for example, when a state exercises its control through its agents or the state has control of the territory in question.[12]

From an internet regulatory perspective, *Perrin v. United Kingdom* presents an interesting case. Perrin was a French citizen living in the UK who was convicted in England of posting indecent images on a US website. Perrin was the largest shareholder of the US site. In his appeal, the question was whether a US site must also be aware of UK law. According to the claim, due to the global nature of the internet, the sender of the message could not be held liable under the laws of all the countries in which the message was made available. The ECtHR dismissed the argumentation and did not find any violation of Article 10 of the European Convention on Human Rights (ECHR).

Territoriality of jurisdictions was not contested in this case, but such a contestation is foreseeable in similar cases due to the worldwide nature of the internet. In a similar case, the ECtHR did not question the competence of the Russian courts to prosecute a hacker for infiltrating the online security system of a US bank. From the national level, a classic case is the *Yahoo* case in France. The American search and listings company Yahoo! was forced to

[12] See *Al-Skeini and others v. United Kingdom*, GC, 7.7.2011, § 149.

stop advertising Nazi memorabilia for sale in France, and its executives faced criminal charges.[13]

These cases are united by the fact that the perpetrator of the crime was under the jurisdiction of a single nation state. In other cases, cooperation between state authorities is required. Despite numerous attempts, only one more comprehensive agreement on cybercrime has been concluded in practice. The only area in which most industrialised nations have come to an agreement is cybercrime. Here, the US, Canada, South Africa and Japan, among many others, signed the Budapest Convention on Cybercrime, which was adopted by the Council of Europe in 2001. However, this convention focuses only on child pornography and copyright infringements.[14]

2.3 Freedom of Speech and Privacy as Central Rights in the Internet

The role of the internet in the interpretation of human rights has focused on two rights: the right to freedom of expression and the right to respect for private life. In general, there is a strong view that these rights are the same offline and online; this does not take into account special circumstances related to the internet and how it has impacted interpretation. Regarding freedom of expression in particular, source neutrality has been recognised already in relation to audiovisual media compared to print media. At the same time, there are differences between media; for example, in relation to the methods of objective and balanced reporting depending on the media in question.

In *Delfi v. Estonia*, the ECtHR for the first time extensively analysed the role of user-generated content in the internet. The Court stated that in addition to the positive aspect of the internet providing a platform for freedom of expression, there was a negative side. It allowed the dissemination of defamatory and other unlawful speech, including hate speech and speech inciting violence, and this can be achieved 'like never before, worldwide, in a matter of seconds, and sometimes remain persistently available online'.[15] So there is a clear understanding of two conflicting consequences of the internet. The Council of

---

13 Catherine Van de Heyning, 'The Boundaries of Jurisdiction in Cybercrime and Constitutional Protection: the European Perspective' in Oresto Pollicino and Graziella Romeo (eds), *The Internet and Constitutional Law: The Protection of Fundamental Rights and Constitutional Adjudication in Europe* (Routledge 2016), 43–47.

14 Benoît Freedman and Isabelle Rorive (2002), 'Regulating Internet Content Through Intermediaries in Europe and the USA', 23 *Zeitschrift für Rechtssoziologie* 1, 41–60.

15 *Delfi v. Estonia*, 16.6.2015, GC, § 110.

Europe has taken several recommendations on the internet and human rights and added a new protocol to the Cybercrime Convention.[16]

Freedom of speech was a key value of the internet from its early years. The digital space was seen as a modern agora, where all people gather to share information. In the beginning, the internet was decentralised and open in nature. The US Supreme Court supported this development, declaring that the internet was within the protection of the First Amendment. The internet has evolved into a digital world dominated by platforms. Nowadays, the biggest issue is the business model of the platforms.[17] In particular, social media platforms do not make money through discussions or take payments directly from users. Platforms and search engines use advertising businesses that collect data and sell ads. They provide an incentive to keep users engaged on their platforms by curating and organising content. These models are something that Zuboff calls 'surveillance capitalism'.[18]

The shift from the internet being the promised land of freedom of speech to the biggest threat to privacy protection has fundamentally changed the human rights-based approach. Since the beginning of the 2000s, the Safe Harbour system has been in force between the EU and the US, and American companies that joined it were deemed suitable to participate in cross-border transfers of personal data. Facebook was part of this system, and its office in Ireland was responsible for data processing in the EU. However, the revelations made by the American data leaker Edward Snowden about the data collection of the US government raised concerns about the protection of European personal data.

Austrian activist Maximilian Schrems also questioned the transatlantic arrangement and referred the matter to the data protection authority. The case eventually progressed through the national court to the EU Court of Justice.

---

[16] The Additional Protocol to the Convention on Cybercrime, concerning the criminalisation of acts of a racist and xenophobic nature committed through computer systems, was opened for signature on 28 January 2003 and entered into force on 1 March 2006; Recommendation CM/Rec(2007)16 to Member States on measures to promote the public service value of the Internet (adopted on 7 November 2007). 16 April 2014 Recommendation CM/Rec(2014)6 of the Committee of Ministers to Member States on a Guide to human rights for Internet users. On 7 March 2018, Recommendation CM/Rec(2018)2 of the Committee of Ministers to Member States on the roles and responsibilities of Internet intermediaries. Recommendation CM/Rec(2022)16 on Combating Hate Speech, adopted on 20 May 2022, by the Committee of Ministers.

[17] José van Dijck, *Platform Mechanism*, in José van Dijck, Thomas Poell and Martijn de Waa (eds), *The Platform Society: Public Values in a Connective World* (Oxford University Press 2018), 31–48.

[18] Shosanna Zuboff, *The Age of Surveillance Capitalism: The Fight for a Human Future at the New Frontier of Power* (Public Affairs 2019).

Due to the first *Schrems* ruling in 2015, the Safe Harbour system failed when the level of data protection was not considered sufficient. Later, the system was replaced by the Privacy Shield system, which in 2016 brought with it, among other things, an American ombudsman institution for European personal data issues. The new system also received criticism, especially because it was still considered to allow leaks for US national security needs. In 2020, the EU Court issued a judgment in the *Schrems II* case, which invalidated the new system. The problems regarding the level of data protection also extend to the model contract terms used by companies approved by the European Commission as transfer mechanisms.

In the Charter of Fundamental Rights of the EU, the protection of personal data is a separately protected fundamental right. This contributed to the EU enacting the General Data Protection Regulation (GDPR) in 2018. Alongside EU regulations (Digital Services Act (DSA) and Digital Markets Act (DMA)) that came into force later, the GDPR significantly regulates data protection-related issues, especially in Europe, but through the Brussels effect, the level of privacy and personal data protection can rise elsewhere as well.[19]

3. FROM COMMUNICATION RIGHTS TO DIGITAL CONSTITUTIONALISM

The development of the global mass media industry has raised questions on how to secure freedom of speech and especially access to information and availability of information. One attempt in the field of media studies was to create the idea of communications rights. Theoretical proposals for these rights were intertwined with other topics in the human rights debate. Communication rights represent one attempt to dismantle the colonial structures of the global mass media. The communication rights debate calmed during the 1990s until the internet and later the platformisation process created new questions on access, availability, privacy and dialogical rights.

The communication right developed as part of the anti-colonial movement and on identifying the differences between the Global North and Global South. UNESCO's 1980 resolution for the New World Information and Communication Order (NWICO) created a framework for understanding communication as a fundamental right (not just free speech) and creating a more balanced global information industry. This initiative was short lived but the idea of communication rights survived. The collapse of the Eastern bloc and the development of the internet created a new kind of political environment

---

19 Anu Bradford, *The Brussels Effect: How the European Union Rules the World* (Oxford University Press 2020).

where the idea of the information society flourished. The World Summit on Information Society (WSIS) in Geneva in 2003 and Tunis in 2005 were turning points in introducing a rights-based approach to internet regulation as well as a revival of the ideas of communication equality.

One of the examples of the communication rights discourse is the Helsinki model.[20] In this model, communication rights include access, availability, privacy and dialogical rights. This approach highlights a slight movement from the more ideological approach in the 1970s and 1980s to more current issues raised by the internet and especially the platform economy. Another noteworthy issue is that during the 2010s, communication rights were combined with digital rights. That does not mean that we need to make a distinction between the internet and other media, or that current communication rights are outdated. Rather, it illustrates that the global information economy and society are practically digitalised.

In addition to the changes in the communication rights debate, several actors from civil society and academia have created different lists of digital rights. Like modern communication rights, these digital rights are a response to challenges from the platform economy, data capitalism and the lack of any international regulation of the internet. Karppinen and Puukko distinguished four different discourses on digital rights:

1. Digital rights as the protection of negative liberties.
2. Positive rights and state obligations.
3. Digital rights as a vehicle of 'informational justice'.
4. Rights and business.[21]

These discourses are presented in different lists and declarations, although it is not necessary to review all of them. The most important factor is that, in addition to the communication rights debate, digital rights enthusiasts see digital rights as complementing human rights that go further and are applicable specifically in the context of the internet.[22]

Another recent trend concerning human rights is digital constitutionalism. This can be divided into three categories according to groups or schools of

---

[20] Marko Ala-Fossi and others, 'Operationalising Communication Rights: The Case of a "Digital Welfare State"' (2019) 8(1) *Internet Policy Review*.

[21] Kari Karppinen and Outi Puukko, 'Four Discourses of Digital Rights: Promises and Problems of Rights-Based Politics' (2020) 10 *Journal of Information Policy* 304–28.

[22] For possible changes in the interpretation of Human Rights when moving from the physical to the virtual world, see Mart Susi, *The Non-Coherence Theory of Digital Human Rights* (Cambridge University Press 2024).

thought. First, techno optimists see constitutionalism in the digital context arising from the internet itself and the rules developed there (*lex digitalis*). The second school's starting point involves international treaties and national laws that slowly expand in the internet and digital environment through new legislation and court cases. The third approach is something between these two, where the various legal and civil society declarations of digital rights, and the like, serve as a model for the future development of a digital constitution.[23]

The final approach to human rights in the digital environment is corporate responsibility.[24] The UN Guiding Principles on Business and Human Rights (Ruggie principles) have provided global standards for evaluating human rights and business activities. In the context of the internet and especially platforms, Meta (formerly Facebook) launched the Oversight Board (OB) as an attempt to comply with the Ruggie principles. The OB refers to principles and Article 19 of the International Covenant on Civil and Political Rights. Other companies have not yet followed, but there have been initiatives for social media councils. Therefore, in addition to state-based human rights monitoring through nation states or different entities (such as the EU and UN), a business-based regulatory system is another possible alternative. However, it remains to be seen whether the OB has a real impact on the practices of Facebook and Instagram.

---

[23] Rikke Frank Jørgensen, 'An Internet Bill of Rights?', in Ian Brown (ed), *Research Handbook on Governance of Internet* (Oxford University Press 2013), 353–72; Edoardo Celeste, 'Digital Constitutionalism: A New Systematic Theorisation' (2019) 33 *International Review of Law, Computers and Technology*, 76–99; Nicolas Suzor, *Lawless* (Cambridge University Press 2019); Matthias Kettemann, *The Normative Order of the Internet* (Oxford University Press 2020); Oreste Pollicino, *Judicial Protection of Fundamental Rights on the Internet: A Road Towards Digital Constitutionalism?* (Bloomsbury 2021); Giovanni de Gregario, *Digital Constitutionalism in Europe – Reframing Rights and Powers in the Algorithmic Society* (Cambridge University Press 2022).

[24] Rikke Frank Jørgensen, 'When Private Actors Govern Human Rights', in Ben Wagner, Matthias C Kettemann and Kilian Vieth (eds), *Research Handbook on Human Rights and Internet Technology* (Edward Elgar 2019) 343–63.

4. ORIGINS OF THE ECTHR NEW FREEDOM OF EXPRESSION DOCTRINE – CAN THE ESTABLISHED GENERAL PRINCIPLES CONTRIBUTE IN THE CONTEXT OF THE METAVERSE

4.1 Adapting to the Transformed Media Landscape

The digital media environment has challenged the established principles that focus on the key role of freedom of expression in a democratic system. Even the concept of democracy and public debate has received new elements. The role of the press has extended to other kinds of influencers, and democracy is no longer limited to those issues related to elections and politicians, but includes other participants; for example, NGOs and the academic community.

The three interlinked concepts of democracy, rule of law and protection of human rights are strongly consistent with interpretations of international treaties; interpretations should be in accordance with the object and purpose of each treaty. At the same time, interpretations are also linked to the idea of interpreting in light of present-day conditions and the Convention being a living instrument. This is often referred to as evolutive and dynamic interpretation. Therefore, when the media is changing, legal interpretations should also follow these changes and take them into account while finding a fair balance between individual rights and public interest.

Until 15 years ago, the ECtHR mostly considered cases related to traditional media, whether print (*Sunday Times v. the UK*, *Observer Guardian v. the UK*, *Von Hannover v. Germany*, *Axel Springer v. Germany*)[25] or broadcast media (*Jersild v. Denmark*, *NIT S.R.L. v. The Republic of Moldova*[26]). In addition to the traditional media category, there are now an increasing number of cases related to social media and the internet.

From a doctrinal perspective, this new continuum of cases is not just adapting original concepts to the new context, but it is also introducing new issues; in particular, it is referring to the digital environment and its particularities that should be taken into account.

In the traditional media approach to freedom of expression, key elements included the public watchdog role that media and journalists have in a

---

[25] *Sunday Times v. the United Kingdom (no.2)*, 26.11.1991; *Observer Guardian v. the United Kingdom*, 26.11.1991; *Von Hannover v. Germany (no.2)*, GC, 7.2.2012; *Axel SpringerAG v. Germany*, GC, 7.2.2012.

[26] *Jersild v. Denmark*, GC, 23.9.1994; *NIT S.R.L. v. The Republic of Moldova*, GC, 5.4.2022.

democratic society, and this principle was related to the possible chilling effect of restrictions on the exercise of freedom of expression and public debate.

In the digital or online environment, one of the essential changes relates to the extension of protected actors. In addition to professional journalists, there are several other important groups that are to be considered under protection. The public watchdog role also applies to NGOs, academic researchers and others acting in this capacity. The role of the internet is considered important in facilitating the dissemination of information and enhancing public access to news. This also means bloggers and popular users of social media may be seen as public watchdogs (*Magyar Helsinki Bizottság v. Hungary*, §168).[27]

Another significant feature of the online environment was established in cases like *Ahmet Yıldırım v. Turkey*[28] and *Delfi AS v. Estonia*. The key element in these cases is the specific nature of online media and what restrictions are appropriate. It is especially difficult in the digital media environment to adopt measures that avoid any collateral effects.

In the famous case of *Delfi AS v. Estonia* (GC 16.6.2015), the focus was on a different type of sharing responsibility and how internet news platforms also have to perform their part in protecting rights under Article 8 of the Convention when the platform is based on user-generated material. In particular, the Court considered how different monitoring systems are in compliance with the Convention requirements. The Court recognised that international instruments manifest (§ 113) 'a certain development in favour of distinguishing between the legal principles regulating the activities of the traditional print and audiovisual media, on the one hand, and Internet-based media operations, on the other'.

The Court noted that because of the particular nature of the internet, the 'duties and responsibilities' that are to be conferred on an internet news portal for the purposes of Article 10 may differ to some degree from those of a traditional publisher in regard to third-party content. The publisher of an internet news portal could be held liable for clearly unlawful messages. So, even in the context of the internet, there were to a certain extent similar types of responsibilities for an online publisher and a traditional publisher.

One of the key arguments was that the risk of harm posed by content and communications on the internet in the exercise and enjoyment of human rights and freedoms is higher than that of the traditional press. The Court even analysed different online monitoring regimes (word-based filter; the notice-and-take-down system) against unlawful speech and the effectiveness of these systems in protecting the rights of others. Sometimes even automatic

---

27 *Magyar Helsinki Bizottság v. Hungary*, GC, 8.11.2016, § 168.
28 *Ahmet Yıldırım v. Turkey*, 18.12.2012, § 52 and 53.

monitoring systems are not sufficient to achieve conformity with obligations under the Convention. The Court noted that an internet news portal may be found liable if it fails to take measures to remove clearly unlawful comments without delay, even without any notifications from the alleged victim or third parties (§ 159). New elements are also surfacing with the extensive use of artificial intelligence. This was first recognised in *Glukhin v. Russia* (ECtHR 4.7.2023),[29] providing signs of controlling political opponents at another level. The Court referred to the concept of the chilling effect. The use of highly intrusive facial recognition technology to identify and arrest participants in peaceful protest actions could have a chilling effect in relation to the rights to freedom of expression and assembly (§ 88).

The development of the Strasbourg case law reflects the evolution of the present-day media environment. There is an established foundation including the fundamental role of freedom of expression in a democratic society and a narrow margin left for the authorities of Member States when imposing restrictions on issues related to public concerns. However, the Court acknowledges essential changes in the internet era compared to traditional media, whether print or audiovisual, and a higher risk of interference that might be seen to be against the right to private life. From the concept of media neutrality, the interpretation of digital rights refers to the distinguishing technique and takes into account specific features of internet-based media platforms.

4.2 Going Beyond the Territorial Approach – Some Reflections on Extraterritorial Protection and Acting 'Regardless of Frontiers'

One of the established features of the case law concerning freedom of expression has been the context and even reference to the historico-political context. European history, and especially eras that included totalitarian regimes, has had a major influence on the interpretative lines taken by the Court. Freedom of expression is closely connected to the defence of democracy and combating oppressive ideologies.

The question of the jurisdiction of the Court is introduced in Article 1 of the Convention. It states that '[t]he High Contracting Parties shall secure to everyone within their jurisdiction the rights and freedoms defined in Section I of the Convention'. Already in the *Loizidou* case,[30] the Court had noted that the concept of jurisdiction under that provision was not restricted to the national territory of the contracting states. The extraterritorial application of human rights

29 *Glukhin v Russia*, 4.7.2023, § 88.

30 *Loizidou v Turkey*, GC, 18.12.1996, § 43 and 44.

treaties has been mainly studied in the context of the ECHR, and cases related to discussions of extraterritoriality were especially related to military actions.

Key judgments and decisions, such as *Bankovic*, *Al-Skeini* and *El-Masri*,[31] have shaped the established doctrine to include issues related to criteria that have to be established for the principles of extraterritoriality to be applied. These cases raised the discussion of whether Member States are responsible for actions taken by military forces or security-related events happening under the control of certain states outside Europe; for example, in Iraq or some secret prisons controlled by those states.

The digital world is clearly also raising questions on territorial applicability and challenging the existing principles of national jurisdiction. One of the most discussed issues is whether there can be such diverse standards on the protection of freedom of expression on different continents. Difficulties especially relate to the fact that all the major tech giants are owned and controlled outside Europe and instead of Article 10 of the Convention, the focus could be on the First Amendment case law in the US. This doctrine accepts very aggressive hate speech, in contrast to the European approach. In addition, China, which also has a solid status in the tech field, is, of course, one of the countries that has a rigorous culture of censorship and does not respect freedom of expression.

In *Ahmet Yıldırım v. Turkey*, the Court considered that national legislation was in direct conflict with the wording 'regardless of frontiers' in Article 10.1 of the Convention (§ 67). The Court referred to section 8 of Law no. 5651. This section is about blocking orders and their implementation. There were several grounds under which the blocking would be possible, in addition to offences mentioned in the criminal code; there were also offences against Atatürk mentioned under Law no. 5816 of 25 July 1951.

The applicant complained of the impossibility of accessing his internet site as a result of a measure ordered in the context of criminal proceedings, which were wholly unrelated to his site. In order to achieve an effective restriction in the *Ahmet Yıldırım* case, extensive restrictions on accessing Google sites were necessary and this led to a significant collateral effect. The ECtHR found that the internet has now become one of the principal means by which individuals exercise their right to freedom of expression and information, providing as it does essential tools for participation in activities and discussions concerning political issues and issues of general interest.

[31] *Banković and Others v. Belgium and Others*, GC, 12.12.2001; *Al-Skeini and Others v. the United Kingdom*, GC, 7.7.2011; *El-Masri v. the former Yugoslav Republic of Macedonia*, GC, 13.12.2012.

The Court has not often referred to the 'regardless of frontiers' phrase in Article 10. The ECHR version is clearly an item of heritage from Article 19 of the Universal Declaration of Human Rights (UDHR). 'Everyone has the right to freedom of opinion and expression; this right includes freedom to hold opinions without interference and to seek, receive and impart information and ideas through any media and regardless of frontiers.' In the Convention, the same formulation is a bit different: 'Everyone has the right to freedom of expression. This right shall include freedom to hold opinions and to receive and impart information and ideas without interference by public authority and regardless of frontiers.'

One significant case developing an interpretation of 'regardless of frontiers' is the case of *Cox v. Turkey* (20.5.2010).[32] The applicant considered that a ban on re-entry to Turkey was in conflict with Article 10. The Court considered (§ 31) that there was interference with the applicant's rights guaranteed under Article 10. It argued that the ban on the applicant's re-entry is materially related to her right to freedom of expression because it disregards the fact that Article 10 rights are enshrined 'regardless of frontiers' and that no distinction can be drawn between the protected freedom of expression of nationals and that of foreigners.

A similar legal argumentation was also presented in the case of *Kirkorov v. Lithuania* (19.3.2024)[33], where the applicant was banned from entering Lithuania; however, the conclusion of the Court was different, finding no violation of Article 10. The applicant had been banned because he was known as a Russian Federation tool of soft power; that is, a part of the Russian propaganda machinery and a supporter of President Putin. The Court found that the ban was necessary in the interests of national security, public safety and/or the prevention of disorder and that it was proportionate to the legitimate aim(s) pursued. This case is an interesting example of combating state-led propaganda and finding a fair balance in restricting tools of soft power.

An application on a complaint against a state that it should be held accountable for failure to act against hate speech outside its jurisdiction has not been successful. One of the rare cases where this was argued before the Court related to Danish cartoons (*Ben El Mahi and others v. Denmark*[34]). Two Moroccan applicants complained that the publication of 12 cartoons had breached their rights. They asserted that according to Article 9 and Article 14 they had been discriminated against. They further complained under Articles 10 and 17 that Denmark had permitted the publication of what the applicants considered to be

---

32 *Cox v Turkey*, 20.5.2010, § 31.

33 *Kirkorov v Lithuanai*, 19.3.2024, § 67.

34 *Ben El Mahi and others v. Denmark,* 5853/06/Decision/Court (Fifth Section), 11/12/2006.

offensive caricatures of the Prophet Muhammad, in particular, one caricature showing him as a terrorist with a bomb in his turban.

The Court considered that the application was inadmissible according to Article 35 § 3 and 4. The argument was based on the fact that there was no jurisdictional link on account of an extraterritorial act. The applicants were living in Morocco and the associations were also operating in Morocco. Only in exceptional circumstances may the acts of contracting states performed outside their territory, or which produce effects there (extraterritorial acts) amount to an exercise by them of their jurisdiction within the meaning of Article 1. One of the principles that allow the application of extraterritorial responsibility is that a state has effective control over the territory. Extraterritorial accountability can be based on the premise that the state cannot circumvent obligations by perpetrating acts outside of its territory that it would not permit on its own territory. These conditions were not met in the circumstances of the application.

5. BACK TO THE FUTURE

Virtual reality is the next step in the development of the internet. The web 2.0 platform brought the internet to all devices and to the masses. At the same time, it laid the foundation for the power of large technology companies. The open and free internet moved into the era of closed platforms. The same technology companies have been developing virtual realities. The threats and opportunities of the current internet will significantly affect the realisation of the internet in the era of virtual reality.

Rights are the same online and offline. However, their implementation has been dependent on the borders of nation states and the jurisdiction of supranational actors. Only a few forms of cybercrime have been the subject of global consensus. Europe has been seen as a representative of the rule-based empire in internet regulation, a counterweight to the market empire of the US and the state-led empire of China. Jurisdictional jurisprudence is developing, but its limits are set by trade policy. Law and politics are increasingly intertwined on the internet, and internet regulation is both trade policy, affecting giant corporations, and the protection of societies and political systems. These conflicts are also moving from the internet of platforms to virtual reality.

Virtual reality and augmented reality also create their own challenges for the realisation of human and fundamental rights. In the initial development, harassment in particular has come to the fore, as activity in a digital environment takes on a whole new meaning in virtual form. The understanding of space and activity is also different when moving from text-based to experience-based reality. At the same time, the importance of artificial intelligence is growing in both the creation of virtual worlds and their experience. This affects fundamental issues in how we understand the realisation of rights as speech, actions, experiences and space.

3. Digital constitutionalism in AI-populated metaverses

Juan Diego Arregui Acosta, Edoardo Celeste and Victor Henriquez Diaz

1. INTRODUCTION

Digital constitutionalism theories, and in particular those embracing a socio-legal approach, represent a helpful theoretical lens to investigate the impact of digital technologies on existing constitutional frameworks.[1] These theories argue that we are currently witnessing a *constitutional moment*, where the constitutional ecosystem is reacting to the challenges of the digital revolution.[2] Digital technologies impact our society in 360 degrees, and our constitutional frameworks, which were often created for analogue societies, struggle to address these issues. Yet, the constitutional dimension does not remain inert; it reacts with a series of normative answers that aim to translate the core principles of contemporary constitutionalism in a way that can speak to the problems of today's societal actors. Adopting a socio-legal approach in this context

---

[1] For a comprehensive mapping of the existing theoretical approaches to digital constitutionalism, see Edoardo Celeste, 'Digital Constitutionalism: A New Systematic Theorisation' (2019) 33 *International Review of Law, Computers & Technology* 76; Marta Maroni, *The Right to Access The Internet: A Critical Analysis of The Constitutionalisation of The Internet* (University of Helsinki 2022), ch 8; Francisco de Abreu Duarte, Giovanni De Gregorio and Angelo Golia, 'Perspectives on Digital Constitutionalism' in Bartosz Brożek, Olia Kanevskaia and Przemysław Pałka (eds), *Research Handbook on Law and Technology* (Edward Elgar 2023); Edoardo Celeste, 'Conceptual Approaches to Digital Constitutionalism: A Counter-Critique' in Indra Spiecker, Laura Mendes and Ricardo Campos (eds), *Digital Constitutionalism. A Normative and Institutional Framework for Conflict Solving under Construction* (Nomos 2024); Edoardo Celeste, 'Digital Constitutionalism: A Socio-legal Approach' (2024) 2 *European Data Protection Law Review* 1.

[2] See Celeste, 'Digital Constitutionalism: A Socio-legal Approach' (n 1).

allows us to appraise the multilevel nature of this process, which we could denote as the *constitutionalisation* of the digital society.[3] Our investigation is not limited to norms traditionally belonging to the pyramid of legal sources; the socio-legal lens broadens our scope of analysis. It is therefore possible to observe the emergence of a multiplicity of normative counteractions not only in traditional constitutional sources, such as constitutional amendments or decisions of constitutional courts, but also beyond the state, such as in the terms of service for digital platforms. This constitutional conglomerate might seem chaotic and uncoordinated at first sight; yet, it is also possible to conceive it as a complex mosaic of overlapping societal layers, each complementing and stimulating each other in adapting existing constitutional frameworks to the digital society.[4]

Digital constitutionalism theories adopting a socio-legal approach allow us to embrace a functional perspective.[5] In this way, our analysis is not limited to traditional constitutional norms and actors, but we investigate what and who play a constitutional *function*, thus including normative sources and societal layers that would not be formally part of the constitutional ecosystem. The first task of the legal scholar is therefore to understand the extent to which new technologies are impacting the existing constitutional framework, broadly intended, as referring to the body of norms regulating the protection of rights and the balancing of power. Second, one can focus on the analysis of the related process of constitutionalisation, which is emerging to address these issues. Here one question relates to the sources, or mix thereof, that include normative responses to the challenges of the digital revolution; while another question directly tackles the substantive content of these counteractions, comparing existing and newly emerged principles. The overall aim is to recompose a mosaic of different norms surfacing at various societal levels. Even mere non-legally binding normative conversations are interesting in this context, as they highlight areas of potential constitutional *anaemia*, where societal lymph no longer runs and new more speaking norms are needed.[6]

---

[3] See Edoardo Celeste, 'The Constitutionalisation of the Digital Ecosystem: Lessons from International Law' in Angelo Jr Golia, Matthias C Kettemann and Raffaela Kunz (eds), *Digital Transformations in Public International Law* (Nomos 2022), 47.

[4] Celeste (n 3). See also Edoardo Celeste, 'Internet Bills of Rights: Generalisation and Re-Specification Towards a Digital Constitution' (2023) 30 *Indiana Journal of Global Legal Studies* 25.

[5] Celeste, 'Digital Constitutionalism: A Socio-legal Approach' (n 1).

[6] See Edoardo Celeste, *Digital Constitutionalism: The Role of Internet Bills of Rights* (Routledge 2022), ch 13.

This chapter will adopt such a socio-legal approach to digital constitutionalism as a lens to analyse the impact on the constitutional ecosystem of a new disruptive technology: AI-populated metaverses. In this chapter, we will not use this term with reference to a specific product or brand, but to denote more generally virtual realities whose development and commercialisation have been recently boosted thanks to the use of AI technologies. Section 2 will briefly reconstruct the main characteristics of AI-populated metaverses that have an impact on the constitutional ecosystem. Section 3 will investigate which fundamental rights are most affected by AI-populated metaverses. Section 4 will analyse where normative responses to face the challenges generated by these new technologies are emerging. Section 5 will study from a substantive perspective to what extent these counteractions are also shaping new constitutional principles, specifically targeting the threats created by AI-populated metaverses.

Our chapter will conclude that metaverses, despite their disruptive nature, are not determining a new wave of constitutional innovation nor targeted constitutional responses. They are rather offering the possibility to consolidate AI-related rights and principles that have emerged over the past few decades, before the current AI hype, thus representing an opportunity for these norms to finally find an effective field of testing.

2. 'NEW BOTTLES': AI-POPULATED METAVERSES

As illustrated elsewhere in this book, the metaverse is not an entirely new technology. Virtual realities, such as those created by video games, date back to the end of the 1990s and early 2000s. For instance, Lineage, EverQuest and Second Life, among others, were launched in 1998, 1999 and 2003, respectively.[7] Lineage was a video game with a medieval fantasy world setting, with three-dimensional characteristics.[8] EverQuest was another 3D fantasy game allowing multiple players to interact simultaneously online.[9] Second Life is a three-dimensional virtual world created by Linden Lab, where users create avatars to interact with other users, including economic exchanges.[10] Yet,

---

7 Viktor Mayer-Schoenberger and John Crowley, 'Napster's Second Life? The Regulatory Challenges of Virtual Worlds' (2005) KSG Working Paper No. RWP05-052, 12, 13.

8 'Lineage/NCSOFT' https://kr.ncsoft.com/en/whatWeCreate/lineage.do accessed 5 May 2025; see also Mayer-Schoenberger and Crowley (n 7).

9 'EverQuest' www.everquest.com accessed 5 May 2025.

10 Jonathan Strickland and Chris Pollette, 'How Second Life Works' (*HowStuffWorks* 8 November 2007) https://computer.howstuffworks.com/internet/social-networking/networks/second-life.htm accessed 5 May 2025.

current metaverses differ from their predecessors in terms of scale and user experience: they are immersive environments enabled by 3D and extended reality technologies, blending physical and digital realms in real time for multiple purposes.[11] Unlike the isolated virtual worlds classically seen in video games, the contemporary concept of the metaverse refers to an interconnected space where users have many more abilities and functionalities.[12] Participants in the metaverse can move freely between virtual spaces and the metaverse itself has a very realistic appearance, thus increasing the level of user engagement.[13] Overall, the metaverse represents a more pervasive reality. A notorious example of the contemporary metaverse is Meta Horizon, a platform that brings together services for users to connect, create avatars, explore worlds, work, and communicate with the help of devices such as headsets.[14] Decentraland is another existing metaverse using the Ethereum blockchain, where users are entitled to own virtual land and transfer it to other users.[15]

2.1 Global Spaces: Constitutional Collisions

If one thinks of the size of contemporary metaverses, these virtual spaces might be considered akin to nation states. In 2009, Mark Zuckerberg compared Facebook to a populated country.[16] As of the first week of 2024, Facebook had three billion active users: essentially the population of the world in 1960 and

---

[11] Commission, 'Communication from the Commission to the European Parliament, the Council, the European Economic and Social Committee and the Committee of the Regions, "An EU initiative on Web 4.0 and virtual worlds: a head start in the next technological transition"' COM (2023) 442 final.

[12] Annelieke Mooij, 'What Is the Metaverse?' in Annelieke Mooij (ed), *Regulating the Metaverse Economy: How to Prevent Money Laundering and the Financing of Terrorism* (Springer Nature Switzerland 2024) https://doi.org/10.1007/978-3-031-46417-1_2 accessed 5 June 2025; see also Fabio Moioli, 'The Metaverse: Don't Confuse It With Virtual Reality' (*Forbes* 11 August 2022) www.forbes.com/councils/forbestechcouncil/2022/08/11/the-metaverse-dont-confuse-it-with-virtual-reality/accessed 5 May 2025; see also Louise Walsh, 'What Is the Metaverse – and Will It Help Us or Harm Us?' (*University of Cambridge* 27 July 2023) https://www.cam.ac.uk/stories/metaverse accessed 5 June 2025.

[13] Mooji (n 12); Moioli (n 12).

[14] Meta, 'Learn More about Meta Horizon: MetaStore' https://www.meta.com/help/quest/2186255054883561/ accessed 5 May 2025; see also Maureen Kochan, 'Parent and Guardian Guide to Meta Horizon Worlds' (*ConnectSafely* 14 November 2024) https://connectsafely.org/horizon/ accessed 30 May 2025.

[15] Esteban Ordano and others, 'Decentraland White Paper 2.0' (2024).

[16] Jonathan Zittrain, 'A Bill of Rights for the Facebook Nation' (2009) *The Chronicle of Higher Education.*

one billion short of half the population today.[17] These figures reinforce the claim that Facebook, now known as Meta, is even more than a big state, it is an entity with its own territory, a platform with its own population (the users) and its own law (the terms of service).[18] Meta's virtual reality – the Metaverse with a capital M – could follow this parallelism with approximately 500,000 users. The dimensions of these virtual spaces in terms of users are therefore not comparable to the video games of the past. Contemporary metaverses are global spaces, transcending national boundaries and linking individuals living in different jurisdictions.

The risk of normative or constitutional collisions therefore becomes an ordinary issue.[19] Contemporary metaverses see users from different countries interacting. This circumstance generates a cross-national space where multiple legal regimes may apply, potentially overlapping and clashing. A constitutional dilemma therefore emerges.[20] What should the fundamental rights standards be to govern such a transnational space? Should the approach of a specific jurisdiction prevail? How can individuals belonging to different constitutional traditions interact in a single virtual space? Terms of service regulating metaverses unavoidably emerge as a bridge between different constitutional dimensions.[21] However, in the context of an absent cosmopolitan law of the metaverse, choosing a specific constitutional approach remains a normative conundrum.

---

17 Statista, 'Number of Monthly Active Facebook Users Worldwide as of 4th Quarter 2022' (*Statista* 21 May 2024) www.statista.com/statistics/264810/number-of-monthly-active-facebook-users-worldwide/ accessed 5 May 2025.

18 Edoardo Celeste, 'Terms of Service and Bills of Rights: New Mechanisms of Constitutionalisation in the Social Media Environment?' (2019) 33 *International Review of Law, Computers & Technology* 122.

19 See Gunther Teubner and Andreas Fischer-Lescano, 'Regime-Collisions: The Vain Search for Legal Unity in the Fragmentation of Global Law' (2004) 25 *Michigan Journal of International Law* 999.

20 See Edoardo Celeste and others, *The Content Governance Dilemma: Digital Constitutionalism, Social Media and the Search for a Global Standard* (Palgrave Macmillan 2023).

21 See Celeste (n 18).

2.2 'Virtual Worlds, but Real Rights': Immersiveness and Tangibility

In January 2024, the UK police investigated for the first time an alleged rape in the metaverse, the immersive virtual reality experience created by Meta.[22] Although not physically injured, the 16-year-old victim 'is said to have been left "distraught" after her avatar in the metaverse was assaulted by several adult men in a virtual "room"'.[23] It is no novelty that digital means may become vehicles of crime, even generating tangible effects. The dichotomy between the virtual nature of online spaces and the still very concrete and real effects on human lives was one of the key points stressed since the outset by IT law pioneers.[24]

Yet, a unique characteristic of virtual reality lies in the immersive experience lived by individuals. The victim of the incident mentioned above was indeed said to have suffered similar psychological consequences as those rape victims suffer in real life. Virtual reality technologies also do not represent the *home of Mind* of the cyberlibertarian tradition, but contexts where real rights are exercised and might be violated.[25] If, on the one hand, they might be compared with virtual spaces of the past, such as video games, on the other hand, they expose individuals to an unprecedented level of immersiveness and tangibility, which significantly reduces the difference of impact between offline actions and those occurring in a virtual reality setting.

---

[22] Nancy Jo Sales, 'A Girl Was Allegedly Raped in the Metaverse. Is This the Beginning of a Dark New Future?' (*The Guardian* 5 January 2024) www.theguardian.com/commentisfree/2024/jan/05/metaverse-sexual-assault-vr-game-online-safety-meta accessed 5 May 2025.

[23] Louise Donovan, 'A Wake-up Call: After Alleged Metaverse Rape, Calls to Protect Women and Girls Grow' (*Fuller Project* 22 January 2024) https://www.linkedin.com/posts/louise-donovan-22a62b57_a-wake-up-call-after-alleged-metaverse-activity-7155370382982615040-yAyS?utm_source=share&utm_medium=member_desktop&rcm=ACoAAGRvgTkBiBplZV8D6pdSkQFWtHsrnsm4juE accessed 6 March 2026.

[24] Diane Rowland, '"Virtual World, Real Rights?": Human Rights and the Internet' in Marco Odello and Silvia Cavandoli (eds), *Emerging Areas of Human Rights in the 21st Century* (Routledge 2011).

[25] John Perry Barlow, *A Declaration of the Independence of Cyberspace* (EFF 1996); Roya Bagheri, 'Virtual Reality: The Real Life Consequences' (2016) 17 *UC Davis Bus LJ* 101; Rowland (n 24).

2.3 Interacting with AI Technologies: the Power of Generation

Contemporary metaverses are populated by avatars, which are characters that can be distinguished as two types.[26] On the one hand, those that correspond to and are partially powered by human users – they constitute alter egos or an extension of human personalities in the virtual world.[27] In the context of contemporary metaverses, these avatars are simultaneously partially powered by AI technologies, which determine some aspects of their interaction. On the other hand, we also have fully AI-powered avatars, which do not represent the alter egos of physical users but are simply fictional characters populating the virtual reality. In this second case, AI technologies not only determine some aspects of the interactions of those avatars, but represent their very 'soul'.[28]

Avatars have become another actor within the sphere of human social interaction.[29] The advent of digital technology had already gradually modified human relations, embedding the human-machine binomial at the societal level, where individuals constantly resort to digital technologies to perform daily tasks.[30] The introduction of AI is further altering this formula due to a particular characteristic of this technology: its generative power.[31] For instance, a digital vending machine, which could be considered the original smart contract, has a limited function; once the price of a product has been paid, the machine will automatically deliver it to the buyer.[32] Even an automatic vacuum cleaner has limited performance due to its *simple-reflex agent* architecture. In other words, all these types of technologies fulfil preset tasks according to a

---

26 Sergio Barta and others, 'Avatar Creation in the Metaverse: A Focus on Event Expectations' (2024) 156 *Computers in Human Behavior* 108192.

27 Alanah Davis and others, 'Avatars, People and Virtual Worlds: Foundations for Research in Metaverses' (2009) 10(2) *Journal of the Association for Information Systems* 93.

28 Joanne Yu and others, 'Artificial Intelligence-generated Virtual Influencer: Examining the Effects of Emotional Display on Engagement User' (2024) 76 *Journal of Retailing and Consumer Services* 103560.

29 Christos Kyrlitsias and Despina Michael-Grigoriou, 'Social Interaction with Agents and Avatars in Immersive Virtual Environments: A Survey' (2021) 2 *Front. Virtual Reality* 786665.

30 Mario Di Nardo, D Forino and T Murino, 'The Evolution of Man-Machine Interaction: The Role of Human in Industry 4.0 paradigm' (2020) 8(1) *Production & Manufacturing Research* 20.

31 Ibid.

32 Jonathan Rohr, 'Smart Contracts in Traditional Contract Law, or: The Law of the Vending Machine' (2019) 67(1) *Cleveland State Law Review* 75.

series of instructions.[33] Conversely, deep learning has enabled generative AI models capable of producing more than a limited set of tasks.[34] In this context, current models can converse with users on at first sight a limitless amount of topics. However, the most advanced type of AI technologies, what is called 'narrow AI', currently has a limited capacity to interact.[35] Current AI systems rely on vast amounts of data and adjust a probabilistic model to deliver an outcome. However, it is expected that technological developments will lead to the discovery of Artificial General Intelligence (AGI).[36] This promise is so convincing that even the newly adopted EU AI Act recognises and defines AGI in its own category.[37]

It is important to understand that the moment we arrive at AGI is when AI avatars acting in the metaverse will gain consciousness, and they will become fully autonomous agents. With increased autonomy and consciousness, the question of the legal personhood and rights of AI avatars becomes even more compelling, as we will explain in more detail below.

---

33 Sebastian Schmid, Daniel Schraunder and Andreas Harth, 'Performance Comparison of Simple Reflex Agents Using Stigmergy with Model-Based Agents in Self-Organizing Transportation', *2021 IEEE International Conference on Autonomic Computing and Self-Organizing Systems Companion (ACSOS-C)* (IEEE 2021).

34 Zhihan Lv, 'Generative Artificial Intelligence in the Metaverse Era' (2023) 3 *Cognitive Robotics* 208.

35 J Page, M Bain, and F Mukhlish, 'The Risks of Low Level Narrow Artificial Intelligence', *2018 IEEE International Conference on Intelligence and Safety for Robotics (ISR)* (IEEE 2018).

36 Nick Bostrom, *Superintelligence: Paths, Dangers, Strategies* (Oxford University Press 2014).

37 Regulation (EU) 2024/1689 of the European Parliament and of the Council of 13 June 2024 laying down harmonized rules on artificial intelligence and amending Regulations (EC) No 300/2008, (EU) No 167/2013, (EU) No 168/2013, (EU) 2018/858, (EU) 2018/1139 and (EU) 2019/2144 and Directives 2014/90/EU, (EU) 2016/797 and (EU) 2020/1828 (Artificial Intelligence Act) (Text with EEA relevance), Art 3(63) establishes the following: '"general-purpose AI model" means an AI model, including where such an AI model is trained with a large amount of data using self-supervision at scale, that displays significant generality and is capable of competently performing a wide range of distinct tasks regardless of the way the model is placed on the market and that can be integrated into a variety of downstream systems or applications, except AI models that are used for research, development or prototyping activities before they are placed on the market'.

3. ARE CONSTITUTIONAL FRAMEWORKS UNDER STRESS? THE IMPACT OF AI-POPULATED METAVERSES

The peculiarities of the new virtual spaces described in the previous section, combined with now long-standing features of digital technologies in a context dominated by private multinationals, generate a series of tensions with existing fundamental rights. Conducting a health check of existing constitutional frameworks allows us to identify areas of stress in relation to four fundamental rights: the right to data protection, to right to privacy, the right to freedom of expression and the right to property.

3.1 The Right to Privacy

Most virtual realities are accessed through Head-Mounted Displays (HMD), such as the Oculus Quest 3 from Meta or the recent Apple Vision Pro.[38] This technology has a wide range of sensors that gather data from the physical environment as well as from users themselves, which are then processed or stored in the cloud servers of the private companies that produced the device.[39] Virtual worlds challenge the current conception of privacy due to the surveillance potential inherent in these technologies. Surveillance in the metaverse mainly has a commercial nature and is not linked to state actors.[40] Virtual worlds can operate as control systems, exacerbating an economic model aimed at surveilling and influencing society using hyperconnectivity as a mechanism to exploit the data collected from users.[41]

The immersive technological nature of virtual environments coupled with machine-learning technologies can undermine the ability of users to preserve

[38] Feifei Shi and others, 'A New Technology Perspective of the Metaverse: Its Essence, Framework and Challenges' (2023) 10(6) *Digital Communications and Networks* 1653.

[39] Vasilis Xynogalas and Mark R Leiser, 'The Metaverse: Searching for Compliance with the General Data Protection Regulation' (2024) 14(2) *International Data Privacy Law* 89; see also Roberto Di Pietro and Stefano Cresci, 'Metaverse: Security and Privacy Issues', *2021 Third IEEE International Conference on Trust, Privacy and Security in Intelligent Systems and Applications (TPS-ISA)* (IEEE 2021).

[40] Andrew McStay, 'The Metaverse: Surveillant Physics, Virtual Realist Governance, and the Missing Commons' (2023) 36 *Philosophy & Technology* 13.

[41] Mariusz Maciejewski, 'Metaverse' (European Parliament Policy Department for Citizens' Rights and Constitutional Affairs 2023), 48.

their right to privacy.[42] It seems that the all-encompassing experience of the metaverse is at odds with the expectation to be *left alone*, inherent in the right to privacy.[43] In this regard, privacy in the metaverse could be deemed to be governed and impacted upon in a multilevel manner: on an external-higher layer by administrators and developers of virtual worlds,[44] and on an internal-lower layer by metaverse users who create content on the platform and administer which other users can access their materials in public and semi-public spaces within the virtual world.[45]

3.2 The Right to Data Protection

Privacy and data protection concerns in contemporary metaverses are closely related and could even be deemed to be intertwined. The threats of surveillance illustrated in the previous section emerge as huge amounts of personal data are needed to guarantee an immersive personalised experience in the metaverse. In particular, virtual realities involve the processing of biometric data. According to the EU GDPR, biometric data are pieces of information obtained through technical processes encompassing physical and behavioural traits which help to identify an individual.[46] Biometric data fall within the scope of special categories of data which demand specific protection due to the sensitive nature of the data.[47] Digital technology tools used by users in virtual reality contexts can track hand, face, eye and body movements.[48] Either separately analysed or altogether, these types of data carry great value due to their functionality; for instance, eye-tracking data can be used to predict an individual's age, race, ethnicity, mental and physical conditions and more.[49]

---

42 Ibid.

43 Adrian Kuenzler, 'Why the Metaverse is Challenging Our Notions of Privacy' (*World Economic Forum* 14 August 2023) www.weforum.org/agenda/2023/08/why-the-metaverse-is-pushing-the-notions-of-what-we-call-privacy/ accessed 5 May 2025.

44 Zefeng Chen and others, 'Metaverse Security and Privacy: An Overview', *2022 IEEE International Conference on Big Data (Big Data)* (IEEE 2022).

45 Ibid.

46 Regulation (EU) 2016/679 of the European Parliament and of the Council of 27 April 2016 on the protection of natural persons with regard to the processing of personal data and on the free movement of such data, and repealing Directive 95/46/EC (General Data Protection Regulation) (Text with EEA relevance), Art 4(14).

47 (EU) 2016/679, Art 9.

48 Xynogalas and Leiser (n 39) 7.

49 Evan Selinger, Ely Altman and Shaun Foster, 'Eye-Tracking in Virtual Reality: A Visceral Notice Approach for Protecting Privacy' (2023) 2 *Privacy*

More generally, data collected can be used in machine learning models to train them as part of development processes and personalised services.[50]

This context may result in potential conflicts and issues with basic data protection principles enshrined in the GDPR. The principle of data minimisation, which requires processing only data that are strictly necessary for the purpose of the processing, could be directly affected. First, one may debate what constitutes *necessary means* in the context of the metaverse. Considering that data is the foundation of any virtual world, it might be challenging to set a limit on which data must actually be processed for the service to be provided.[51] The vast amounts of data seamlessly processed within the device and being constantly overwritten to give a realistic experience might be deemed as non-compliant with the principle of data minimisation, especially in light of the main purpose of the processing and considering that users can execute manifold activities in the metaverse.[52] This is apparent in the case of users that may not be interested in a fully immersive metaverse experience,[53] for example, an individual using an HMD device, like the Apple Vision Pro Max, as a computer to write an essay. The user does not need to be constantly tracked and monitored to fulfil this task. Nonetheless, these features are embedded in the product, hence creating tensions with the principle of data minimisation.

In this same vein, we can raise the question of whether the metaverse would comply with the principle of purpose limitation. Data protection policies must be drafted in a concrete and specific manner to inform the user of the use of their data.[54] Nonetheless, despite customisation being an apparent solution, it will be challenging to have in advance an exhaustive list of all the purposes and uses of the data, due to the massive amount of information collected and processed in virtual realities.[55]

Studies Journal 1, 5.

[50] Kamal Balogun, 'Personalizing the Metaverse: How AI Shapes Your Virtual World' (*Medium* 13 December 2023) https://kamalgood.medium.com/personalizing-the-metaverse-how-ai-shapes-your-virtual-world-829901850cb7 accessed 5 May 2025.

[51] Xynogalas and Leiser (n 39).

[52] Metaort, 'GDPR Challenges in the Metaverse: Is the Law Ready for New Technology?' (*Medium* 21 June 2024), https://medium.com/@amirhashemi-pwut/gdpr-challenges-in-the-metaverse-is-the-law-ready-for-new-technology-d5b14c4d3eb6 accessed 5 May 2025.

[53] Leon Anidjar, Nizan Geslevich Packing and Argyri Panezi, 'The Matrix of Privacy: Data Infrastructure in the AI-Powered Metaverse' (2023) 18 *Harvard Law & Policy Review* 59, 81.

[54] Xynogalas and Leiser (n 39).

[55] Nikolaus Forgó, Stefanie Hanold and Benjamin Schutze, 'The Principle of Purpose Limitation and Big Data' (2017) in Marcelo Corrales, Mark Fenwick and

3.3 Freedom of Expression

Similar to what happens more generally on digital platforms, metaverses have a twofold effect on freedom of expression. On the one hand, they can act as a catalyst for this right; while, on the other hand, they might foster the potential to violate and compress individual affordances. Metaverses indeed increase corporate control over freedom of expression on top of that exercised by state authorities, especially in non-democratic states. Big tech companies have direct access to an immense amount of information, with considerable content moderation power regarding what is shown, how and to what extent.[56] Content moderation rules usually follow specific national or regional guidelines or norms.[57] However, the metaverse challenges this classical territorial distinction, and companies offering such immersive services could go to the extreme of removing content for the sake of compliance in all jurisdictions, thereby taking a toll on freedom of expression.[58] Likewise, metaverses exacerbate the potential for manipulating content, which could have a direct effect on democratic societies. Misinformation, disinformation, hate speech, and propaganda find a new mechanism in virtual experiences to influence users.[59] Therefore, there appears to be a very fine line between limiting content for societal good and compressing the fundamental right to freedom of expression.[60]

3.4 The Right to Property

Another tension emerges in relation to the applicability of the right to property in the context of metaverses. Generally, developers of virtual games are deemed the copyright holders vis-à-vis user-generated content (UGC).[61] There

---

Nikolaus Forgó (eds), *New Technology, Big Data and the Law. Perspectives in Law, Business and Innovation* (Springer Singapore 2017).

[56] Mateus de Oliveira Fornasier, 'Freedom of Expression and the Metaverse: On the Importance of Content Creation for the Emergence of a Complex Environment' (2024) 10(1) *Revista de Investigações Constitucionais* e236.

[57] Emmie Hine, 'Content Moderation in the Metaverse Could Be a New Frontier to Attack Freedom of Expression' (2023) 36 *Philosophy & Technology* 43; Celeste and others (n 20).

[58] Eric Goldman, 'Content Moderation Remedies' (2021) 28(1) *Michigan Technology Law Review* 1.

[59] Tom Wheeler, 'Who Will Make the Rules for the Metaverse' (2022) M-RCBG Associate Working Paper Series No. 195, 5.

[60] Irene Kitsara and Jennie Steinhagen (eds), *The Metaverse and its Impacts on Human Rights, the Rule of Law and Democracy* (Council of Europe 2024), 10.

[61] Amy Thomas, 'Merit and Monetisation: A Study of Video Game User-Generated Content Policies' (2023) 12 *Internet Policy Review* https://policyreview

is no univocal approach to this matter of property as companies rely on end users' licence agreements, which change from one platform to another. For instance, Minecraft stresses that the content created by users within the virtual world is the property of the users.[62] Second Life has a similar approach.[63] Nevertheless, since the platforms own the software and licence it to the users, the former de facto use this immaterial property without enjoying a right to the property itself. And they do so to train AI models and profit from them, with no benefit to those individuals producing the content.

This problem also generates an issue for those who invest in virtual realities, with the uncertainty of not knowing the destiny of properties purchased in metaverses. It is indeed interesting that there is a growing trend to invest in virtual worlds in cryptocurrency, NFTs and real estate.[64] PwC, JP Morgan, HSBC and Samsung are investing in plots of land in virtual realities, such as Decentraland or the Sandbox, where the cheapest plot of land available costs 13,000 US dollars.[65]

4. CONSTITUTIONALISING THE METAVERSE: REACTIONS FROM THE CONSTITUTIONAL ECOSYSTEM

Digital constitutionalism theories argue that the challenges generated by the digital revolution in the constitutional ecosystem are in turn drivers of a series of normative counteractions emerging at multiple societal levels. In the past, the courts played an important role within this complex process of constitutionalisation, translating core constitutional principles and guiding private

.info/articles/analysis/merit-and-monetisation-video-game-user-generated-content-policies accessed 5 June 2025.

62 Minecraft, 'End(ER)-User License Agreement (EULA)' (*Minecraft.net* 13 July 2023) www.minecraft.net/en-us/eula accessed 5 May 2025.

63 Linden Lab, 'Second Life Terms and Conditions' (*Linden Lab* 2 May 2024) https://lindenlab.com/legal/second-life-terms-and-conditions accessed 5 May 2025.

64 Kalin Bracken, 'What Is Metaverse Real Estate? An Expert Explains' (*World Economic Forum* 8 November 2022) https://www.weforum.org/stories/2022/11/property-buying-in-the-metaverse-is-the-future/ accessed 7 February 2026; João Marinotti, 'Can You Legally Own Things in the Metaverse? This Law Professor Says No' (*World Economic Forum*, 6 May 2022) https://www.weforum.org/stories/2022/05/can-you-own-anything-in-the-metaverse-a-law-professor-explains/ accessed 29 May 2025.

65 Bernard Marr, 'How to Buy Land & Real Estate in the Metaverse' (*Forbes* 23 March 2022) http://www.forbes.com/sites/bernardmarr/2022/03/23/how-to-buy-land--real-estate-in-the-metaverse accessed 5 May 2025.

companies. We could expect that the courts will approach metaverses by analogy building on the case law developed in relation to social media platforms.[66] Yet, in the absence of specific judicial decisions, we can observe that the first normative counteractions to issues generated by metaverses are emerging in the terms of service and policy documents of the digital platforms.

4.1 Private Constitutions? The Vagueness of Terms of Service

Generally speaking, the private internal rules of these companies can play a constitutional function. Indeed, from a socio-legal perspective, we can observe that these norms directly shape users' online affordances in terms of exercising fundamental rights.[67] They determine the extent to which individuals can exercise their constitutional freedoms in these virtual spaces. This is not because state constitutional law does not apply; it is due to the fact that, in the absence of a single global constitutional law to regulate online content or specific international rules to reconcile constitutional collisions, terms of service play what we could metaphorically call a syncretic function: they bring unity to a reality that is characterised by the simultaneous overlap of multiple constitutional regimes.

Only a few digital platforms commercialising virtual realities have adopted specific terms of service for their metaverses. Despite having adopted specific rules, an analysis of these new norms does not reveal the emergence of new tailored rules for virtual realities. Meta adopted a Code of Conduct for Virtual Experiences highlighting the company's goal to 'build community', which would allow people to share views, ideas, experiences and also express disagreement.[68] Meta manifests the expectation that participants in virtual experiences respect the platform's values of 'voice, safety, authenticity, dignity and privacy'. Nonetheless, the Code does not elaborate these values any further, making basic considerations regarding the prohibition of illegal actions, such as exploitation, abuse, human trafficking, smuggling, non-consensual intimate activity, violation of intellectual property rights, unlawful selling, etc.[69] Interestingly, the Code stresses that within the virtual experiences there can be

---

66 Edoardo Celeste, 'Packingham v North Carolina: A Constitutional Right to Social Media?' (2018) 17 *Cork Online Law Review* 116; Edoardo Celeste, 'Digital Punishment: Social Media Exclusion and the Constitutionalising Role of National Courts' (2021) 35 *International Review of Law, Computers & Technology* 162.

67 Celeste (n 18); Luca Belli and Jamila Venturini, 'Private Ordering and the Rise of Terms of Service as Cyber-Regulation' (2016) 5(4) *Internet Policy Review*.

68 Meta, 'Code of Conduct for Virtual Experiences' www.meta.com/at/en/legal/quest/code-of-conduct-for-virtual-experiences/ accessed 5 May 2025.

69 Ibid.

public spaces which may not accept behaviour that could be deemed acceptable in a *closed* experience with a limited number of users. Finally, some governance rules emerge, distinguishing the role of creators, administrators and developers, with Meta acting with ultimate disciplinary functions.[70]

Minecraft's Usage Guidelines similarly fall short of developing innovative constitutional norms regarding its virtual world.[71] The section entitled 'Essential Guidelines' states a list of actions not accepted on the platform, such as unlawful, deceptive, obscene, harmful or abusive behaviours by users, without, however, further defining these terms nor elaborating the rights of users.[72] Minecraft more generally refers to the Xbox Community Standards, which apply to all players. These norms intend to promote values such as diversity, safety, inclusiveness, and no hate. The Standards intend to promote a respect for the law, community safety, inclusiveness, and exclude harmful behaviour, among other principles. They alert users not to 'engage in any activity that could significantly affect the safety, *fundamental rights* or well-being of users' (emphasis added).[73] However, no concrete articulation or specification on fundamental rights is given.

4.2 Policy Strategies: a Sectoral Approach

The new nature of metaverses is evident also from examining policy strategies in the field, all still in their infancy in terms of tailored constitutional principles. The EU has adopted an initiative on Web 4.0 and virtual worlds, recognising virtual reality as a key component of Europe's strategy for the 'Digital Decade'.[74] Virtual realities are expected to have a profound impact on social relations, and the EU, in line with the Council of Europe, acknowledges that the issue of fundamental rights is crucial in this context.[75]

In February 2024, the EU launched a pilot project focusing on addressing the future governance of virtual worlds and Web 4.0.[76] However, no specific action addressing virtual realities has been adopted for the moment at

70 Ibid.

71 Minecraft, 'Minecraft Usage Guidelines' (*Minecraft.net* 23 June 2023) www.minecraft.net/en-gb/usage-guidelines accessed 5 May 2025.

72 Ibid., section 'Essential Guidelines'.

73 Xbox, 'Xbox Community Standards' (*Xbox.com* May 2024) https://www.xbox.com/de-AT/legal/community-standards accessed 7 February 2026.

74 European Commission (n 11), 2.

75 Council of Europe, 'The Metaverse' (2023) <https://rm.coe.int/leaflet-metaverse-en/1680ac8cac> accessed 5 May 2025.

76 'Pilot Project: A Space for the Metaverse – Virtual World and the Transition to Web 4.0: Shaping Europe's Digital Future' (*European Commission* 13 February

EU level, thus relying on existing sectoral legislation. Indeed, the European Commission has stressed that some of its current legislative efforts, including the GDPR, DSA, DMA, Data Governance Act, Data Act, AI Act, Markets in Crypto Assets (MiCA) Act, the Regulation on the EU Trade Mark, the European Accessibility Act, the Web Accessibility Directive, and the Directive on Copyright in the Digital Single Market, already cover various aspects of virtual realities.[77] In addition, nine actions have been proposed including skills development, promotion of guiding principles, developing toolboxes, as well as standards engaging with multi-stakeholder governance.

The lack of a single regulation or set of policies for virtual worlds seems to be a common situation worldwide. The UK is also approaching the regulation of the Metaverse in a sectoral manner.[78] The Online Safety Bill has recently been passed to protect vulnerable populations from hard and illegal online content. Likewise, the UK's Data Protection Act is also expected to apply to virtual worlds.

5. CONSTITUTIONAL INNOVATION? THE CONSOLIDATION OF VIRTUAL REALITY RIGHTS

A coherent policy and regulatory approach to the metaverse, which would offer an appropriate response to the constitutional challenges created by such a technology, is currently lacking. We are not seeing the emergence of a wave of constitutional innovation.[79] Some of the constitutional issues analysed in Section 2, such as potential infringements of basic data protection principles, can indeed be addressed through extending existing constitutional principles to the virtual reality environment. This would involve the adoption of a sectoral approach, where principles applicable to metaverses are dispersed among several pieces of regulation.

2024) <https://digital-strategy.ec.europa.eu/en/funding/pilot-project-space-metaverse-virtual-world-and-transition-web-40> accessed 5 May 2025.

77 European Commission (n 11), 5.

78 Camomile Shumba, 'UK's New Online Safety Bill Applies to the Metaverse, Lawmakers Agree' (*Coindesk* 13 July 2023) www.coindesk.com/policy/2023/07/13/uks-new-online-safety-bill-applies-to-the-metaverse-lawmakers-agree/ accessed 5 May 2025; see also Jack Boreham, 'UK Adopts Online Safety Legislation Extending to the Metaverse: Safeguarding in the Digital Sphere' (*Digital Twin Insider* 20 September 2023) https://digitaltwininsider.com/2023/09/20/uk-adopts-online-safety-legislation-extending-to-the-metaverse-safeguarding-in-the-digital-sphere/ accessed 5 May 2025.

79 See Celeste (n 6).

What we can conversely address is a further consolidation of principles that emerge to address broader societal issues generated by the advent of digital technologies. The mutated social interactions with AI-powered avatars characterising current virtual realities have not produced a constitutional revolution, but rather help establish and further promote discussion about emerging digital rights.

5.1 Human in the Loop

The Data Protection Directive of 1995 already included the first iteration of the principle of *the human in the loop* in its Article 15, as a legacy of the French data protection law adopted in the 1970s.[80] This provision referred to the involvement of human supervision in automated decision-making processes, which could affect individuals' rights. The aim was to prevent machines from becoming the rulers of significant aspects of our societies. Article 22 of the GDPR reproduces the content of Article 15 while strengthening accountability in the data controller's decision-making. The EU Ethical Guidelines for AI[81] included the principle of the human in the loop as a key requirement to ensure adequate oversight, and a provision on the matter was also enshrined in Article 14 of the new AI Act.[82]

The principle of the human in the loop construes in direct opposition to the datafication of human beings and the reduction of our unique characteristics to mere data fed to an algorithm.[83] The claims for a system with human oversight and participation are based on the robustness offered by the human-machine duo in terms of results. Considering the metaverse as a technology that combines data and AI in real time, it is expected that this right might play a significant role in the context of virtual worlds. Born in the field of data protection, the right to the human in the loop might be considered a core principle in relation to the development of virtual realities, thus preventing AI alone from taking decisions that will be able to significantly affect individual rights

---

80 See Edoardo Celeste and Giovanni De Gregorio, 'Digital Humanism: The Constitutional Message of the GDPR' (2022) 3 *Global Privacy Law Review* 4.

81 European Commission: Directorate-General for Communications Networks, Content and Technology and Grupa ekspertów wysokiego szczebla ds. sztucznej inteligencji, 'Ethics Guidelines for Trustworthy AI' (EU Publications Office 2019) https://data.europa.eu/doi/10.2759/346720 accessed 7 February 2026.

82 Regulation (EU) 2024/1689 (n 37), Art 14.

83 Antoinette Rouvroy, 'Technology, Virtuality and Utopia: Governmentality in an Age of Autonomic Computing' in Mireille Hildebrandt and Antoinette Rouvroy (eds), *Law, Human Agency and Autonomic Computing: The Philosophy of Law Meets the Philosophy of Technology* (Routledge 2011), 119.

without human oversight. We are certainly not witnessing the emergence of a novel right, but virtual realities contribute to reinforcing the position of this principle, which was not so often put into practice in the past as a central norm in the framework of contemporary digital rights.

5.2 Epistemic Rights in Human-Machine Interactions

The requirement that individuals *know* when they are interacting with artificial intelligence systems was included in the EU Declaration on Digital Rights and Principles of 2022, a non-binding document which advocated for the application of epistemic rights, intended as *the rights to know*, to be applied across several digital technologies.[84] The positivisation of such epistemic demands occurred through the AI Act, which introduced an obligation of transparency for providers, according to which, individuals must be informed when they are interacting with an AI system, unless this is apparent from the context.[85]

Considering that current metaverses offer immersive experiences characterised by a seamless combination of virtual and real worlds, it becomes challenging to put such epistemic rights into practice. Which basic obligations must be respected in virtual worlds should be determined to allow users to know when they are interacting with partially or fully AI-powered avatars. Similar to the right to a human in the loop, we see that the operational aspects of the implementation of this principle pose significant challenges. However, from a constitutional perspective, this might represent an opportunity to further consolidate and refine the scope of a right to know in the context of AI applications.

5.3 Rights of AI Avatars?

Already back in the 2000s, Koster published a Declaration of Rights of Avatars, conceiving avatars as an expression of real-life people in the online sphere, and thus supporting the application of human rights to avatars.[86] In a similar vein, we have assumed that human rights extend to the online projection of human users. A different question is that of whether virtual artificial

---

[84] European Declaration on Digital Rights and Principles for the Digital Decade 2023/C 23/01, Chapter II.

[85] Regulation (EU) 2024/1689 (n 37), Art 50.

[86] Raph Koster, 'Declaring the Rights of Players' (*Raph's Website* 27 August 2000) http://www.raphkoster.com/games/essays/declaring-the-rights-of-players/ accessed 5 May 2025.

agents are afforded similar entitlements.[87] The European Parliament drafted a proposal to recognise *electronic personhood*; however, this idea sparked little interest and it was not included in the recent AI Act.[88]

According to the 'Will Theory' of rights, an entity's capacity for independent decision-making is closely linked to its rights.[89] In light of this approach, the more autonomous and conscious AI avatars become, the more compelling the question of the recognition of their rights will be. However, according to 'Interest Theory',[90] rights are bestowed in order to safeguard an entity's interests, regardless of its consciousness or autonomy, the parameter being the possibility that these interests be harmed or benefited. In this sense, it is possible to claim that AI avatars have certain *interests*, such as being protected from harm or abuse, although these are externally imposed by their human designers. Following this line of reasoning, the personhood of AI avatars could be conceived as similar to the recognition of Nature or other non-human persons as subjects of rights.[91]

The particular quality of AI-powered avatars is their appearance or, even more generally, their conceptual association to human or living beings. From a constitutional perspective, this aspect requires consideration. As such, a violation of the fundamental rights of a fully AI-powered avatar is not legally

87 See Lorena Arismendy Mengual, 'A Legal Status for Avatars in the Metaverse from a Private Law Perspective' (2024) InDret 2.2024 102, 112; see also Souichirou Kozuka, 'The Avatar Law and (Cyber) Transnational Contracts' (2023) 28(3–4) *Uniform Law Review* 281; Tiffany Day, 'Avatar Rights in a Constitutionless World' (2009) 32(1) *Hastings Communications and Entertainment Law Journal* 137 ff; see also Joanna J Bryson, Mihailis E Diamantis and Thomas D Grant, 'Of, for, and by the People: the Legal Lacuna of Synthetic Persons' (2017) 25(3) *Artificial Intelligence and Law* 273.

88 European Parliament resolution of 16 February 2017 with recommendations to the Commission on Civil Law Rules on Robotics (2015/2103(INL)) [2018] OJ C 252/239.

89 Ori Herstein, 'Legal Rights' in Edward N Zalta and Uri Nodelman (eds), *The Stanford Encyclopedia of Philosophy* (Winter 2023 ed, Metaphysics Research Lab, Stanford University 2023).

90 Ibid.

91 See Rafi Youatt, 'Personhood and the Rights of Nature: The New Subjects of Contemporary Earth Politics' (2017) 11(1) *International Political Sociology* 39. See also the case of the orangutan Sandra, whose personhood was recognised by an Argentinian court, *Asociacion De Funcionarios y Abogados por los Derechos de los animales y otros contra GCBA sobre amparo, A2174-2015/0, 21 October 2015*; see also Pedro R David, 'Notes on the Case of Orangutan Sandra, the Non-Human Subject of Rights' in Helmut Kury and Sławomir Redo (eds), *Crime Prevention and Justice in 2030* (Springer International Publishing 2021).

relevant. Yet, the psychological effect or the ideological meaning of violating the rights of a virtual being having the appearance of a human or living being might still violate the principle of human dignity or environmental protection and thus ideally be prohibited. Moreover, despite such actions happening in a virtual world, there could be tangible effects on the behaviour of other users witnessing a fundamental rights violation. In this sense, protecting the rights of AI-powered avatars could also be a mechanism to better conceptualise and preserve fundamental societal values.

This area of legal reflection therefore combines the perspectives of the consolidation of existing fundamental rights, when this concerns human beings, and aspects of potential constitutional innovations, should a limited protection of avatars' rights be recognised in the future as a mechanism to avoid circumventions of the principle of human dignity or environmental protection.

6. CONCLUSION

Adopting a socio-legal approach to digital constitutionalism as a lens for analysing the impact of AI-populated metaverses on the constitutional ecosystem allows us to go beyond formal legal transformations. The law traditionally lags behind societal developments; however, a functional perspective is helpful in a comprehensive study of the complex process of the constitutionalisation of the digital society that is currently underway at multiple societal levels.

Metaverses represent disruptive technologies. They inherit the global nature of social media, where individuals from different jurisdictions interact, thus generating similar normative dilemmas on which rules to apply in the case of a collision of different regulatory approaches. Yet, unlike traditional online platforms, AI technologies employed in the metaverse offer a fully immersive and more tangible user experience, blurring the distinction between physical and virtual worlds even more. Human users interact through alter-ego avatars both among themselves and with fully AI-powered virtual characters.

The unprecedented use of AI technologies in the context of metaverses is the driver of most of the challenges emerging in the constitutional ecosystem. Yet, these threats are not dissimilar from those analysed in the context of traditional social media platforms and in the digital society more generally. What changes is the scale of the phenomenon. The fully immersive experiences in metaverses represent an unprecedented potential to violate individual privacy, process sensitive data for other purposes or compress the freedom of expression through opaque content moderation practices. Problems associated with the exploitation of properties created in the metaverse are also not new, as they also characterised virtual games in the past, but they now reach a more significant magnitude and impact, as they are de facto used by virtual reality providers to train their AI systems.

This lack of novelty in terms of areas of constitutional impact generated by the widespread diffusion of metaverses is reflected in the still scarce specific normative responses generated so far. Courts, which have played an important constitutionalising role over the past few years, have not yet had the opportunity to adopt a position on metaverse-related issues. Some digital platforms have introduced ad hoc terms of service, which, however, do not include any tailored norms. The EU has emphasised the need to monitor these technologies, while still maintaining a sectoral approach, thus developing norms which are transversally applicable across various technologies.

The advent of metaverses does not generate a new wave of constitutional innovation but contributes to further consolidating and testing newly developed AI rights. On the one hand, existing digital rights, such as the right to privacy and data protection, are required to play a substantive role in ensuring that metaverses do not become a way to circumvent existing constitutional guarantees. On the other hand, we are witnessing a consolidation of rights developed to face the challenges generated by the use of AI technologies. The principle of *the human in the loop* becomes a cornerstone in an environment where machines can take impactful decisions on human users. The new right to know if users are interacting with fully AI-powered avatars, recently also enshrined in the EU AI Act, finds a natural field of application in the metaverses, where its effective implementation can be progressively tested. The legal-ethical-philosophical question related to the personality of AI avatars and their consequent potential to enjoy fundamental rights is exposed to unprecedented scrutiny. Here, rather than witnessing the emergence of new rights, the issue revolves around the need to preserve human dignity in the virtual world and to prevent that, through the compression of the rights of characters with human appearance, despite the absence of a concrete effect on a conscious human being, there might be a violation perpetrated on the concept of human beings in a more general and abstract way.

4. Intellectual property in the metaverse: when a virtual force meets an intangible object

Philippe Jougleux

1. INTRODUCTION

A medium is an extension of our senses, wrote McLuhan.[1] If his theory of the senses is not without substantial criticism, in its naïve causality between media and advances in society,[2] it has the merit to enlighten at least a correlation between medium and biology. Let us assume that oral cultures favoured dialogues, while the post-Nuremberg era, based on visual perception, is by nature more individualistic. Therefore, a distinction is proposed between *hot* and *cold* media: while the first category is defined by its rich sensory data level, the second is characterised by the high degree of interaction between the communicants.

What would McLuhan say then about the development of virtual worlds? This umbrella notion regroups all kinds of online platforms, from multiplayer games to shared virtual reality environments, where a new form of communication is developed based on enhanced interaction through avatars. Here comes a paradox: this new medium should be qualified as *hot* in this topology, as the users' senses are bombarded by images and sounds, but at the same time, it offers a degree of interaction that no other medium was able to until now. This combination of a high level of interaction and a hot medium makes the metaverse an unstoppable virtual force in the sense that the feeling prevails that this medium will gradually conquer the market and people's everyday lives through gaming applications in 2D or 3D (using a virtual reality set) or in

1 Marshall McLuhan, *Understanding Media: The Extensions of Man* (McGraw-Hill 1964), 77.

2 Alexander Fedorov and Victoria Kolesnichenko, 'Marshall McLuhan and Umberto Eco as Theorists of Media Education' in *Representations of Canada. Vol. 8* (Volgograd State University 2013), 74–82.

the context of office meetings.[3] In parallel, intellectual property law has gained a new statute in this digital age as a substantial part of the legal regime relating to digital behaviours. Most immaterial objects, as we will see, are protected by one or another legal framework of intellectual property law. Therefore, we assist with a contemporary version of the classic thought experiment: 'What happens when an irresistible force meets an immovable object' here becomes 'What happens when an unstoppable virtual force meets an immovable intangible object.' On the one hand, it could be argued that intellectual property law is not ready to alter its core principles to adapt to the virtualisation of the cultural economy. On the other hand, metaverse makers seem completely indifferent to the thorny legal issues relating to respect for intellectual property.

This chapter will analyse this opposition. It aims to propose a general overview of the application of the general principles of intellectual property in virtual worlds, highlighting the finding that, although intellectual property generally applies to virtual environments, new issues and some requirements for clarification are still expected from this specific legal framework. As it is not possible to study all the components of EU intellectual property law, the chapter will focus on its main components: copyright, trademark and patent laws.

First of all, original creations in the metaverse are regulated mainly by copyright law (Section 2). Using European copyright law as a reference point, the study will show how legal protection extends to virtual worlds and will pose the question of the virtual creation of works of the mind by the user. The issue is dealt with from the perspective of the authorship of User Generated Content (UGC), but also by discussing the validity of the clauses, which are very popular in practice, that restrict the acknowledgement of authorship to UGC.

Subsequently, the same issue is analysed from the perspective of industrial property law (mainly trademark and patent law, Section 3). It is not possible to deny the existence of trademark/copyright and patent/copyright interfaces,[4] which means that a general overview of intellectual property issues relating to virtual worlds also needs to encompass a discussion of trademarks and patents.

2. COPYRIGHT LAW IN THE METAVERSE AND THE QUEST FOR REAL ORIGINALITY

Although in most national legal traditions, copyright law has emerged in relationship with specific tangible media, the European Court of Justice (ECJ) has

---

3 See for instance Meta, 'Meta Horizon Workrooms' https://forwork.meta.com/horizon-workrooms/ accessed 21 May 2025.

4 Laura A Heymann, 'The Trademark/Copyright Divide' (2007) 60 *SMU L Rev* 55.

gradually imposed a dematerialised system of copyright law.[5] This evolution greatly facilitates the management of issues of copyright law relating to virtual worlds, specifically regarding the definition and the scope of copyright (2.1). However, the rise of virtual worlds poses specific legal challenges in copyright law: the issue of the ownership of user-generated creations (2.2), the issue of the liability of the virtual world's provider in the case of a copyright infringement by a user (2.3), and, in a more practical tone, the issue of the validity of various contractual mechanisms of copyright transfers usually inserted in the terms of use in virtual worlds (2.4).

2.1 Rightsholder's Prerogatives in Virtual Worlds

Undoubtedly, virtual objects, appearances (skins), virtual landscapes and architecture are protected as works of the mind in copyright law, assuming they demonstrate sufficient originality, without the need for registration.[6]

The mechanisms of the virtual world, as software, should also be protected as such. However, it should be mentioned that their protection is autonomous of that conferred to software. According to the ECJ case *BSA*,[7] the 'look and feel', and generally speaking, the graphical consequences of software, are not by themselves part of the software, and therefore not regulated by the relevant *lex specialis*. The virtual world would be protected as an artistic creation, regulated by the main legal regime of copyright law.

The virtual character of a work of mind does not pose serious legal issues in copyright law. The US *Pacman* case law[8] can be used as a reference in this context. In the context of a dispute on the illegal reproduction of the emblematic video game character Pacman, the defence argued that the character itself was not protected, as it does not appear as the picture in any physical medium (at the time, the memory's limitations of the hardware led to the conceptualisation of the character as a mathematical shape in the code). The Court rejected this argument, considering that the stability of access to the character (each time the game started, the user had access to the same character) was enough to characterise a 'fixation'.

---

5 Jonathan Griffiths, 'Dematerialization, Pragmatism and the European Copyright Revolution' (2013) 33(4) *Oxford Journal of Legal Studies* 767.

6 Thomas Margoni, 'The Harmonisation of EU Copyright Law: the Originality Standard' in Mark Perry (ed), *Global Governance of Intellectual Property in the 21st Century: Reflecting Policy Through Change* (Springer Cham 2016).

7 Case C-393/09 *Bezpečnostní softwarová asociace – Svaz softwarové ochrany v. Ministerstvo kultury* [2010] ECR I-13971.

8 *Atari Inc v. North American Philips Consumer Electronics Corp* 672 F.2d 607 (7th Cir 1982).

Another objection against the protection of virtual worlds by copyright law would be the recourse to the concept of a closed list of works. The issue has not been explicitly settled by the European courts whether the traditional criteria of the closed list, used mainly in common law countries,[9] perdures in European copyright law. The theory of the closed list approach asserts that only some recognised forms of artistic creation are protected by copyright law.

However, this theory is implicitly rejected by the ECJ in two cases. In *Brompton Bicycle*,[10] in 2020, the Court decided that no distinction should occur between works of huge or minor artistic quality, and only one criterion should apply to decide whether the work is protected: originality. Similarly, in *Levola*,[11] the ECJ (refusing protection as a work for the taste of a cheese) held as a fundamental principle that a work is protected from the moment it is original and can be objectively assessed. Consequently, any original work available through the senses of vision and hearing should be included in the protection.

Furthermore, special attention must be given to AI-generated work or AI-enabled creations. Copyright law does not protect mere ideas, only original execution. When the execution of the creative decisions is taken by AI, the work may not receive protection. While the notion of 'prompting art' or 'prompting engineering' has emerged to describe the way the user interacts with the machine,[12] it is almost certain that the act of prompting itself does not fulfil the condition of original expression. Nevertheless, it should also be noted that EU copyright law encompasses an anthropocentric approach to copyright, and human intervention is implicitly placed as a core condition of the protection.[13]

Therefore, even if copyright law is sometimes seen as a *creature of the statute*, nothing in its principles will make obstacles to its application to virtual

---

[9] Nishant Thakur and Sandra Anil Varkey, 'Closed List Approach Versus Open-ended Approach in Subject-matter Copyright' (*SCC Times Online* 28 March 2021) www.scconline.com/blog/post/2021/03/28/copyright-2/ accessed 21 May 2025.

[10] Case C-833/18 *SI and Brompton Bicycle Ltd v. Chedech / Get2Get* [2020] ECLI:EU:C:2020:461.

[11] Case C-310/17 *Levola Hengelo BV v. Smilde Foods BV* [2018] ECLI:EU:C:2018:899.

[12] Ike Stevens, 'The Art of Prompting: Why "Prompt Engineering" Is a Skill of the Future' (*Medium* 18 September 2022) https://ikestevens27.medium.com/the-art-of-prompting-why-prompt-engineering-is-a-skill-of-the-future-bbe404c86e64 accessed 21 May 2025.

[13] P Bernt Hugenholtz and João Pedro Quintais, 'Copyright and Artificial Creation: Does EU Copyright Law Protect AI-Assisted Output?' (2021) 52(9) *IIC-International Review of Intellectual Property and Competition Law* 1190.

worlds. As already noted above, the dematerialisation of the medium has entailed a complex redefinition of the rightsholder's prerogatives from a control of the medium to a control of access to the work.[14]

In EU legislation, the rightsholder's prerogatives have been defined in an extended way, facilitating their adaptation to the context of the virtual world. For example, the notion of communication to the public is defined as 'the exclusive right to authorize or prohibit any communication to the public of their works, by wire or wireless means, including the making available to the public of their works in such a way that members of the public may access them from a place and at a time individually chosen by them'.[15] The notion has been refined by the ECJ through numerous requests for clarifications from the Member States on diverse aspects of the rights.[16]

Of main interest in the context of virtual worlds is the *Rafael Hoteles* case.[17] The right is divided into two distinct analyses: the existence of a communication, and a new public. The existence of communication is implied by the online characteristic of the virtual world and the concept of public is apprehended in abstracto. This means that it does not matter in practice how many users are present on a specific server open to the public; the access itself encompasses the notion of a new public (nevertheless, the conclusion would be different on a closed server open only to some friends and family).

In this context, streaming on video-sharing platforms, such as YouTube or Twitch, of events that occurred in virtual worlds is deemed to be seen as a retransmission. That is to say that this streaming by itself is an act of reproduction to the public and, in an ideal world, the platform should obtain a licence agreement from the virtual world producer.[18]

Furthermore, the reproduction of pre-existing works inside a virtual world is also covered by this right. For instance, the famous video game and virtual world Fortnite organised the Fortnite Soundwave Series, which is basically a concert in a virtual context. There is no doubt that this digital context does not

---

[14] Eleni-Tatiani Synodinou, 'Time and Access to Copyright-Protected Works in the Digital Age' (2024) 55(6) *IIC-International Review of Intellectual Property and Competition Law* 1.

[15] Art 3(1) of Directive 2001/29/EC of the European Parliament and of the Council of 22 May 2001 on the harmonisation of certain aspects of copyright and related rights in the information society [2001] OJ L167/10.

[16] Justin Koo, *The Right of Communication to the Public in EU Copyright Law* (Haart Publishing 2020).

[17] Case C-306/05 *Sociedad General de Autores y Editores de España (SGAE) v. Rafael Hoteles SA* [2006] ECR I-11519.

[18] Despoina Farmaki, *The Interpretation of Copyright Protection in Video Game Streaming in Europe* (DPhil thesis, Brunel University London 2023).

affect the core mechanisms of copyright law: the virtual concert belongs to the category of communication to the public.

There were even discussions relating to the frontier of the notion of protected work. More specifically, the intensive use in games such as Fortnite of characteristic references to modern pop culture constitutes a resilience test to copyright law. The style itself, as an idea, is not protected, but a specific expression of this idea may be protected if it is judged original. For instance, when the virtual world reproduces a series of movements, such as some dance steps, providing the players with the option to use them with their avatar, is the creator of these steps entitled to sue for copyright law infringement? This issue was posed in the US, but the lawsuit was definitively stopped in 2023, after a settlement.[19] In EU copyright law, originality is defined as the personal intellectual effort of the creator.[20] Nevertheless, this effort must surpass a minimum threshold to constitute a message by itself. In this context, for instance, a mere movement, even an iconic one, such as Bolt's victory pose after winning the 100-metre sprint, will not be protected. On the contrary, a complete choreography could be protected by copyright law, and its insertion in a virtual world without consent would infringe the rightholder's prerogatives.

However, this dematerialisation of copyright law is not complete. In particular, the distribution right, defined as the right to control the first distribution in the EU market, differs from the other rightsholder's prerogatives, as it does not concern the work of the mind itself, but its incorporation in a specific medium. Consequently, as stated by the ECJ in the *Allposters* case,[21] the change of medium means that a new distribution right is involved. Furthermore, the distribution right is normally exhausted after the first sale in the EU. However, as there is no equivalent exhaustion of the right of distribution in the digital world, and since access to the protected work is seen more as a service than a purchase of a good,[22] the rightsholder does not lose control of the distribution of the dematerialised work of the mind. Concretely, this means that any market of virtual goods (i.e., a magical object acquired by a player in a virtual gaming

---

19 Bill Donahue, 'Choreographer Ends Copyright Case Against "Fortnite" Maker Epic Games Over Dance Moves' (*Billboard* 14 February 2024) www.billboard.com/business/legal/fortnite-dance-choreographer-ends-epic-games-copyright-lawsuit-1235607331/ accessed 21 May 2025.

20 Case C-145/10 *Eva-Maria Painer v. Standard Verlags GmbH and Others* [2011] ECR I-12533.

21 Case C-419/13 *Art & Allposters International BV v. Stichting Pictoright* [2015] ECLI:EU:C:2015:27.

22 Case C-263/18 *Nederlands Uitgeversverbond and Groep Algemene Uitgevers v. Tom Kabinet Internet BV and Others* [2019] ECLI:EU:C:2019:1111.

world) is void, as a second-hand market of purely digital goods is just not possible from the perspective of copyright law.

2.2 User-generated Creations in the Metaverse, or the Virtual Distinction between Collaborative and Derivative Works

One of the most important, albeit thorny, issues regarding the application of copyright law in the virtual world concerns the legal regime of User Generated Content.[23] If, in the real world, a photographer takes a picture of a person, the relationship between legal systems is clearly defined: while the photographer enjoys the protection of copyright law, the person may be entitled to protection through personal data protection. In a virtual context, however, the mere portrait of a user is by itself a work of the mind, potentially. It can use some unique combination of 'skins' or customisable appearance and thus produce an original construct. Therefore, virtual photography would be the combination of two creative intents. Normally, this legal issue is solved in copyright law through the notions of collaborative and derivative works.

The term 'derivative work' does not exist in the Berne Convention, which only stipulates that 'Translations, adaptations, arrangements of music and other alterations of a literary or artistic work shall be protected as original works without prejudice to the copyright in the original work.'

In some legal systems such as in the USA, the right to produce derivative work is considered an autonomous prerogative of the author of the pre-existing work.[24] In the EU, however, a holistic concept of the right of reproduction has been adopted that includes any kind of reproduction regardless of the shape, format or medium. It has been argued that ontologically the derivative right differs from the right of reproduction,[25] but in practice, the European notion of the right of reproduction will fully encompass the derivative right.

---

[23] For instance, see: Greg Lastowka, 'User-generated Content and Virtual Worlds' (2008) 10(4) *Vanderbilt Journal of Entertainment & Technology Law* 893; Randy Finch and Jamie C Yang, 'Rights to User Generated Content in a VR World' (2016) 5(1) *NTUT Journal of Intellectual Property Law and Management* 53; Mira Burri-Nenova, 'User Created Content in Virtual Worlds and Cultural Diversity' in Christoph B Graber and Mira Burri-Nenova (eds), *Governance of Digital Game Environments and Cultural Diversity* (Edward Elgar Publishing 2010).

[24] US Copyright Office, 'Circular 14: Copyright in Derivative Works and Compilations' www.copyright.gov/circs/circ14.pdf accessed 23 May 2025.

[25] Daniel J Gervais, 'The Derivative Right, or Why Copyright Law Protects Foxes Better than Hedgehogs' (2013) 15 *Vanderbilt Journal of Entertainment and Technology Law* 785.

Therefore, when a user or a player in a virtual world has come with a substantial intellectual investment, the question of the authorship of this creation can be solved either through the notion of joint work or of derivative work. In the first case, it means that the creator of the virtual world obtains a right to the user's virtual creation, while, in the second case, the creation belongs in full to the user, assuming that the user has acquired the derivative right.

On paper, the distinction between collaborative and derivative works is clear and straightforward. While collaborative or joint works involve the participation, through substantial involvement, of two or more authors, the notion of derivative work, on the contrary, refers to the use of pre-existing work in a new and independent creation. Nevertheless, the frontiers are blurred in practice in some circumstances due to the extensive jurisprudential interpretation of the notion of collaborative work. For instance, a famous video game, Grand Theft Auto V, proposes to the players the option to use an in-game movie editor, to create their own movies. The user has a lot of options to work as a film director, but is limited to the décor of the town and the personages created by the game producer. At first glance, it appears that the video is a derivative work, as the creative choices entirely belong to the user. Nonetheless, the creative choices heavily depend on the available tools and options from the provider, who plays, in this context, an indirect but substantial role in the creation.

The concept of joint work is not harmonised in EU law, but some fundamental underlying principles are revealed by numerous national case laws.[26] The results show that for joint work to exist, it is not necessary for collaborations to coexist chronologically or geographically, or even of the same extent. Furthermore, both notions heavily rely on the concept of substantive contribution, which is by definition analysed through the prism of the notion of originality. Indeed, only original contributions are deemed to be considered part of a joint effort of creation, while only original modifications of a pre-existing work are seen as derivative works.

Therefore, the more important distinction between joint works and derivative works lies in the notion of the achievement of the work. However, this notion is not legislatively defined or discussed in case law. Pablo Picasso may have said 'To finish a work? To finish a picture? What nonsense! To finish it means to be through with it, to kill it, to rid it of its soul, to give it its final blow the coup de grace for the painter as well as for the picture.'[27] Metaphorically, a virtual world could be seen as a theatre stage: the users improvise a work,

---

26 See for instance in the UK: *Martin v. Kogan* [2017] EWHC 2927 (IPEC).

27 Although this citation is largely attributed to Picasso, its exact source is unknown.

based on the general indications and the clues left on the stage, and the results come from both efforts.

In conclusion, the concept of joint works should not be automatically discarded from the analysis, depending on the specific context of the creation, but a large majority of UGC will belong to the concept of derivative work. Interestingly, in some specific circumstances, the court is prone to accept both concepts simultaneously. In the case of *Greene et al. v. Ablon*[28] in the USA, the Court found the 2002 book was both a joint work by Greene and Ablon and a derivative work based on Greene's 1998 book.

2.3 UGCs and Statutory Exceptions in Virtual Worlds

As analysed above, the legal nature of UGC will only in some exceptional circumstances be one of joint authorship. Most of the time, UGC will be identified as derivative work. The qualification of UGC as derivative work implies, as we have seen above, that the user has to ask for permission from the rightsholder of the pre-existing work. This mechanism is to be interpreted as a regime of strict liability: regardless of the creativity, artistic intention, or economic value of the UGC, its creator violates the right of reproduction of the first author assuming their consent has not been obtained prior to the publication of the UGC. For instance, the famous artist Jeff Koons has been condemned for his series of sculptures that reproduced classic photographs, both in the USA[29] and in France.[30]

One option for the user would be to rely on exceptions to the rightsholder's prerogatives as mechanisms of the exemption of liability. In the USA, the fair-use exception will protect any UGC that passes the test of 'transformation'.[31] In Canada, a specific statutory exception in favour of non-commercial UGC has been enacted.[32] In the EU, no specific statutory exception in favour of UGC exists, even if a lot of discussions revolve around the idea of a new statutory exception on the model of the exception of private copying, that would

28 *Greene v. Ablon* No 13-2369 (1st Cir 2015) (Lipez, J.).

29 *Rogers v. Koons* 960 F.2d 301 (2d Cir 1992).

30 Cour d'Appel de Paris, 23 février 2021 (19/09059).

31 See the case *Cariou v. Prince* No 11-1197 (2d Cir. 2013), where it is explained that the law does not require that a secondary use comment on the original artist or work, or popular culture, but only that a reasonable observer finds the work to be transformative.

32 See Section 29.21 of the Canadian Copyright Act, *Copyright Act*, RSC 1985 c C-42).

include an obligation to pay equitable remuneration.[33] Therefore, two existing statutory exceptions may be of interest in this context: the quotation and the parody exceptions.

The quotation exception has a relatively broad scope under EU copyright law.[34] Contrary to appearances, this exception is not limited to literary works and is not used for criticism only, but also to review pre-existing work. In addition, the quotation is not mandatorily short. The extent of the amount quoted depends on the prism of the principle of proportionality of the intended purpose. As the ECJ highlighted,[35] this exception works as a basic instrument of balance between copyright law and freedom of expression, protecting from liability the user who legitimately uses a pre-existing work as a medium to express something different, assuming that proper attribution to the original author is made. Therefore, the use of the virtual world as the décor of their creation by the user will be justified by this exception, which will protect them from liability.

In parallel, the exception of parody is useful in practice to protect the UGC against action on the basis of liability from third parties in cases where the UGC constitutes a reference to a popular cultural work. This exception has also been broadly interpreted by the ECJ in the *Deckmyn* case.[36] The court considers that for the exception to apply, the second work does not need to constitute a parody of the first, but it is also accepted for the first work to be used as material for the parody of something else. The most fundamental criterion here is not the humorous intent, which as a notion is subjective and difficult to appreciate, but the objective result of transformation: are the modifications substantial enough to allow an independent viewer to understand at first sight the different nature of the second work? The humorous intent can then be deduced from the substantial modifications.

---

33 Martin Senftleben, 'User Generated Content: Towards a New Use Privilege in EU Copyright Law' in Tanya Aplin (ed), *Research Handbook on Intellectual Property and Digital Technologies* (Edward Elgar Publishing 2020).

34 Stavroula Karapapa 'The Quotation Exception under EU Copyright Law: Paving the Way for User Rights' in Eleonora Rosati (ed), *The Routledge Handbook of EU Copyright Law* (Routledge 2021).

35 Case C-469/17 *Funke Medien NRW GmbH v. Bundesrepublik Deutschland* [2019] ECLI:EU:C:2019:623; Case C-476/17 *Pelham GmbH and Others v. Ralf Hütter and Florian Schneider-Esleben* [2019] ECLI:EU:C:2019:624; and Case C-516/17 *Spiegel Online GmbH v. Volker Beck* [2019] ECLI:EU:C:2019:625.

36 Case C-201/13 *Johan Deckmyn and Vrijheidsfonds VZW v. Helena Vandersteen and Others* [2014] ECLI:EU:C:2014:2132.

2.4 The Validity of Licensing Agreements Requiring Players to Waive their Intellectual Property Rights

This fragile equilibrium between the virtual world's creator right to allow the UGC and the exceptions provided to protect the user's freedom of expression is in practice greatly affected by contract law. Lawful users of virtual worlds are contractually bound by the terms and conditions of the platform that hosts the world. In a virtual world, it can be advanced that the provider of the virtual world implicitly consents to the creation of derivative works by technically allowing (and often encouraging) the user to be creative. From this perspective, the UGC would be legal without any need for recourse to the mechanism of statutory exceptions. However, in practice, the contractual framework governing most virtual worlds is extremely restrictive regarding the users' rights and freedoms. More specifically, the issue of copyright waiver as a condition for gaining access to a virtual world is substantial.[37]

For example, in the Roblox host agreement[38] it is indicated that:

> You hereby grant to Roblox an unlimited, non-exclusive, perpetual, worldwide, irrevocable, royalty-free licence to exercise all rights of whatever kind or nature now or hereafter protected by the copyright laws of the United States of America and similar laws in all foreign countries in and to the Event and any taping of the Event.

Or, in the terms of use in Second Life, it is stipulated that:

> ...you hereby grant to Linden Lab, and you agree to grant to Linden Lab, the non-exclusive, unrestricted, unconditional, unlimited, worldwide, irrevocable, perpetual, and cost-free right and license to use, copy, record, distribute, reproduce, disclose, modify, display, publicly perform, transmit, publish, broadcast, translate, make derivative works of, and sell, re-sell or sublicense (through multiple levels) (with respect to each Product or otherwise on the Service as permitted by you through your interactions with the Service), and otherwise exploit in any manner whatsoever, all or any portion of your User Content (and derivative works thereof), for any purpose whatsoever in all formats, on or through any media, software, formula, or medium now known or hereafter developed, and with any technology or devices now known or hereafter developed, and to advertise, market, and promote the same.[39]

---

37 Erez Reuveni, 'On Virtual Worlds: Copyright and Contract Law at the Dawn of the Virtual Age' (2007) 82(2) *Indiana Law Journal* 261.

38 Roblox, 'Host Agreement' https://en.help.roblox.com/hc/en-us/articles/15765085259284-Host-Agreement accessed 21 May 2025.

39 Second Life, 'Second Life Terms and Conditions' (*Second Life* 31 July 2017) https://secondlife.com/app/tos/tos.php accessed 21 May 2025.

Some remarks must be formulated on this practice. First, from the perspective of consumer law, any terms and conditions that would have resulted in fully depriving the user of the benefit of copyright law would be so extreme that it would fall into the category of an abusive clause. Second, the mere licences to the platform can also be problematic. Indeed, the EU Directive on Copyright in the Digital Single Market[40] has posed a new fundamental principle of EU copyright law: the principle of fair remuneration of the author. Article 18 states that:

> Member States shall ensure that where authors and performers license or transfer their exclusive rights for the exploitation of their works or other subject matter, they are entitled to receive appropriate and proportionate remuneration.

The concept of appropriate and proportionate remuneration implies here that, contrary to the terms usually incorporated in most virtual worlds, any commercial exploitation of a protected creation by the user of the platform should lead to the payment of a fair reparation.

Furthermore, the 'omnibus Directive'[41] of 2019 amended the Directive on consumer rights and added that, in the case of withdrawal from the consumer, the trader shall refrain from using any content which was provided or created by them,[42] and also make available the content to the consumer at their request.[43] It could be argued that this article implicitly consecrates the principle of ownership by the user of their content.

However, this principle is limited by four wide exceptions,[44] and mainly the content must have a utility outside of the virtual world. The principle is also

---

40 Directive (EU) 2019/790 of the European Parliament and of the Council of 17 April 2019 on copyright and related rights in the Digital Single Market and amending Directives 96/9/EC and 2001/29/EC [2019] OJ L130/92.

41 Directive (EU) 2019/2161 of the European Parliament and of the Council of 27 November 2019 amending Council Directive 93/13/EEC and Directives 98/6/EC, 2005/29/EC and 2011/83/EU of the European Parliament and of the Council as regards the better enforcement and modernisation of Union consumer protection rules [2019] OJ L328/7.

42 Art 13(5) of Directive 2011/83/EU of the European Parliament and of the Council of 25 October 2011 on consumer rights, amending Council Directive 93/13/EEC and Directive 1999/44/EC of the European Parliament and of the Council and repealing Council Directive 85/577/EEC and Directive 97/7/EC of the European Parliament and of the Council [2011] OJ L304/64 ('Directive 2011/83/EU').

43 Art 13(6) of Directive 2011/83/EU, ibid.

44 The principle does not apply when the content '(a) has no utility outside the context of the digital content or digital service supplied by the trader;

restricted by the antagonistic principle that the trader may prevent any further use of the digital content or digital service by the consumer. Therefore, such a right exists only in cases where digital content may exist independently of the specific virtual world proposed by the trader (e.g., a 3D model that is interoperable with other virtual worlds).

3. INDUSTRIAL PROPERTY OF THE METAVERSE AND INSIDE THE METAVERSE

Industrial property ontologically differs from copyright law as it requires prior registration, but also industrial property is based on the philosophy of the exploitation of a mark, sign or patent in the real world. The adaptation of trademark and patent laws to virtual world uses may turn out to be more difficult (3.1). One very specific difficulty that needs to be analysed concerns the application of the principle of territoriality in the context of multiverses (3.2).

3.1 The Influence of Patent and Trademark Laws in Virtual Worlds

Brands are, by nature, immaterial objects and nothing could travel with more ease in virtual worlds. However, trademark law is built on a fragile equilibrium between the protection of the legitimate interest of the brand's owner and the freedom of expression. Virtual items, for instance, a virtual Ferrari, would pose trademark law issues that an average user may not expect.[45] Following the same reasoning adopted above for copyright law (see Section 2.1), it appears that the brand's owner enjoys in the virtual world the full protection provided by trademark law in the real world.

Nevertheless, trademark laws may be seen as less ready than copyright law for pure enforcement in a virtual world. More specifically, the issue of the protection of purely virtual goods as trademarks is still unclear.[46] In this context, the guidelines issued by the EU Intellectual Property Office (EUIPO) are of

---

(b) only relates to the consumer's activity when using the digital content or digital service supplied by the trader;

(c) has been aggregated with other data by the trader and cannot be disaggregated or only with disproportionate efforts; or

(d) has been generated jointly by the consumer and others, and other consumers are able to continue to make use of the content'.

45 Priyal Chandrakar, 'An Analysis on Law and Metaverse' (2022) 2(1) *Indian Journal of Integrated Research in Law* 1.

46 Sharon K Lowry, 'Property Rights in Virtual Reality: All's Fair in Life and Warcraft' (2008) 15(1) *Tex Wesleyan Law Review* 109.

tremendous importance.[47] The EUIPO considers that virtual goods may be registered as trademarks, assuming sufficient description is provided (e.g., a 'virtual good' by itself is not enough. But the trademark may be referred to as 'virtual clothing' if it is a digital file used to dress an avatar). A specific class (class 9) has been created specifically for virtual goods, which are protected independently of their potential function by analogy in the real world. For example, virtual clothing will be registered under class 9 and not under the class corresponding to the trademark of real clothing.

Therefore, the road has been opened to the enforcement of trademark law in the context of virtual worlds. This does not mean that any use of a real brand in a virtual world is deemed to be illegal. The protection provided by trademark law is restricted to the uses that designate a specific service or good through the prism of the principle of 'speciality'. In this context, the classic issue of a potential conflict between trademark law and freedom of expression is solved by restrictively interpreting the scope of the trademark's protection.[48] Practically, any use of the trademark outside of an economic context, such as a reference inside the metaverse by a simple user, will not infringe the owner's rights (unless the good or activity related to the sign is itself inside the metaverse).

In parallel, virtual worlds and virtual realities are heavily dependent on technical innovation. For a virtual world to happen, some resource management features need to be installed and massive collaboration between users achieved. In virtual reality (VR), specifically, all technology is still emergent, with persistent obstacles such as VR sickness (headaches, eyestrain, and potential drowsiness, mainly caused by a conflict between visual and vestibular cues, which are cues that are related to the individual's perception of movement and position).[49]

Any invention that would emulate motion or temporarily neutralise in any other way the VR sickness would take a major step in this sector. Until now, IT companies such as Meta have already, for instance, patented algorithms for

---

[47] EUIPO guidelines on the registration of virtual goods and NFTs can be found on EUIPO, 'Trade mark and Design guidelines' (2025) https://guidelines.euipo.europa.eu/ accessed 21 May 2025.

[48] Michal Bohaczewski, 'Conflicts Between Trade Mark Rights and Freedom of Expression Under EU Trade Mark Law: Reality or Illusion?' (2020) 51 *IIC International Review of Intellectual Property and Competition Law* 856.

[49] Eunhee Chang, Hyun T Kim and Byounghyun Yoo, 'Virtual Reality Sickness: A Review of Causes and Measurements' (2020) 36(17) *International Journal of Human–Computer Interaction* 1658.

generating and moving virtual shapes and scenes in a VR environment based on hand gestures, head motion, or the line of sight of the user.[50]

This finding, however, has to be relativised by three legal principles.

First, the theory of essential facility[51] has a role to play here. Although patent law has been conceived as a means to motivate investors, many critics have expressed the contemporary abusive use of this mechanism through the monopolisation of concepts, depending on competition law. In the EU, in exceptional circumstances, it is nowadays accepted that the refusal of a rightsholder of intellectual property to grant a licence could amount to a violation of the principles of competition law.[52] In other words, leading IT companies in the field of virtual worlds should be aware that abusive strategies of control in this new technology will induce significant legal risks, especially if monopolistic tendencies are detected.

Second, it is important to go back to the definition of invention in EU patent law. According to EU law, a patentable invention must have a technical character (and not be merely a method), possess industrial application, show novelty (must be new, meaning it cannot be part of the state of the art), and most of all indicate an inventive step (a reasoning that is not obvious to a person skilled in the art). Meanwhile, the topic of virtual worlds has for a long time been largely influenced by sci-fi[53] and it could be interesting to discuss whether an idea that is largely accepted in the realm of sci-fi can be nevertheless new and show an inventive step from the perspective of patent law. Hugo Gernsback, one of the 'fathers' of science fiction, believed that works of science fiction are analogous to patents, in the sense that both sci-fi and patents aim to disclose information about new inventions to the public.[54] It could be accepted that an imaginary invention, sufficiently described in detail, and largely accepted by the public, would have the effect of bearing a real patent to apply this invention.

---

50 Michael Fainberg and Mohammad Zaryab, 'Patenting the Metaverse' (*National Law Review* 25 March 2022) https://www.natlawreview.com/article/patenting-metaverse accessed 24 April 2025.

51 Gregory J Werden, 'The Law and Economics of the Essential Facility Doctrine' (1987) 32 *Saint Louis University Law Journal* 433.

52 James Turney, 'Defining the Limits of the EU Essential Facilities Doctrine on Intellectual Property Rights: the Primacy of Securing Optimal Innovation' (2005) 3(2) *Nw J Tech and Intell Prop* 179.

53 Stanley G Weinbaum, *Pygmalion's Spectacles* (1935), is considered one of the first novels on the topic of virtual reality.

54 Camilla A Hrdy and Daniel H Brean, 'The Patent Law Origins of Science Fiction' (2022) 47 *Columbia Journal of Law & the Arts* 1.

Third, we must remember that software per se cannot be patented. The US Supreme Court decision in *Alice Corp v. CLS Bank*[55] also explained that mere abstract ideas are not methods, and even implementing these ideas on a computer is not enough to transform them into patentable subject matter. The European approach is even stricter.[56] However, the exclusion does not apply to computer programs having a technical character. In this context, technical character requires a 'further technical effect', defined as 'a technical effect going beyond the "normal" physical interactions between the program (software) and the computer (hardware) on which it is run'.[57] Therefore, it can be argued that the virtual context of software deprives it of a technical effect. Nonetheless, software running in a virtual environment may still pretend to possess the copyright law protection (see previous section).

To conclude, it is also possible to discuss the possibility of virtual invention, but its patentability is arguable. For instance, in the famous multiplayer game Minecraft developed by Microsoft, players have absolute freedom to interfere with their virtual environment and some of them have created interesting virtual inventions, such as an automatic bridge builder or a working calculator.[58] Would it be possible to patent an invention in the metaverse itself? Normally, as a virtual invention has no effect in the real world, such an assumption should be rejected. However, it has been argued that the broad appreciation by the courts of the concept of 'technical effect' makes it permissible to patent virtual tools producing technical effects.[59]

3.2 Intellectual Property's Principle of Territoriality and the Metaverse

Copyright law benefits from a comparative advantage over industrial property: most of the core principles of the legal regime have been harmonised through

---

55 *Alice Corp v. C.L.S. Bank International*, 573 US 208 (2014).

56 Art 52(2)(c) and (3) of the Convention on the Grant of European Patents (European Patent Convention) (signed 5 October 1973, entered into force 7 October 1977) 1065 UNTS 199.

57 European Patent Office, 'Guidelines for Examination in the European Patent Office' (2025), chapter II – Inventions – 3.6 'Programs for computers'.

58 Rupesh Nair, 'The Craziest Minecraft Inventions Players Have Managed to Pull Off' (*Essentially Sports* 8 April 2021) www.essentiallysports.com/the-craziest-minecraft-inventions-players-have-managed-to-pull-off-esports-news/ accessed 24 April 2025.

59 Iony Randrianirina, 'Patent Law & Metaverse', Metaverse & Law Conference (Lyon, France 21–22 April 2023) https://hal.science/hal-04314534/document accessed 24 April 2025.

the International Berne Convention. In parallel, industrial property needs registration with a national office. Therefore, while in theory all intellectual property law is regulated by the principle of territoriality, the issue of the choice of law and jurisdiction is posed with more acuity for industrial property. For instance, trademarks may be protected differently and even belong to different entities.

Legislation around jurisdiction in the metaverse is still developing.[60] The issue is that the virtual world gives the illusion of a new digital space, independent from geographical restrictions, and this leads to the myth of an independent cyberspace.[61] But the user interacts in a specific location, through a server hosted in a specific place, which belongs to a national company.

For instance, in the USA, in the case of *Bragg v. Linden Research, Inc*,[62] a user participating in the Second Life virtual world was entitled to sue in his personal jurisdiction, since, as the Court noted, the company had engaged in nationwide marketing efforts to publicise its virtual world and therefore met the requirement of 'minimum contact'. In the EU, the issue is governed by the Brussels I Regulation, as interpreted by the ECJ.[63] The ECJ has developed the mosaic approach,[64] and interprets the place of a harmful event as both the place where the event giving rise to the damage took place and the place where the damage occurred. Therefore, several Member States will arguably have jurisdiction over an intellectual property infringement claim related to the metaverse, such as the place from which the infringing work in the metaverse may be accessed, or the location where the event giving rise to the damage takes place.[65] However, this is only true for a claim for reparation. On the contrary, injunctions for cessation of infringement will be governed by the rule of the domicile of the defendant.[66]

---

60 Maria Kalyvaki, 'Navigating the Metaverse Business and Legal Challenges: Intellectual Property, Privacy, and Jurisdiction' (2023) 3(1) *Journal of Metaverse* 87.

61 Rolf H Weber, *Regulatory Models for the Online World* (Brill 2021), 25.

62 *Bragg v. Linden Research Inc* 487 F Supp 2d 593 (ED Pa 2007).

63 Case C-68/93 *Shevill and others v. Presse Alliance* [1995] ECR I-00415.

64 Cases C-509/09 and C-161/10 *eDate Advertising GmbH and Others v. X and Société MGN Ltd* [2011] ECR I-10269.

65 Cheng L Saw and Samuel ZW Chan, 'The Subsistence and Enforcement of Copyright and Trade Mark Rights in the Metaverse' (2024) 19(4) *Journal of Intellectual Property Law and Practice* 371.

66 Cedric Vanleenhove, 'The European Court of Justice in Bolagsupplysningen: The Brussels I Recast Regulation's Jurisdictional Rules for Online Infringement of Personality Rights Further Clarified' (2018) 34(3) *Computer Law & Security Review* 640.

4. CONCLUSION

The opposition between the logic of the virtual world and the mechanisms of intellectual property law should not be overestimated. By definition, virtual worlds are not the unstoppable virtual force predicted in this introduction, in the sense that the legal framework on the protection of digital content cannot be ignored. At the same time, neither is intellectual property an 'immovable intangible object' as it rests on the fragile equilibrium between conflicting interests. The thorny legal issue of UGC, assimilated to derivative works by principle, is the principal obstacle to the harmonious integration of copyright law into virtual worlds. While copyright law has largely anticipated the emergence of virtual worlds by adapting in general to a dematerialised world of creation, patent and trademark laws encounter more difficulties. This needs more attention, as now more than ever a holistic approach to intellectual property is required to solve the multiple legal challenges stemming from the emergence of multiverses.

5. Language rights in the metaverse: the implications of translingual metaverse communication

Maarit Koponen, Rui Sousa-Silva and Antonio Pareja-Lora

1. INTRODUCTION

The term *metaverse* has attracted particular attention with the rebranding of Facebook in 2020, before the social media network launched a transformative programme in 2021 to offer a metaverse-based work platform involving social, learning, collaboration, and gaming experiences.[1] However, the term has been used at least since the 1990s.[2] Initially employed in literature, it became subsequently applied in other contexts, such as education, to refer to how learners use technology to socialise and engage with each other.[3] Over the years, however, the concepts of technology and particularly the metaverse have continued to evolve dramatically. But what is the metaverse, and how does it relate to language rights? Visions of the metaverse or virtual worlds, where people interact on a three-dimensional online platform through virtual reality (VR), augmented reality (AR) or even extended reality (XR), often posit that the interaction is mediated by translation technology that allows people to communicate seamlessly in real time across language barriers.[4] In these visions, such technology would remove language barriers and guarantee the realisation of rights regardless of the user's language. However, while translation tech-

[1] Facebook, 'Introducing Horizon Workrooms: Remote Collaboration Reimagined' (2021) https://about.fb.com/news/2021/08/introducing-horizon-workrooms-remote-collaboration-reimagined/ accessed 17 February 2026.

[2] Davy Tsz Kit Ng, 'What Is the Metaverse? Definitions, Technologies and the Community of Inquiry' (2022) 38 *Australasian Journal of Educational Technology* 190.

[3] Ibid.

[4] OECD, Global Scenarios 2035 (2021) 14.

nology has the potential to support inclusion by enabling communication and increasing linguistic accessibility, it can also exacerbate exclusion due to the unequal availability and quality of systems for different languages.

In this chapter, we examine how human rights intersect with language rights and reflect on the potential role of technology in supporting linguistic accessibility and the realisation of rights in the metaverse. We first define the concept of metaverse as used in this chapter and examine questions of law, ethics and responsibility in the metaverse. We then outline how language technology is used for (automatic) translation and interpreting, discussing both the current state and more speculative views of translingual communication in the metaverse. After a brief overview of relevant language rights, we then examine the potential implications of the metaverse on these rights. Finally, we conclude with some recommendations for the development of the metaverse in light of language rights.

2. DEFINING THE CONCEPT OF THE METAVERSE

Huynh-The et al. describe the sound technical structure underlying the metaverse, in that an entirely 3D immersive experience produced by merging advanced technologies is offered to users so that they can interact and collaborate in the virtual world.[5] In this immersive experience, virtuality and reality are fused[6] to offer users a distinctive, albeit integrated, user-generated experience.[7] Over time, the gap between the virtual space and the real space is expected to be gradually bridged;[8] especially as a result of AR, and the two will become increasingly integrated, and hence indistinguishable. AR glasses are an example of how this integration will be unveiled, to offer a range of opportunities in the personal, industrial, public and societal spheres.[9]

---

[5] Thien Huynh-The et al., 'Artificial Intelligence for the Metaverse: A Survey' (2023) 117 *Engineering Applications of Artificial Intelligence* 105581, 3.

[6] Feifei Shi and others, 'A New Technology Perspective of the Metaverse: Its Essence, Framework and Challenges' (2023) *Digital Communications and Networks* S2352864823000524.

[7] Yun Kyung Oh, Jisu Yi and Jongdae Kim, 'What Enhances or Worsens the User-Generated Metaverse Experience? An Application of BERTopic to Roblox User EWOM' (2024) 34 *Internet Research* 1800.

[8] Shasha Yu and Fiona Carroll, 'Insights into the Next Generation of Policing: Understanding the Impact of Technology on the Police Force in the Digital Age' in Reza Montasari (ed), *Artificial Intelligence and National Security* (Springer 2022).

[9] Commission, 'Communication from the Commission to the European Parliament, the Council, the European Economic and Social Committee and the

While the concept has been repurposed across disciplines, it is worth examining from a linguistics perspective. Although the term *metaverse* has been defined by Dionisio et al.[10] based on the prefix *meta* (in the sense of 'beyond') and the suffix *verse* (to mean 'universe'),[11] we contend that building on the morphology of the word, as well as on its lexicographic, dictionary definition, the lemma *verse* stands for *universe*, whereas the prefix *meta*[12] is meant to invoke change and going beyond the ordinary limits of the universe. In this sense, the concept is here repurposed to mean a new form of seeing and experiencing the universe that moves within and beyond the virtual world(s), and where the physical and the virtual are seamlessly integrated.

Technological developments in recent decades, notably in language technology, have paved the way for new virtual worlds, which have initially attempted to mimic the *real* physical world in the *virtual* environment.[13] However, as predicted by Perlin,[14] technology has evolved to become integrated with our senses, which enables users to speak not only through technology, but more importantly to technology.[15] This subtle change has had a major impact on the metaverse. Users no longer simply replicate physical world actions and interactions in the virtual world, but more importantly, become immersed in the metaverse and replicate in the physical world the actions and interactions of the virtual world(s). Consequently, the two worlds have become blended. The metaverse is hence no longer shaped by virtual realities, but instead shapes our physical world by augmenting its virtues and its vices, and by changing it significantly. This is already visible in how generative AI is changing language, action and interaction.

Committee of the Regions, "An EU initiative on Web 4.0 and virtual worlds: a head start in the next technological transition"' COM (2023) 442 final.

[10] John David N Dionisio, William G Burns III and Richard Gilbert, '3D Virtual Worlds and the Metaverse: Current Status and Future Possibilities' (2013) 45 *ACM Computing Surveys* 1.

[11] Ng (n 2).

[12] 'meta, prefix' (*Cambridge Dictionary* 2024) https://dictionary.cambridge.org/dictionary/english/meta accessed 6 February 2026.

[13] Thomas J Holt and Adam M Bossler, *Cybercrime in Progress: Theory and Prevention of Technology-Enabled Offenses* (Routledge 2016).

[14] Ken Perlin, 'Future Reality: How Emerging Technologies Will Change Language Itself' (2016) 36 *IEEE Computer Graphics and Applications* 84.

[15] Dave Sayers and others, 'The Dawn of the Human-Machine Era: A Forecast of New and Emerging Language Technologies' (*Report for EU COST Action CA19102 'Language In The Human-Machine Era'* 2021) https://jyx.jyu.fi/handle/123456789/75737 accessed 6 February 2026.

Consequently, for the purposes of this chapter, we build upon Ng's framework[16] to define the metaverse as a new form of emerging virtual world, where social interaction, boosted by advanced computing and powerful hardware platforms, builds upon the immersive context provided by the most recent advances in (language) technology. The computing power currently available allows language to be processed in a way that realistically simulates human interaction. More importantly, it also provides users with decentralisation: in the metaverse, users no longer depend on a centralised authority to establish what they can or cannot do. This leads to the ultimate aim of the metaverse: socialisation. In the metaverse, users have the power to fully socialise with others; not only to engage in online discussions, but also to collaborate with other users, produce and create entertaining content, experience new scenarios and solve problems in real-life settings.[17] They can also build their own identity (even multiple identities), including their true identity (that they are not allowed to assume in the real, physical world), their alternate identity (that they are incapable of assuming in the offline world), or even fake identities (which they want to – and can – assume in the metaverse). As they are given the opportunity to create their own virtual spaces, users can express and actualise themselves in unprecedented ways.[18] In the metaverse, they can be what they are, but also what they would like to be and, more importantly, socially interact in previously unthinkable ways. This includes repurposing language rights, whatever its advantages and disadvantages may be, especially in translation scenarios.

3. LAW, ETHICS AND RESPONSIBILITY IN THE METAVERSE

A much-desired feature of metaverse-related technologies is increasing the development of humanisation skills across different fields by encouraging sociability, affection and emotional understanding and sympathy among users in technology-mediated communication. However, so far, this potential has not been fully realised, despite all attempts made,[19] largely because technology-mediated communication acts as a barrier to said humanisation. Conversely, examples of the disadvantages of the metaverse abound, including trespassing on user rights and freedoms, deceiving and ignoring citizens'

16 Ng (n 2).
17 Ibid.
18 Oh, Yi and Kim (n 7).
19 Maria Gonzalez-Moreno and others, 'Improving Humanization through Metaverse-Related Technologies: A Systematic Review' (2023) 12 *Electronics* 1727.

choices, or failing to grant accessibility and affordability to all, instead of only those who have sufficient financial, technical and technological resources. The seamlessly interconnected metaverse has a noticeable impact on how people interact, how they live and work, and create and share content. The metaverse thus increasingly mirrors *real* physical life in its virtues and vices.[20]

From a social perspective, the possibilities offered by the metaverse are endless, thanks to the new forms of interaction and collaboration among citizens and the new immersive cultural experiences provided. The simulation scenarios offered by the metaverse make it possible to simulate emergency scenarios and consequently provide better health services; in the education sector, they support more engaging forms of education and training based on more experiential learning processes; and in the public services sector, new forms of engaging with people emerge which enable more personalised administrative services (including providing remote assistance in remote and rural areas). On a larger scale, the metaverse makes it possible to improve life in communities; for example, via the preservation or reconstruction of cultural heritage, in as much as this contributes to enhancing democratic participation, since citizens have new more engaging opportunities to have a voice in public affairs.[21] Unsurprisingly, therefore, these virtual worlds are situated at the intersection of law, ethics, and responsibility.

In the legal arena, digital worlds have long faced unlawful activities. Starting by mimicking real-life criminal activities in virtual spaces,[22] cybercriminals have meanwhile devised new offences that not only replicate real crime in virtual worlds but also augment it. Nevertheless, developments in the metaverse also bring significant challenges to fundamental human rights and, in the EU, to shared values such as user safety, confidence, empowerment, and respect for people's rights. In that sense, users need to be granted the right to privacy protection, protection against cyber-violence, hate speech and exclusion, as well as all forms of disinformation.

The emerging metaverse is also likely to result in new ethical challenges, related in particular to the misuse of personal data to improve communication in the metaverse. While, from a legal perspective, personal data are handled by the General Data Protection Regulation (GDPR), legal conformity does not necessarily equate with ethical compliance. One example is that companies operating in the EU are required to observe the provisions of the GDPR, but often deceivingly obtain holders' consent to secure their data, analytics and information. The problem, in this case, is not whether the data holder has

---

20 Adrien Basdevant, Camille François and Rémi Ronfard, *Mission Exploratoire Sur Les Métavers* (Gouvernement de France 2022).

21 Commission (n 9).

22 Holt and Bossler (n 13).

granted access to their data, but rather whether the access is based on genuinely informed consent.

The metaverse consequently raises the issues of responsibility and liability, not only due to the risk that lower EU social standards might be imposed on users of virtual worlds,[23] but also due to issues related to instruction, assessment, planning and preserving languages.[24] Despite these challenges, the interoperability potential offered by the metaverse enables users to benefit from freedom of choice, while championing sustainability, inclusion and accessibility – all of which underlie the technological developments in the metaverse.[25]

In the EU, a robust legislative framework already exists that applies to the virtual worlds and to the development of the metaverse, including the Digital Services Act, the Digital Markets Act, the Data Governance Act, the AI Act (which aims to address the emerging risks arising from AI, while promoting trustworthy AI), the aforementioned GDPR, among others (e.g., the EU consumer law). Altogether, these aim to mitigate the risks underlying the development of the metaverse, although it is very likely that some risks will remain high. One example of these risks is access to the metaverse by people with disabilities or linguistic limitations, which will doubtless remain a challenge, despite the European Accessibility Act and the Web Accessibility Directive.

4. TRANSLINGUAL COMMUNICATION IN THE METAVERSE

While virtual worlds have no physical barriers or frontiers preventing people from communicating and socialising, the physical world's language barriers may persist, as they originate from the multilingualism and multiculturalism characterising international environments, including the metaverse. Automated translation has been offered as a solution to this problem. In 2000, Lehman-Wilzig envisioned synchronous automated translation systems that would make instantaneous communication possible between people speaking different languages.[26] Since then, advances first in neural machine translation technology (NMT), which forms the basis of popular tools like Google Translate, and more recently in generative AI based on large language models,

---

23 Commission (n 9).

24 Patriann Smith, 'Black Immigrants in the United States: Transraciolinguistic Justice for Imagined Futures in a Global Metaverse' (2022) 42 *Annual Review of Applied Linguistics* 109.

25 Commission (n 9).

26 Sam Lehman-Wilzig, 'The Tower of Babel vs the Power of Babble: Future Political, Economic and Cultural Consequences of Synchronous, Automated Translation Systems' (2000) 2 *New Media & Society* 467.

such as ChatGPT, have brought this idea closer.[27] Translation technology is already widely used and integrated into websites, social media and chatbots. In the metaverse, users come from different backgrounds and speak different languages, and the natural way for them to communicate is to use their native languages.[28] While some studies promote establishing a common language in the metaverse as a solution,[29] this would jeopardise diversity and the inclusion of languages, cultures, identities and people(s). Hence, 'translation is essential, in collaboration with artificial intelligence, for the development and success of interaction and communication in the metaverse'[30] and '[t]he demand for automatic translation in virtual worlds is as strong as in the real world'[31] – perhaps even stronger.

The Virtual Babel project has already shown how a non-verbal-context-aware automated translation system can help users of the popular virtual world Second Life to understand messages in foreign languages, allowing them to communicate and socialise.[32] A recent systematic review of studies involving automated translation of communication and interaction in the metaverse revealed that while NMT approaches provide 'better linguistic solutions when dealing with complex issues in translation, such as context, ambiguity [or] interpretation', the number of languages covered is insufficient, and particularly when a minority or under-resourced language is involved in the translation pair, numerous syntactic and semantic errors and inaccuracies emerge. This inadequate level of precision in the translations leads to a notable lack of quality in the conversations. As González Vallejo argues, 'the metaverse must offer an inclusive experience and [help to preserve] languages in a virtual world, to address racism and overcome racialization'.[33]

Real-time communication and socialising between metaverse users across different languages requires developing an AI-based universal translation system, an 'instantaneous speech-to-speech translation across all languages

27 See e.g., Sai Cheong Siu, 'Revolutionising Translation with AI: Unravelling Neural Machine Translation and Generative Pre-Trained Large Language Models' in Yuhong Peng, Huihui Huang and Defeng Li (eds), *New Advances in Translation Technology* (Springer Nature Singapore 2024).

28 Ying Zhang and Nguyen Bach, 'Virtual Babel: Towards Context-Aware Machine Translation in Virtual Worlds', *Proceedings of Machine Translation Summit XII: Posters* (2009).

29 Rubén González Vallejo, 'Metaverse and Translation Studies: Analysis of Machine Translation' (2023) 2 *Metaverse Basic and Applied Research* 38.

30 Ibid., 1.

31 Zhang and Bach (n 28), 2.

32 Ibid., 2.

33 González Vallejo (n 29), 2.

[...]; the ability to communicate with anyone in any language', as Meta's Mark Zuckerberg has defined the goal of the company's No Language Left Behind programme.[34] However, today's AI-based speech translation systems are not equipped to serve the thousands of languages and their diverse varieties utilised around the world mainly due to the shortage of suitable language resources for model training,[35] and challenges of variation in spoken languages and their dialects. Currently, the common approach is still to convert speech to text for translating and then back to speech, which delays responses excessively.[36] Accordingly, the aim (and the challenge) is to develop models that translate speech-to-speech directly, without intermediate processes.[37] In addition to the translation process being quicker, such technology could enable translation for languages and language varieties without standardised writing systems.[38]

Furthermore, sensory accessibility[39] also needs to be considered. Some attention has indeed been paid to making the metaverse inclusive for blind and visually impaired people.[40] However, while some work has addressed

---

34 Andre Syafrony and Vica Ananta Kusuma, 'Universal Language Translator: Is This the Future or the Doom of Language Learning?' (2022) 2 *Jurnal Humaya: Jurnal Hukum, Humaniora, Masyarakat, dan Budaya* 93.

35 Cf. Pratik Joshi and others, 'The State and Fate of Linguistic Diversity and Inclusion in the NLP World', *Proceedings of the 58th Annual Meeting of the Association for Computational Linguistics* (Association for Computational Linguistics 2020).

36 Hirofumi Inaguma and others, 'UnitY: Two-Pass Direct Speech-to-Speech Translation with Discrete Units', *Proceedings of the 61st Annual Meeting of the Association for Computational Linguistics (Volume 1: Long Papers)* (Association for Computational Linguistics 2023) 15655.

37 Peng-Jen Chen and others, 'Speech-to-Speech Translation for a Real-World Unwritten Language', *Findings of the Association for Computational Linguistics: ACL 2023* (Association for Computational Linguistics 2023); Inaguma and others (n 36); Jeongsoo Choi and others, 'AV2AV: Direct Audio-Visual Speech to Audio-Visual Speech Translation with Unified Audio-Visual Speech Representation', *2024 IEEE/CVF Conference on Computer Vision and Pattern Recognition (CVPR)* (IEEE 2024).

38 Syafrony and Kusuma (n 34).

39 Cf. Maija Hirvonen and Tuija Kinnunen, 'Accessibility and Linguistic Rights' in Kaisa Koskinen and Nike K Pokorn (eds), *The Routledge Handbook of Translation and Ethics* (Routledge 2021).

40 Callum Parker and others, 'Towards an Inclusive and Accessible Metaverse', *Extended Abstracts of the 2023 CHI Conference on Human Factors in Computing Systems* (ACM 2023).

recognising and processing sign language within virtual systems,[41] less attention appears to have been paid to sign language generation in order to achieve full inclusion of the deaf and hard-of-hearing community in virtual systems in general. Although some sources provide recommendations or suggestions in order to make virtual systems more inclusive,[42] actual implementation of these recommendations in the metaverse appears distant since current virtual avatars offer relatively limited freedom of movement for hands and arms, and limited facial expression, which does not allow for proper sign language to be used in virtual scenarios.

Despite improvements, translation systems still face many challenges to becoming fully operational and helpful in the potentially highly multicultural and multilingual metaverse domain, where languages are spoken spontaneously, with unrestricted vocabulary and register. These challenges include the need for translation systems to address numerous cultural issues, and translation in the metaverse may require 'extensive culturalisation of content, including certain non-verbal elements such as icons and layouts, to make the presentation more suitable for the target audience'.[43] Nowadays, such culturalisation may also involve inclusion criteria, such as readability for people with special needs or plain language in legal texts for a general audience, or unbiasing when dealing with gender-biased language. These aspects need to be addressed seamlessly for cross-lingual, cross-cultural communication to succeed in the metaverse.

Studies focusing on visual culture in the metaverse show that virtual worlds are created and shaped by their users; sometimes replicating reality and real objects and designing new, imagined realities and objects, which may further

---

41 Natalie Hollain, Martha Larson and Floris Roelofsen, 'Analyzing the Potential of Linguistic Features for Sign Spotting: A Look at Approximative Features', *Proceedings of the Second International Workshop on Automatic Translation for Signed and Spoken Languages* (EAMT 2023); Mario Perez-Enriquez, Jose Luis Lopez-Cuadrado and Israel Gonzalez-Carrasco, 'Platform for Accessible Online Learning', *Proceedings of the XXIV International Conference on Human Computer Interaction* (ACM 2024).

42 Dhruv Jain and others, 'Towards Sound Accessibility in Virtual Reality', *Proceedings of the 2021 International Conference on Multimodal Interaction* (ACM 2021); Irene Mazza and others, 'Poster: An Exploratory Analysis to Elicit Requirements for Avatar-Based Interfaces Aimed at the Deaf Community', *Proceedings of the 15th Biannual Conference of the Italian SIGCHI Chapter* (ACM 2023).

43 Sam Berner, '"Lost in Translation": Cross-Lingual Communication, and Virtual Academic Communities', *5th Annual Conference on World Wide Web Applications* (2003), 8.

complicate and diversify the visual culture of the metaverse.[44] However, users belonging to a different culture (and hence also translation systems) may perceive or conceptualise other users' creations in a different way. Therefore, localisation (in this case, from the culturalisation perspective) is essential in the metaverse. However, the automation of localisation, including the localisation of visual elements, such as digital 3D objects, images, and non-standardised icons, remains a problem that future technology will hopefully help solve.

Culture-aware translation can be viewed as part of the wider, more complex problem of pragmatics-aware translation, which characterises (or should characterise) human translation, but not necessarily current translation technology. Pragmatics-aware translation has to handle or interpret correctly not only cultural aspects, but also other kinds of contextual information and knowledge.[45] Such information includes implicit and explicit context-aware, circumstantial references like time, date, season, and location, or multimodal references in sign language, as well as higher-level rules and protocols, like politeness and proper ways of addressing the hearer.[46] Finally, the meaning of a speech act, referring to the actual meaning or intention of the speaker, may differ from what is being said.[47] While current translation systems appear to address the circumstantial references with relative success, they still struggle with the higher-level figurative and implicit uses of language, which may hinder the intention of the speaker especially in less common language pairs. Furthermore, aspects such as politeness and implied meanings vary across groups of people or geographical language varieties, making their use and translation challenging even for native speakers and experienced human translators. While research on the metaverse is still scarce, general theoretical perspectives highlight the significance of pragmatic issues, such as the participation structure, the

44 Hsiao-Cheng Sandrine Han, 'Visual Culture Versus Virtual Culture: When the Visual Culture Is All Made by Virtual World Users' (2017) 1 *International Journal of Virtual and Augmented Reality* 60.

45 Cf. George Yule, *Pragmatics* (21st ed, OUP 2014).

46 Rachel Mapson, 'Im/Politeness and Interpreting' in Rebecca Tipton and Louisa Desilla (eds), *The Routledge Handbook of Translation and Pragmatics* (Routledge 2019); Christopher Stone, 'Pointing, Telling and Showing – Multimodal Deictic Enrichment during in-Vision News Sign Language Translation' in Tipton and Desilla, ibid.

47 Silvia Bruti, 'Speech Acts and Translation' in Tipton and Desilla, ibid.; Carlos de Pablos-Ortega, '"I'm so Sorry to Disturb You but I Wonder If I Could Have Your Autograph" versus ¿Me Firma Un Autógrafo Por Favor? – Contrastive (in)Directness in Subtitling' in Tipton andDesilla, ibid.

medium and other circumstances of communication,[48] as well as the impact of context and contextualisation.[49] Questions of difference, context and audience are raised also by the impact of multimodality; for example, in the form of advertisements,[50] and the translation of 2D works into 3D galleries and other forms of virtual art.[51]

Regarding languages and the metaverse, perhaps the main challenge for future technology is the issue of augmentation. In visions of the metaverse, translation systems combined with facial augmentation technology,[52] full sense integration and more realistic avatars with improved freedom of movement and facial expressions can provide an actual feeling of reality. In this scenario, communication flows seamlessly, independent of the language spoken by the metaverse users, since this technology should enable the instantaneous and accurate interpreting of each speaker's speech into the hearer(s) language (where the 'No Language Left Behind' principle should apply), who would not even notice that the speaker is using a different language (variety). This scenario, which we will refer to as translingual metaverse communication, may have implications for the users' language rights, which we will examine next.

5. DEFINING LANGUAGE RIGHTS

Language rights refer to 'all rights related to the learning and use of languages', while language varieties, such as regional dialects, are sometimes included under the broader term linguistic rights.[53] Arguments for language rights are grounded, on the one hand, on an instrumental view of language as enabling access to information, communication and societal participation, and on the other hand, on views emphasising the importance of language for the identity, autonomy and dignity of an individual.[54] The instrumental view also

---

48 Daria Dayter, Miriam A Locher and Thomas C Messerli, *Pragmatics in Translation: Mediality, Participation and Relational Work* (CUP 2023).

49 Rebecca Tipton and Louisa Desilla (eds), *The Routledge Handbook of Translation and Pragmatics* (Routledge 2019).

50 Cristina Valdés, 'Advertising Translation and Pragmatics' in Tipton and Desilla, ibid.

51 Patrick Lichty, 'The Translation of Art in Virtual Worlds' in Mark Grimshaw-Aagaard (ed), *The Oxford Handbook of Virtuality* (OUP 2014).

52 Sayers and others (n 15).

53 Tove Skutnabb-Kangas, 'Linguistic Human Rights' in Carol A Chapelle (ed), *The Encyclopedia of Applied Linguistics* (Blackwell Publishing 2012), 1.

54 Stephen May, 'Multilingualism and Language Rights' in Chapelle, ibid.; Jacqueline Mowbray, 'Translation as Marginalisation? International Law, Translation and the Status of Linguistic Minorities' in Gabriel González Núñez

connects to accessibility: linguistic aspects of access have recently been raised alongside more traditional, physical, social, sensory and cognitive aspects of accessibility.[55] Some identity perspectives appear to rely on a deterministic, essentialised linking of language and (ethnic) identity, while others argue that language is not a determining factor of identity, although still significant.[56] The key aspects are the right for members of linguistic minorities to maintain their membership in that culture and for members of the community to control ongoing linguistic and cultural change and development.[57]

International law and treaties can grant rights to languages themselves, as is the case with the European Charter for Regional or Minority Languages, which stipulates measures to promote minority languages.[58] More commonly, however, language rights are granted collectively to speakers of minority languages; for example, in the Council of Europe's Framework Convention for the Protection of National Minorities, the United Nations Declaration on the Rights of Indigenous Peoples, and the UN Convention on the Rights of Persons with Disabilities, which has important provisions for the use of signed languages.[59] These collective rights include, for example, the right to use one's own language when interacting with public services and authorities, and participating in political, cultural, social and economic life.[60] Such rights tend to be limited to officially recognised national or regional language minorities, while migrants and refugees are generally not afforded the same status.[61] Linguistic rights that apply to all individuals can also be derived from general human rights instruments, such as the United Nations' Universal Declaration of Human Rights, International Covenant on Economic, Social and Cultural Rights and International Covenant on Civil and Political Rights.[62] These include specific rights like the right to translation and interpreting at criminal proceedings (Directive 2010/64/EU of the European Parliament and of the Council of 20 October 2010) or as a way to access medical services to guarantee the right to health.[63] As a minimum, speakers of all languages should have the right to use their preferred language in the private sphere, without

and Reine Meylaerts (eds), *Translation and Public Policy: Interdisciplinary Perspectives and Case Studies* (Routledge 2017).

55 Hirvonen and Kinnunen (n 39).

56 May (n 54).

57 Ibid.

58 Skutnabb-Kangas (n 53). See also Mowbray (n 54).

59 Skutnabb-Kangas (n 53).

60 Mowbray (n 54). See also Hirvonen and Kinnunen (n 39).

61 May (n 54).

62 Skutnabb-Kangas (n 53).

63 Mowbray (n 54).

discrimination or the interference of the state[64] – whether those speakers can go about without social discrimination or interference is a different matter. Following the interpretation of Skutnabb-Kangas,[65] our discussion aims to address implications not only for members of officially recognised linguistic minorities in a given society, but more broadly all non-dominant language groups.

6. IMPLICATIONS FOR LANGUAGE RIGHTS FROM TRANSLINGUAL METAVERSE COMMUNICATION

The instantaneous accurate translingual metaverse communication envisioned in Section 4 would make it possible for all users to communicate with others independent of the language spoken by each participant in the interaction, and provide everyone access to the same information, discussions, collaborations and entertainment in the metaverse. This would allow all individuals in multilingual communities to socialise and communicate without giving preference to any specific language.[66] The multilingualism enabled by technology could broaden access for minority language speakers to public services, healthcare and educational opportunities and empower speakers of minority languages to participate in public discussion, political and civic activity, and decision-making.[67] It can be argued that, in this manner, translingual metaverse communication would support the realisation of the right to use one's own language and the connected rights to information and to participation in political, civic, cultural, social and economic life. This idealised vision, however, comes with some caveats.

One key consideration involves the quality offered by translingual metaverse communication. While the technology has improved and will likely continue to develop, the potential for translation errors cannot be fully eliminated in translingual metaverse communication. Misunderstandings and miscommunications caused by faulty translations can have potentially severe consequences

---

64 Skutnabb-Kangas (n 53).

65 Ibid.

66 Cf. Lehman-Wilzig (n 26).

67 Petra Lea Láncos, 'The Role of Language Technologies in Promoting the Participation of Linguistic Minorities in Social, Political and Economic Life' (2021) 14 *Foreign Policy Review* 73; Olga Torres-Hostench, 'Europe, Multilingualism and Machine Translation' in Dorothy Kenny (ed), *Machine Translation for Everyone: Empowering Users in the Age of Artificial Intelligence* (Language Science Press 2022); Luis Cabrera, 'Babel Fish Democracy? Prospects for Addressing Democratic Language Barriers through Machine Translation and Interpretation' (2024) 68 *American Journal of Political Science* 767.

including physical injury or even death, damage to property, financial damage and legal consequences.[68] Quality issues are often also downplayed in popularised accounts of translation technology, which tend to frame it as infallible, nearly magical, and treat errors as unexpected aberrations, if they are even mentioned.[69] Reflecting such accounts, unrealistic views that '[i]n practice, artificial intelligence can perform even better than humans in many narrow sectors such as translation'[70] can lead to a situation where service providers – public or private – decide that automated translation alone is sufficient for serving speakers of some languages in the metaverse (on the grounds that technology is good enough to get a gist of the text), while speakers of dominant languages are offered human-created content and direct communication. Since translation quality is generally poorer for under-resourced languages, overreliance on translation technology places members of already disadvantaged groups at a further disadvantage.[71] In this way, translingual metaverse communication could have adverse implications for the equal treatment of languages and their speakers.

A second consideration relates to the fact that people's way of expressing themselves through language affects how others perceive them. For example, literally translating expressions from one language to another, as is sometimes done by people speaking a foreign language, can lead the hearers to make unfairly negative assumptions about the speaker's intelligence, credibility or honesty.[72] Similar issues could arise in translingual metaverse communication, if the technology cannot account for pragmatic and cultural differences. Furthermore, the language models behind translation technology have been observed to replicate and even exacerbate biases and harmful stereotypes found in the training data, and even to introduce biased or offensive features

---

[68] Maarit Koponen and Mary Nurminen, 'Risk Management for Content Delivery via Raw Machine Translation' in Marion Winters, Sharon Deane-Cox and Ursula Böser (eds), *Translation, Interpreting and Technological Change: Innovations in Research, Practice and Training* (Bloomsbury 2024).

[69] Lucas Nunes Vieira, 'Machine Translation in the News: A Framing Analysis of the Written Press' (2020) 9 *Translation Spaces* 98.

[70] Steering Group of the Artificial Intelligence Programme, *Finland's Age of Artificial Intelligence* (Ministry of Economic Affairs and Employment 2017), 64.

[71] Lucas Nunes Vieira, Minako O'Hagan and Carol O'Sullivan, 'Understanding the Societal Impacts of Machine Translation: A Critical Review of the Literature on Medical and Legal Use Cases' (2020) 24 *Information Communication and Society* 1515; Laura Weidinger and others, 'Taxonomy of Risks Posed by Language Models', *2022 ACM Conference on Fairness, Accountability, and Transparency* (ACM 2022).

[72] Cf. Yael Peled, 'Language Barriers and Epistemic Injustice in Healthcare Settings' (2018) 32 *Bioethics* 360.

in translations when no corresponding feature is present in the source.[73] Particularly if the participants in the interaction have an unrealistic impression of translation technology as an infallibly accurate and neutral representation of what was said and have an insufficient understanding of the role of cultural and pragmatic aspects, they blame perceived oddities or inconsistencies on the speaker rather than the technology. In this way, technology can also have an adverse impact on people's right to self-expression.

From the identity perspective, one central idea is that members of a linguistic community have the right to control the development of their language.[74] While translingual metaverse communication can support language revitalisation and preservation efforts by allowing people to use the minority language, there is the risk that the language produced by the speakers themselves could become overpowered by automatically translated discourse, which tends to reflect the cultural, pragmatic and discourse practices of the source language.[75] Being exposed to overwhelming amounts of such language could especially lead minority languages that lack an established standard form to develop according to the features of the source language (and the technology) rather than on its own terms. The seamless integration of translingual metaverse communication could also reduce and even hide linguistic (and cultural) diversity, lowering the general awareness of minority languages (or even accents) and decreasing interest in learning them.[76]

Another perspective relates to the broader nature of the metaverse where the users can not only choose to represent their true identity (for which the ability to use their own minority language could be beneficial), but also to misrepresent themselves with a fake identity. For example, someone could pose as a member of a minority language community in order to produce harmful or deceitful content, including offensive and disrespectful comments, gain an unfair advantage, or produce disinformation.[77] Recent generative AI systems make it easy for anyone to instantly produce harmful content in any language. Even good intentions can lead to harmful impacts. For example, when nearly half of the Wikipedia articles in the Scots language were found to have been written by a user who had no knowledge of Scots, and therefore did not reflect

---

73 Weidinger and others (n 71).

74 May (n 54).

75 Nora Aranberri and Uxoa Iñurrieta, 'When Minoritized Languages Encounter MT: Perceptions and Expectations of the Basque Community' (2024) 41 *Journal of Specialised Translation* 179.

76 Lehman-Wilzig (n 26).

77 Rui Sousa-Silva, '"We Attempted to Deliver Your Package": Forensic Translation in the Fight Against Cross-Border Cybercrime' (2024) 37 *International Journal for the Semiotics of Law* 1323.

the actual grammar and vocabulary of the language, the Scots-speaking community raised concerns about this misrepresentation of their language, which contributed to a perception that it is not a real language.[78]

7. RECOMMENDATIONS FOR TRANSLINGUAL METAVERSE COMMUNICATION

In this chapter, we have aimed at examining how translingual communication may be enabled by the metaverse and what implications this may have for language rights. While some implications may be positive, the potential negatives must also be considered. In general, some guiding principles are required to design a desirable and fair metaverse, all of which have a direct or indirect impact on language rights: freedom of choice, sustainability, humanisation and human-centricity, health, education, safety and security, transparency, and inclusion.[79] These values can be granted in the metaverse by improving and promoting its fair and just development. In this discussion, we aim to draft some recommendations with a view specifically to upholding language rights.

For language rights, the potential major ethical challenge of the metaverse is equality and accessibility. If technological developments are driven by demand, companies are likely to invest more in more widely spoken languages. Conversely, little investment is likely to be made in under-resourced languages, where support is most needed. As a result, the citizens who are most likely to need the metaverse are the ones who are most likely to struggle with access to it, either due to unequal availability of solutions for their languages, or due to their cost being insurmountable.[80] Furthermore, the virtual environment could form obstacles to blind or deaf people. Consequently, the metaverse may remain only accessible to the chosen few. Achieving the goal of translingual metaverse communication entails raising the quality of the output of translation systems to match real human-like quality. However, this will likely require new hybrid approaches or innovations that improve accuracy but do not increase response delays, particularly for the kind of spontaneous, unrestricted and colloquial communication that is likely to occur in a multilingual metaverse. To truly support diversity, identity and inclusion in this communication, technological development needs to take into account different languages (and language variants), sensory accessibility, as well as cost.

---

[78] Stephen Harrison, 'What Happens to Scots Wikipedia Now?' (*Slate* 2020) https://slate.com/technology/2020/09/scots-wikipedia-language-american-teenager.html accessed 6 February 2026.

[79] Commission (n 9).

[80] Sayers and others (n 15).

Considering the potentially adverse effects of automatically translated discourse on the preservation and development of languages, particularly minority or endangered languages, some have even proposed that language and translation technology solutions should not be made publicly available until they can be demonstrated to reach a sufficient level of quality.[81] However, it is not straightforward how such a level would be defined and assessed,[82] and members of linguistic minorities themselves may find less than perfect translations useful for instrumental communication purposes. In any case, the linguistic communities should have a say in how technology is developed and used for their language.

Seamless and instantaneous translingual metaverse communication may mean that users do not even realise that they are not interacting directly with the other person in a shared language but speaking to each other through technology. As discussed in Section 6, this can lead to problems such as misunderstanding, misrepresenting, or misjudging the other person. Therefore, transparency is needed: users need to be made aware if and when information or interactions are being translated automatically, similar to current practices of placing disclaimers on machine-translated websites or documents.[83] However, such disclaimers may run counter to the very goals of metaverse developers, who aim to provide seamless integrated systems where users cannot tell physical from virtual worlds. This may thus entail a broader focus on AI literacy, including raising awareness not only of how translation systems work, but also what problems may arise, and how to use this technology in a responsible manner.[84] For example, it may be necessary to recognise that automated translation as the only solution is not appropriate for certain high-risk situations, such as healthcare or legal settings.

Another concern is the question of liability. Where does responsibility lie if miscommunications caused by the technology lead to harm? One issue is the generation of translation errors and hallucinations (i.e., factually false information that is presented to users as truthful), which may lead to critical miscommunication events, particularly when interlocutors do not have control over the information. Moreover, generative AI relies on large language models that feed on vast amounts of often unacknowledged training data, which means that users run the risk of inadvertently infringing copyright and intellectual property. Until now, providers of machine translation tools and developers of

---

81 Lynne Bowker, 'Translation Technology and Ethics' in Kaisa Koskinen and Nike K Pokorn (eds), *The Routledge Handbook of Translation and Ethics* (Routledge 2021).

82 Bowker, ibid.; see also Weidinger and others (n 71).

83 Cf. Koponen and Nurminen (n 68).

84 Vieira, O'Hagan and O'Sullivan (n 71).

generative AI systems have warded off any responsibility by presenting users with a disclaimer of how their systems build upon AI, and therefore are not guaranteed to be fully accurate. It is thus safe to assume that any responsibility resulting from the use of such systems lies with the user. All these issues need to be resolved before translingual metaverse communication can become sufficiently reliable for users to communicate seamlessly in the metaverse.

In the EU, one of the main aims of the Artificial Intelligence Act is to promote trustworthy AI, providing a solid first step to providing the right to safety and inclusion for metaverse users. The Act's approach to prohibiting social scoring, whereby people are classified according to their personal characteristics or behaviour, as well as the need to officially register systems designed to provide assistance in legal interpretation and the application of the law, are demonstrative of the Union's good intentions and will help shape the future of the metaverse. The AI Act is a high-stakes attempt to strike a balance between safety and fundamental rights, on the one hand, and decentralisation, on the other. Decentralisation being one of the major basic tenets of the metaverse that allows users to communicate freely and independently of a central controlling authority; a careful approach by regulatory authorities is required to ensure a balance between the potentially conflicting concepts of guaranteeing safety and granting all forms of fundamental rights, including language rights, and offering individuals the power to choose how to communicate. As users are granted decentralised control, they will have the opportunity to infringe the rights of others, in which case a technological, political or legal authority will be called upon to resolve conflicting interests. That balance can be difficult to achieve and is likely to be imperfect, and depending on how such authority is exerted in the metaverse, the consequences may be dire. Nevertheless, the democratisation potential of the metaverse is invaluable, given the freedom of choice that it will offer users and the power that they are given to enforce their own rights, while also standing up for the rights of others.

Finally, the development and use of the technology needed for translingual metaverse communication intersects with wider societal and even global issues, including environmental and economic sustainability. Environmental concerns involve the energy consumption, emissions, and use of natural resources required for building hardware and managing software.[85] Developing the language models needed for the approximately 6,000 to 7,000 languages and additional language varieties spoken in the world also entails vast economic investment, with further costs arising from keeping the solutions up to date,

[85] See e.g., Emily M Bender and others, 'On the Dangers of Stochastic Parrots: Can Language Models Be Too Big?', *Proceedings of the 2021 ACM Conference on Fairness, Accountability, and Transparency* (ACM 2021); Weidinger and others (n 71).

integrated and interoperating in the metaverse. Instead of competing development by multiple (private and public) actors, joint efforts by companies and governments might be needed to support the fair and sustainable development of translingual metaverse communication.

8. CONCLUSION

In the previous discussions, we have envisioned a form of translingual communication enabled by instantaneous automatic translation seamlessly integrated into the metaverse. While this scenario remains speculative for now, the necessary technological building blocks already exist or are being developed. We therefore contend that future implementation of these technologies in the metaverse is foreseeable. It is likely that, in the near future, technology will move from large language models, which exacerbate and maximise the most evident language patterns of the vast majority of speakers, to medium-sized models. These will hopefully more accurately represent the diversity of languages, regardless of the statistical weight of those features, which is strikingly different from technology-shaped language use.

Although we posit translingual metaverse communication as possible, even likely, it is not our intention to argue that it is recommended or desirable in all possible communication scenarios. While such technology-enabled communication could be well suited to allow people to use their own (or preferred) language in the private sphere, in interactions between citizens and public services the risk of misunderstandings as outlined in Section 6 may be much greater. Furthermore, as noted, translingual metaverse communication could have negative impacts on language as part of culture and identity. Upholding language rights in the metaverse is therefore a multifaceted issue. With careful consideration of the implications, caveats and recommendations outlined here, translingual metaverse communication could one day allow world citizens to communicate across languages in a seamlessly integrated technological environment, yet with the imperfections that punctuate humanisation.

ACKNOWLEDGEMENTS

The work of Maarit Koponen is partially funded by the Strategic Research Council (SRC) established within the Research Council of Finland – funding agreements 352577 (University of Eastern Finland) and 352557 (DECA consortium coordinator University of Helsinki). The work of Rui Sousa-Silva is funded from national funds by the Fundação para a Ciência e a Tecnologia, I.P. (FCT), project UID/00022, CLUP – Centre for Linguistics of the University of Porto (DOI: https://doi.org/10.54499/UID/00022/2025). The work of Antonio Pareja-Lora is partially funded by the Spanish Ministry of Science and Innovation, Knowledge Generation Programme, via the PRAGMACOR ('Corpus pragmatics and telephone interpreting: analysis of face threatening acts in telephone interpreting') project grant, with ref. n.º PID2021-127196NA-I00. The collaboration has been facilitated by the COST Action 'Language in the Human–Machine Era' LITHME (CA19102), funded by COST (European Cooperation in Science and Technology).

6. Virtual public spaces

Riku Neuvonen

Virtual reality and the metaverse have been advertised as public spaces by tech companies.[1] In this context, space is conceptualised as being a meeting point for avatars and enabling activities that are different from those in physical reality. Spaces as places have a significant function for societies, especially places that are intended for meetings, activities and communicating.

Traditionally, these places are open to everyone, which makes them public places.[2] They have a public function as public forums. In this chapter, I will analyse how virtual worlds could be understood as public places and based on what the criteria are. I will utilise legal geography, theoretical approaches to the internet and private places as public places, and communication rights to establish a viewpoint on how these places function as public places.

The internet has been considered a public space in many approaches from different disciplines. A public space is by definition a place that is open to the public; that is, everyone, and is not dependent on relationships with companies or memberships. Public places are places to be in the public and for public activities. Therefore, these places are open and transparent. Public places can be used for the functions of public life and the public sphere – for public debates, demonstrations, and meetings, but also for public appearances. Public spaces function as spaces for both public and private activities.

Public places are difficult to define in practice because even publicly owned places might have access restrictions or a certain place might be designated for a certain purpose. Then there is a kind of grey zone between public places and private areas. Along with the public space, there are semi-public spaces and private spaces. Semi-public spaces refer to public administration facilities or commercial facilities, such as shopping centres. We all have free access to

1 In this chapter, the concept of space is more concrete and related to physical space (places) than to the concepts of space used in social theory. See Henri Lefebvre, 'The Production of Space', in Jen Jack Gieseking and others (eds), *The People, Place, and Space Reader* (Routledge 1991).

2 Setha M. Low, *Why Public Space Matters* (Oxford University Press 2023).

these places, but the owner of the space has the right to close it and prevent people from entering.

The problem of public spaces can be approached from the viewpoint of geography, and especially in jurisprudence these issues are related to legal geography. From the legal geography viewpoint, spaces are such that they can be drawn on a map or measured.[3] Transferring the spatial concept to the virtual world requires a different approach. For example, the buyer of a virtual island owns the right to the digital form of the island, whereas an owner of a real island owns the island. The digital form can be changed, and it exists only virtually.

As mentioned, the public space is by definition freely accessible to everyone. Access to semi-public places can be limited to some extent. A third category is private space where the intensity of privacy can vary; for example, from the yard to the interior of the apartment, or from the lobby of an office building to the workrooms behind locked doors. These divisions apply to the built environment. Outside the built environment, space can be private or public, but in some countries, for example, in Nordic countries, everyone has the right to access that space to walk or even pick berries.[4]

In a legal context, space is often absolute; that is, it is viewed as physical and measurable and can be represented on a map.[5] Location, distances, and how the geometric patterns that structure the space drawn on the map are named are essential. Legally, the space must be able to be located and determined with such precision and permanence that it is possible to derive rights and obligations. Most space is owned, and ownership must be demonstrable, most often with the help of a map, boundary posts, and coordinates.

The internet, and especially virtual applications, are by definition virtual. This leads to several problems when applying definitions of physical space to virtual environments. However, my starting point is that the idea of the internet as a public space is fundamentally misleading. The internet was developed by public institutions, such as the military and universities.[6] However, access

---

3 Nicholas Blomley, 'Learning from Larry: Pragmatism and Habits of Legal Space', in Irus Braverman and others (eds), *The Expanding Spaces of Law: A Timely Legal Geography* (Stanford University Press 2014), 78.

4 Riku Neuvonen, 'Kenelle kaupunkitila kuuluu? Kaupunkien julkiset tilat oikeuksien verkostona', in Pia Bäcklund, Jouni Häkli and Harry Schulman (eds), *Kansalaiset kaupunkia kehittämässä* (Tampere University Press 2017). There are similar rights, e.g., in Sweden, Scotland and Switzerland.

5 John Agnew, *Place and Politics* (Allen and Unwin 1987), 13.

6 Manuel Castells, *The Network Society: A Cross-Cultural Perspective* (Edward Elgar 2004); Janet Abbate, *Inventing the Internet* (MIT Press 1999).

to the internet requires devices and connections offered by private companies.[7] Similarly, many services, such as hosting services, were commercial from the beginning. Using the internet also requires special software, an internet browser, or an application that is designed for a certain task.

Following the breakthrough of the internet in the 1990s, cyberutopists and cyberlibertarians believed in an open internet, but now the internet is closed, and phenomena such as cyberfeudalism and cybercolonialism abound.[8] This stems from the situation in which all virtual applications and software, as well as connections and hardware, are offered by private companies. The contemporary internet is based mostly on a platform economy, meaning that platforms, search engines, and cloud services have privatised internet space. From the viewpoint of content, social media services and, for example, streaming services, have monopolised access to content. The consequence is that unlike the 2D internet, the 3D virtual world will be built on private and commercial grounds.

In this chapter, the key issue is access to virtual applications. In this context, the argumentation is based on access to internet-related discussions and analogies made from this. Another issue is the definition of virtual public space. The definitions of spaces in the chapter are based on legal geographical concepts that are applied to the digital environment. In this respect, the matter concerns hypothetical scenarios.

My approach is based on the Helsinki model of communication rights.[9] Communication rights have transformed into digital rights and subsequently epistemic rights. The history of communication rights dates from the 1960s and 1970s, but interest in such rights increased during the development of the internet and especially the platform economy. There are many similarities between digital rights and epistemic rights, and therefore the terms are reasonably interchangeable. My choice to use the term 'communication rights' is based on the Helsinki model being analytical and clear when applied in virtual environments.

According to the Helsinki model of communication rights, these rights can be defined as access, availability, dialogue and privacy. Access means all citizens have equal access to communication channels and the public sphere. Availability refers to different contents and communication channels being available without major obstacles, such as restrictions or even high prices. Dialogical rights refer to the idea of the public sphere in a way that citizens

---

7 See Anne Peacock, *Human Rights and the Digital Divide* (Routledge 2019).

8 See Monica Horten, *The Closing of the Net* (Polity Press 2016) and Yanis Varoufakis, *Technofeudalism: What Killed* Capitalism (The Bodley Head 2023).

9 Marko Ala-Fossi and others, 'Operationalising Communication Rights: The Case of a "Digital Welfare State"' (2019) 8(1) *Internet Policy Review*.

must have real opportunities to participate in social debates, receive information and hold opinions. Privacy guarantees that everyone is safe from unlawful intrusions, and all gathered and processed data are handled carefully. These communication rights are intertwined and align with human rights. Therefore, communication rights as a viewpoint offer a valuable way to analyse virtual environments from the perspective of different rights.

PUBLIC PLACES AND EXERCISING HUMAN RIGHTS

The internet is a constellation of networks. Therefore, it has enabled the idea of a networked public that can enjoy rights and use networks as a channel for protests. Public places are important for the enjoyment of political rights, especially freedom of assembly, which includes the right to demonstrate. This approach applies similarly to the networked public.[10] Freedom of assembly is connected closely to freedom of speech and general democratic rights to participate in public discussion. Freedom of assembly is one of the key aspects regarding access and dialogical rights.

Access to places that are public or have another importance strengthens the function of freedom of assembly. Freedom of assembly is an empty right if assemblies cannot be held in places that are socially significant. The second category comprises cultural rights. Cultural rights are necessary to promote availability, and these rights are also important for the enjoyment of dialogical rights. Culture as part of society is significant for the function of the public sphere. The UN Special Rapporteur in the field of cultural rights, Karima Bennoune, has stated that public places are necessary for the exercise of various cultural rights, and everyone should have access to such places.[11]

However, cultural rights are closely tied to freedom of speech and the exercise of freedom of assembly in a virtual environment requires access. Therefore, we can make delimitations in our approach and focus on the freedom of speech doctrine regarding public places. Another reason for this approach is that practically all human rights treaties and national constitutions protect freedom of speech, but in some countries, for example, the US, freedom of assembly is more closely connected to freedom of speech but is a right on its own. On the other hand, in some countries, for example, in Finland, the doctrine regarding freedom of assembly and cultural rights is similar to freedom of speech, which is also the case in many decisions by the European Court of Human Rights

---

10 Tetyana Lokot, 'Social Media and Protest: Contextualising the Affordances of Networked Publics', in Edoardo Celeste, Amélie Heldt and Clara Iglesias Keller (eds), *Constitutionalising Social Media* (Bloomsbury Publishing 2022).

11 UNGA, 'Report of the Special Rapporteur in the field of cultural rights' (30 July 2019) UN Doc A/74/255.

(ECtHR). Similarly, not all treaties and constitutions recognise cultural rights as a category of rights. This means that there is far more legislation and court practice considering freedom of speech and public places in a context that is parallel to virtual environments, and in many issues, doctrine and interpretation are close enough.

Analysing human rights in a virtual environment requires defining the legal status of the virtual environment. The viewpoint in this chapter is from public spaces. Therefore, it is necessary to determine which human rights are most commonly applied in the context of public places. To keep the approach concise, we need to analyse rights from the virtual perspective by applying the concepts of communication rights.

Virtuality adds another layer to the analysis because the completely artificial environment exists only in networks. All activities in the virtual environment require specific devices, software, connections, and platforms (applications). All these requirements process and store information about the user. The more developed the virtual environment is, the more data is needed, and therefore it is possible that different operators can obtain knowledge of every blink of an eye. Some adult platforms will process and store more sensitive information.

Public spaces as places for public and societal activities are as old as humankind. The early internet was compared to the agora.[12] The agora was a central public place in ancient Greek city-states. The most famous agora was in Athens, where the athletic, artistic, business, social, spiritual, and political life of the city happened. Therefore, the agora as a concept has many positive attributes. This is especially the case because Athens has been considered the birthplace of modern democracy and philosophy. The agora was a physical place where members of the polis (citizens of the city-state, i.e., free and equal men) had the opportunity to engage in dialogue with each other. Hierarchy and violence had no place in the agora.[13] Places like the agora were accessible at least to all citizens, and citizens were able to engage in dialogue on societal and cultural issues as well as present themselves in public.

Traditionally, structures and borderlines have given public space its unique form as a space. Libraries have doors and walls, and the ancient agora of Athens was surrounded by buildings and hills. In the virtual world, structures and borders are virtual. In theory, a virtual place can be in different dimensions and avatars can fly like fairies and wear togas. Some kind of idealisation

[12] Anne Wells Branscomb, *Who Owns Information? From Privacy to Public Access* (HarperCollins Publishers 1994).

[13] Niklas Damiris and Helga Wild, 'The Internet: A New Agora?', in Jaques Berleur and Diane Whitehouse (eds), *An Ethical Global Information Society* (Springer Nature Link 1997), 309.

of the agora can be seen in the development of the public sphere in the 19th century.

In classic approaches, Jürgen Habermas identifies coffee-houses and salons as places of civic society to participate in opinion making, in other words dialogue.[14] It is also noteworthy that coffee-houses were meeting places for the bourgeois class and freedom of speech advocates, such as John Stuart Mill, who were educated people who wrote for other educated people. Some might argue that in that sense, such a public sphere also resembled the agora. For the majority of people, both the agora and the coffee-house were beyond access. Similarly, the availability of newspapers, books and communication channels was limited.

The definition of the public sphere by Jürgen Habermas presupposes a few principles. First, access to public debate needs to be free and open to everybody. This criterion is similar to the definition of access in the communication rights approach. Second, all participants in a public debate must be considered equal and no subjects and topics are to be excluded from the debate. Third, the result of public deliberation is to be judged only on the basis of the best arguments and the aim of the debate is consensus and unanimity.[15] The aim is access to a sphere where dialogue can be possible.

The idea that the internet has formed a public sphere was promoted by early thinkers of digitalisation.[16] One of the key components is the concept of the network society, which was introduced in *The Network Society* by Jan van Dijk, first in Dutch in 1991, and later in English in 1999. The network society has been replaced or complemented by social networks of physical communications. In the first edition of his book, van Dijk predicted that modern society is shaping to become a network society. In the latest edition from 2020, he states that the transformation has already happened.[17] The downside is that people without access to networks will become second-class citizens.[18] Manuel Castells has argued that the internet has created links between highly concentrated media businesses and diverted audiences – in other words, created a network society.[19] Castells goes much further than van Dijk, arguing

---

14 Jürgen Habermas, *The Structural Transformation of the Public Sphere. An Inquiry into a Category of Bourgeois Society* (Thomas Burger trans., MIT Press 1991).

15 Ibid., 36–37.

16 Diana Saco, *Cybering Democracy: Public Space and the Internet* (University of Minnesota Press 2002).

17 Jan van Dijk, *The Network Society* (4th ed., SAGE 2020).

18 Ibid., 199–200.

19 Manuel Castells, *The Network Society: A Cross-Cultural Perspective* (Edward Elgar 2004).

that networks are already the basic units of our lives. The network society requires access to provide available content and opportunities for dialogue. From this perspective, freedom of speech and other human rights are in jeopardy without normative and technical guarantees.

The idea that the internet has created a golden age for freedom of speech and similarly how the internet has formed a public sphere similar to the ancient agora or Roman forum have been echoed by both cyberutopians and human rights promoters. The internet has been seen as a society in itself, a global community that creates its own global public spheres.[20] However, web 2.0 and especially platforms have changed attitudes and reality. Platforms, such as search engines and social media platforms, represent a model in which one big platform has a dominant position.[21]

In practical terms, Google is the dominant search engine and all social media platforms have their own functions, but very little competition. Therefore, Facebook is the agora or forum of a certain kind of communication, LinkedIn is a meeting place for professionals, Instagram is for sharing photos, and TikTok is for short videos, while X does not have the same societal impact that Twitter had before the rebrand. Meta Corporation (formerly known as Facebook) has spent billions of dollars to develop its Metaverse. Similarly, Microsoft has its own virtual meeting room conceptions, and gaming firms are also searching for the killer app of virtual reality. This means that virtual reality in the form of the metaverse will be created by corporations, which will (again) endanger utopias of the public sphere and challenge human rights.

ACCESS TO VIRTUAL REALITY AS A RIGHT

The UN Special Rapporteur Frank La Rue has stated that access to the internet is essential to enjoy freedom of speech. He has also emphasised the idea that states must have a positive obligation to promote universal access to the internet or else the internet will only be accessible to elites.[22] This would lead to a digital divide both inside states and between states. Therefore, he has demanded concrete political action to guarantee that the benefits of the digital society are evenly distributed.

---

20 Ingolf Pernice, 'Global Constitutionalism and the Internet: Taking People Seriously', *HIIG Discussion Paper Series No. 2015-01*, 6.

21 See for different angles Peter Lewis and Jordan Guiao (eds), *The Public Square Project: Reimagining Our Digital Future* (Melbourne University Publishing 2021).

22 UNHRC and Frank La Rue, 'Report of the Special Rapporteur on the promotion and protection of the right to freedom of opinion and expression' (27 May 2011) UN Doc A/HRC/17/27/Add.1, 60.

This approach is connected to ideas of the internet as the modern agora. The same logic was behind the landmark US Supreme Court decision *Reno v. American Civil Liberties Union* in 1997, in which the Court stated that the internet was a new medium for worldwide human communication. Such approaches were typical during the early stages of the internet, when it still had a somewhat open and competitive nature. The turning point for the internet was the rise of the platform economy, which has meant a less open and less competitive digital environment. There is practically one global search engine and several specialised social media platforms. 'The winner takes it all' has characterised the platform era of internet development.

This has been a consequence of a narrative that Daniel McCarthy has called the attempt to utilise human rights language to promote liberal democracy and capitalism.[23] This has been characteristic especially of the US and is connected to the economic *laissez-faire* concept of the marketplace of ideas and the report by the UN Special Rapporteur. Both emphasise the idea that all speakers and users of the internet are equal, and that the internet is democratic. Therefore, all problems are caused by individuals and freedom of speech as an absolute right will flourish in a digital environment. So, access to the internet can be categorised as a human right and the state should promote access but at the same time avoid over-regulation.[24] Private internet companies and especially gatekeepers such as Google and Meta have actively promoted human rights discourses and the benefits of fewer state regulations.[25]

The ECtHR has interpreted access to the internet in the landmark case of *Yıldırım v. Turkey*.[26] The Court states that national constitutions and the European Convention on Human Rights (ECHR) guarantee freedom of expression and particularly the freedom to receive ideas and information is applicable regarding access to the internet. The right to access information and communication encompasses the right of individuals to participate in the information society.[27] This obligates states to guarantee their citizens access to the internet. Therefore, the ECtHR combines access to the internet with the

---

23 Daniel McCarthy, *Power, Information Technology, and International Relations Theory* (Springer 2015), 101.

24 Marta Maroni, *The Right to Access the Internet: A Critical Analysis of the Constitutionalisation of the Internet* (Faculty of Law 2022), 71–91.

25 Rikke Frank Jørgensen, 'What Platforms Mean When They Talk About Human Rights' (2017) 9(3) *Policy & Internet* 340.

26 *Ahmet Yıldırım v. Turkey* ECHR 2012-VI 505. See also *Kalda v. Estonia*, App no 17429/10 (ECtHR, 19 January 2016) and *Jankovskis v. Lithuania*, App no 21575/08 (ECtHR 17 January 2017).

27 Peacock (n 7), 78–80.

right to impart and receive information, and exclusion from the internet is a violation of freedom of speech.[28]

It is also noteworthy that in the case of *Animal Defenders International v. UK*, the ECtHR regarded internet social media as a comparable alternative to pamphleteering and television broadcasting.[29] In the case, on the basis of national law, an advertisement was banned from being shown on television because it was interpreted as a political advertisement. Political advertising was very limited. Instead, the advertisement was shown on the internet. According to the ECtHR, the internet and social media are even more powerful media than television. Therefore, advertising is not prohibited in general, except by one method of transmission. This case demonstrates that the internet and social media were already powerful media in 2012. It is clear that 12 years later, they have become even more powerful and important. Therefore, social media and the internet are alternatives for exercising human rights, especially freedom of speech. Following that argument, virtual worlds could be considered public spaces similar to physical public spaces. This has significant consequences for the need for access to the internet and virtual worlds.

Freedom of speech is not the only human and constitutional right to consider. Freedom of assembly guaranteed in Article 11 of the ECHR has case law that could be interpreted also in virtual worlds. Articles 10 and 11 often protect similar activities and are therefore in concurrence. Neither right implicates a specific space for the exercise of rights.[30] It is noteworthy that freedom of speech is practically an absolute right in US judgments, and there is no wide margin for appreciation. In Europe, by contrast, fundamental rights and human rights are more commonly weighted and balanced. Therefore, it is possible in Europe for property rights and free speech rights to exist simultaneously in the same space.

PRIVATE SPACES AS PUBLIC FORUMS

In legal geography, there are a few examples of how public space has increased with private space. In New York, a private developer gains more building rights if part of the space is public space open to everyone.[31] In the digital

[28] Maroni (n 24), 84.

[29] *Animal Defenders International v. United Kingdom* [GC] ECHR 2013-II (extracts) 203.

[30] *Tuskia and Others v. Georgia*, App no 14237/07 (ECtHR 11 October 2018), para 72; *Ekrem Can and Others v. Turkey*, App no 10613/10 (ECtHR 8 March 2022), para 91.

[31] Jerold S. Kayden, *Privately Owned Public Space: The New York City Experience* (John Wiley and Sons 2000).

space, offering a similar incentive to companies could solve issues of access and availability. Despite this, the virtual space is based on private commercial activity, enhanced by the private control of rules and even laws.

The distinctions between public and private highlight possible solutions when analysing virtual spaces. Public places have a long history. As noted, the internet has been compared to the ancient agora, which was a place for ancient Greeks to exercise their rights as citizens. The use of the forum as a metaphor has a similar genealogy. The forum was the Roman version of the agora, a place where public life happened. Even the most famous forum, Forum Romanum in Rome, was formed quite eclectically from other younger forums in Roman towns, and they were clearly open and transparent spaces for public life and other activities of society.[32] Later, town squares had a similar function as places for political, social, and cultural activities. Therefore, metaphors of the agora and forum suggest that these places have a public nature.[33]

Private places are defined as being the opposite of public places. Private places are places where human beings can enjoy privacy, regardless of how privacy has been understood in different times. A private place is also a synonym for a privately owned place, which means that the owner has the right to control access and use. The current platforms and practically all initiatives for the metaverse assume that internet applications, such as platforms and virtual worlds, are privately owned.

The key question is whether these private virtual worlds could be considered as semi-public or public places and have public functions. Public places that have importance for society have a public function as part of the public sphere and public life. That was the core function of agoras, forums, and town squares. The ECtHR has stated that access to the internet is part of the right to impart and receive information. In addition, the Strasbourg Court considers the internet and social media as alternatives and extensions to the heritage media, even to the extent that a ban on an advertisement on television is acceptable because the advertisement can be published on the internet. From the perspective of spaces, case law from both sides of the Atlantic references the public function doctrine; that is, the doctrine of public forums. This doctrine can be divided into US and European approaches.

In the US, the Supreme Court case *Marsh v. Alabama* is the key case regarding public forum doctrine.[34] The Gulf Shipbuilding Corporation owned a town called Chickasaw, which was considered a company town, namely a

---

[32] See for different uses and models of forums Antonio López Garcia (ed), *Running Rome and Its Empire: The Places of Roman* (Routledge 2024).

[33] Cass R. Sunstein, '#Republic: Divided Democracy in the Age of Social Media', *#Republic* (Princeton University Press 2018).

[34] *Marsh v. Alabama*, 326 US 501 (1946).

town where the main employer is a big company that literally owns the whole town or at least major parts of it. In this town, Jehovah's Witness Grace Marsh attempted to distribute religious material on the sidewalk. Marsh was convicted of criminal trespass by the state of Alabama.

The Court argued that even though the company owned the town, it was open for use by the public. The incident happened near a post office, and this kind of business is freely accessible and open to people in the area and those passing through. Therefore, a company town does not have the same rights as a private homeowner. In addition, conflicts between property rights and constitutional rights should typically be resolved in favour of the latter. The Supreme Court gave its view on how this space was used and intended for use. The town was open and had businesses with a public interest, such as the post office. Therefore, the space was accessible to everyone and could be used for the exercise of constitutional rights, and furthermore, it was part of the public sphere of this town and its neighbourhood. In other words, the space was a forum with public functions.

This doctrine was applied to a shopping mall in the US Supreme Court case of *Logan Valley*.[35] In this case, the Court decided that peaceful picketing by a labour union in a privately owned shopping mall was protected under the First Amendment. The key point in the decision was that the shopping mall is a space that is generally open to the public and constitutes a business area for the local community. The owner of the private shopping mall has the right to regulate and govern access to the property and its use, but these rights cannot be exercised to violate freedom of speech. Shopping malls are more physically bounded than company towns, as they usually have doors and walls. Nevertheless, in this case, the function as an accessible space and function as a collective space for the community makes it a place usable for exercising constitutional rights. This interpretation highlights the function as a key element of the public forum.

A change in interpretation occurred in the US Supreme Court case of *Lloyd*.[36] The Court was divided, but it stated that a prohibition against distributing antiwar leaflets and protesting against the drafts for the Vietnam War was not a violation of the First Amendment. The Court argued that the distribution of leaflets and protesting against the will of the owner could be a violation of the owner's right to property.[37] The difference between this and the case of *Marsh v. Alabama* was that a company town has all the attributes of a municipality – it is a public place by nature, and the difference compared to *Logan*

35 *Food Employees v. Logan Valley Plaza Inc*, 391 US 308 (1968).
36 *Lloyd Corp Ltd v. Tanner*, 407 US 551 (1972).
37 Especially the Fifth and Fourteenth Amendments.

Valley was that in the *Logan Valley* case, the protest was against the owners of one particular store. Therefore, the argument was that the leaflets and the protest were not related to the activities of the shopping mall. Following that argument and constituting the public function and public forum, it is necessary that activities are related to the typical activities of the space in question. Finally, in the case of *Hudgens v. NLRB*, the Supreme Court found that picketing in a shopping mall by labour union members was not protected under the First Amendment.[38] The Court confirmed the earlier doctrine that the constitutional protection of freedom of speech only applies in relation to citizens and federal or state governments – a vertical relation instead of a horizontal one.[39] *Hudgens* overruled the case of *Logan Valley* but not the case of *Marsh*.

The final episode in US jurisprudence in the public function saga is the *PruneYard* judgment.[40] In this case, activists were asking passersby to sign a petition against a United Nations resolution in a privately owned shopping centre. The Court stated that at the state level, permitting citizens to exercise their right to free speech did not violate the property rights of the shopping mall owner. In addition, shopping mall owners have the right and opportunity to dissociate themselves from messages expressed in their shopping mall. The *PruneYard* case means that private places can have the character of public places if that right is provided at the state level and the private places have some kind of public function. Presumably, the estimation of the public function is based on the criteria applied in *Marsh*; that is, accessibility and the activities of the place are intended for the public to some degree.

The starting point in the ECHR is that member states are bound to respect rights guaranteed in it. However, the ECtHR has stated that sometimes positive obligations to protect and promote human rights might have horizontal effects between private parties.[41] This is possible if the Court finds that the state had a positive obligation to protect the rights of private individuals against the interference of other private parties.

It is interesting that from the viewpoint of the public function doctrine, the ECtHR has taken into account the US Supreme Court cases relating to shopping malls. In the case law of the Strasbourg Court, the most important case in this view is *Appleby*.[42] The Court argued that freedom of speech guaranteed in Article 10 of the ECHR does not recognise a specific place or forum for the exercise of free speech. In the *Appleby* case, the applicants were distributing

---

38 *Hudgens v. NLRB*, 424 US 507 (1976).

39 Cass R. Sunstein, *Democracy and the Problem of Free Speech* (The Free Press 1993), 44.

40 *Pruneyard Shopping Center v. Robins*, 447 US 74 (1980).

41 See Laurens Lavrysen, *Human Rights in a Positive State* (Intersentia 2016).

42 *Appleby and Others v. the United Kingdom* ECHR 2013-IV 185.

leaflets in a supermarket, which excluded them from the entrance area and passageways. The Court stated that the state did not violate Article 10 when it did not guarantee the free speech rights of activists in the supermarket and nearby area, which was also owned by a private company. Similar to the *Animal Defenders International* case, the Court argued that the applicants had other venues to exercise their freedom of speech.[43]

At the national level, a significant case is the *Fraport* decision in the German Constitutional Court.[44] In this case, activists were distributing leaflets at Frankfurt airport. The company that owns the airport banned the activists from the premises of the airport. However, the company was majority publicly owned. Despite this, the Court emphasised that in German constitutional law, constitutional rights have a direct or indirect effect on private relations and private actors. In this case it was a question of the indirect horizontal effect. The Court stated that freedom of assembly guaranteed the right to hold assemblies in places open to general traffic. The airport was also a special space for communicating messages to people. Therefore, the privately owned airport was a public forum in the same sense as traditional public places.[45]

These European cases demonstrate that constitutional rights are increasingly applied in relations between private parties. This is a direct horizontal effect of the constitutional rights (*Drittwirkung*) doctrine developed in German constitutional law, but it applies also in other jurisdictions. In Europe, the horizontal effect has been applied in various contexts, but the US and several other jurisdictions do not recognise the doctrine. In the context of private places, the *Drittwirkung* doctrine has been used as a public forum doctrine in cases where privately owned places are open to the public and have some kind of public function similar to public places. Therefore, we have precedents of the claim that some corners of the internet and some places in the virtual world could be considered public places, and thus public forums.[46] However, this requires more analytical and analogical analysis on what is required for such an assessment.

CONCLUSIONS

In this chapter, I have analysed how the internet has been interpreted as a public place, and in particular, how the discussion over access to the internet has

43 Peacock (n 7), 123–25.

44 BVerfG 22 February 2011, 1 BvR 699/06, Fraport.

45 Matthias C. Kettemann, *The Normative Order of the Internet: A Theory of Rule and Regulation Online* (Oxford University Press 2020), 152.

46 Anni Carlsson, *Constitutional Protection of Freedom of Expression in the Age of Social Media* (Uppsala University 2024), 451–55.

formed the right to access the internet. Similar approaches could be adapted in the case of virtual worlds. I have also adapted the public function doctrine to analyse how primarily private virtual worlds could be interpreted as places with public functions that allow wider access and opportunities to exercise constitutional and human rights.[47] This chapter provides different aspects and ideas on the question of public virtual places. This conclusion will provide some criteria and viewpoints to make assessments, but it is clear that more detailed and analytical research is needed.

Virtual worlds can be described as public spaces if they meet certain criteria. First, a virtual world has to have some kind of public function. If a virtual place is just for gaming, commercial interests, or clearly private matters, it has limited or zero public function. From the perspective of human rights and society, such functions are connected to the public sphere and democratic decision-making or public services, such as the post office in the *Marsh* case. Second, the public space must be accessible – at least in principle – to everyone. Forums and meeting places are intended for public use and are accessible to almost everyone. If virtual spaces are accessible to everyone and function like an agora, forum, or town square, they are intended to fulfil some kind of public function. The intention to create accessible space could constitute it as a public space and enable the application of human and constitutional rights.

Definitions comprise one crucial aspect of analysis. Using metaphors such as the agora or forum, the space in question is connected to political, societal and cultural life. The agora was central for citizens of the city-state, which constituted a political unit. The forum, at least in the Roman Republic, was central to state activities and the public life (politics) of Roman citizens. Such metaphors lead to the concept of a public sphere that is accessible; it is a place where information is available and dialogue on different topics is possible for citizens, members and constitutive elements of the political community. However, regarding the internet and especially platforms, people are not citizens but users and customers. This kind of vocabulary moves people from the world of public law to the world of private law. Instead of rights, we deal instead with contracts and courts. A truly public nature requires that access is guaranteed to everyone, not just clients.

Of course, it is important to notice that in the virtual world, forums and agoras are not literally similar spaces as they were in the ancient world. However, the connotation of these concepts is strong, and *forum* in particular is used to describe an open meeting place. On the internet, forum is used in the context of discussion forums, such as Bulletin Board Software (BBS), Usenet news and IRC (Internet Relay Chat), which were open and accessible by nature.

47 Ali Madanipour, *Rethinking Public Space* (Edward Elgar Publishing 2023).

Another important feature was that these different ways to communicate supplemented each other. This meant that if a user was banned from one forum, he or she could definitely find a new forum. In the platform age, the range of choices has decreased and, for example, Twitter was synonymous with important political discussion until it transformed into X. Similarly, Instagram is arguably the most significant platform for sharing images. According to the ECtHR *Animal Defenders International* case, the internet is a more powerful medium than broadcasting, and therefore it is a supplement to broadcasting. But what is a supplement to the internet and platforms? The internet is a more important medium now than it was 12 years ago, but it is less open and accessible, and platforms have become de facto monopolies. Virtual reality is still waiting for its big breakthrough, but it is already necessary to publicly discuss how to avoid the pitfalls of the platform economy.

I have adopted the viewpoint of communication rights to assess how private spaces could function as public spaces. The communication rights approach provides a few key aspects for evaluating the different facets of the public sphere and public space. Real access to the internet and virtual spaces is the most important feature. If access is restricted or access costs too much, it shuts many groups out of the political and societal sphere. Availability supports access and dialogue, ensuring that different content is available for those who have access and as material for public discourse. From my viewpoint, dialogue is the goal of different rights and also the reason why we need access and availability. The internet as a medium has become the most powerful forum for dialogue, but at the same time, the internet and platforms represent the greatest danger to public discourse. If and when virtual reality creates new spaces for opinion formation, it will be necessary for dialogue to be diverse and ensure different voices and content are not blocked by restrictions or cost.

Finally, from a communication rights perspective, it is important that privacy is a right, not a currency as in the platform economy.[48] Platforms process the data of users and use it as merchandise to guarantee profits. In virtual reality, it is possible to detect every blink of an eye and muscle movement. Therefore, in the virtual world there might well be private spaces, but equipment and software collect far more information than platforms do currently. Without privacy, there is no room for other rights.

However, despite the hype surrounding the metaverse and virtual games, there has been quite slow progress and more talk than killer apps. As has been seen with Artificial Intelligence (AI), the breakthrough could be very fast and unprecedented. Similarly, practically no one foresaw how some platforms

---

[48] Shoshana Zuboff, *The Age of Surveillance Capitalism: The Fight for a Human Future at the New Frontier of Power* (PublicAffairs 2019).

would develop into the giants they are today. For that reason, it is necessary to debate virtual reality before it is captured by corporations. Public space is one of the most important features of the public sphere and dialogue. There is a need for a public virtual space and, from the viewpoint of rights, to make such a space possible.

PART II

LEGAL SUBJECTS IN VIRTUAL WORLDS

7. The experience of virtual worlds – believability, immersion, and embodiment

Jean Du Toit and Wian Erlank

INTRODUCTION

This chapter will first investigate the individual's experience of virtual worlds by specifically looking at the concept of *level of immersion / believability* as articulated through the philosophical concept of *embodiment* to ask whether engagement with a virtual world leads to a loss of the sense of self and one's experience of a physical body. It is posited that, while one cannot escape or negate a fundamental degree of embodiment, the virtual allows for an elasticity of one's embodied experience of a world. Technological artefacts, such as VR headsets, have the ability to reshape and contort, filter and block off, remould and reorganise, transfigure and recalibrate, and otherwise modify one's embodied experience in various ways.

The experience of entering a three-dimensional digital production (or reproduction) of a navigable space via virtual reality (VR) – or an HMD (head-mounted display) and DG (data gloves) – is one that is increasingly shared by a larger contingent of the public. These technologies, once only prevalent in the imaginative realm of science fiction, have entered – to various extents – the realm of consumer electronics. The addition of 8K displays, image stabilisation technologies, more advanced processors, and the potential to integrate artificial intelligence (AI) in the future, suggests that critical reflection is needed to make sense of the legal and experiential aspects of these contemporaneous developments, both of which are addressed in this chapter.

Next, this chapter will touch on some of the legal implications of such experiential modifications via technological artefacts (while taking into consideration specific cutting-edge developments in the field, such as AI avatars).[1] This topic is especially important as our society is increasingly digitised, with Stephenson's view of a metaverse in *Snow Crash*[2] and Cline's *Ready Player One*[3] guiding and informing our arguments. When it comes to AI and avatars, such conceptualisations of embodiment[4] guide the user's ability to know when and if they are actually interacting with an AI or with a flesh-and-blood person.

The affective as part of the experiential becomes important here. We have seen that trust in the unique persona behind even an anonymous avatar is of extreme importance to users of virtual worlds, and it is expected that a shift from human-to-human relationships, when an avatar changes hands and is now in the control of a new user, will have a direct negative bearing on experiences online.[5] Additionally, the level of immersion[6] or believability (in the 'reality' of the virtual environment) experienced by a player or user in the virtual world (and eventually, possibly the metaverse)[7] will have a direct bearing on the suspension of disbelief that a person needs to undertake.

The aim of this chapter is to analyse the experience of virtual worlds in the context of law by centring the concept of embodiment. We posit that embodiment plays a crucial role in the evolving understanding of how individuals perceive and interact with virtual objects and artificially intelligent agents, and that embodiment constitutes an important point of consideration in sketching specific legal implications for the digital age. The more immersive the environment and the more users feel embodied within it, the stronger the argument for recognising embodiment in terms of its legal ramifications since embodied characteristics shape the individual's (altered) experience of space and time,

---

1 As a more developed version of the traditional NPC AI that we have seen to date.

2 Neal Stephenson, *Snow Crash* (Bantam Books 1992).

3 Ernest Cline, *Ready Player One* (Random House 2012).

4 Embodiment is understood in phenomenology as not just having a body but living through it, striving to describe how we experience our bodies from the first-person perspective as both subject and object.

5 See, e.g., Wian Erlank, 'Law and Property in Virtual Worlds' in Jonathan Marc Blitz and Woodrow Barfield (eds), *Research Handbook on the Law of Virtual and Augmented Reality* (Edward Elgar 2018), 642.

6 See Wian Erlank, *Property in Virtual Worlds* (LLD thesis, University of Stellenbosch 2012), 43–46, 265–267. Erlank (n 5), 637–641, 652–653, 660.

7 See in general Wian Erlank, 'NFTs – Buyer's Remorse and a Flash in the Pan? Some Thoughts on the Nature and Usefulness of NFTs in Virtual Worlds and the Metaverse' (2024) 36(2) *South African Mercantile Law Journal* 187, section 3 The Metaverse.

bodily integrity and avatars, and informs contemporary understandings of the virtual object in terms of property law.

The insights of phenomenologists and philosophers of technology, as well as legal scholars, are invaluable in this regard. A central argument as regards the character of the body in relation to subjectivity is provided by Maurice Merleau-Ponty, an important early 20th century phenomenologist. In terms of technology, Don Ihde[8] contends that making use of any artefact entails a transformation of the user's experience. This suggests that 'an invariant feature of all human-technology relations is … an *amplification-reduction* structure'.[9] Consider the use of a mobile phone. While certain bodily senses are enhanced (such as browsing the internet and thus being able to see news events unfold that take place far away), so other senses are withdrawn (struggling to walk while using said smartphone or colliding with an obstacle). For Ihde, artefacts embody technics in specific ways as a symbiosis of artefact and user, and this symbiosis entails that 'the use of instruments is always non-neutral, in the sense that such use inevitably involves a transformation of the user's experience'.[10] Said transformation has salient implications that relate to rights in the virtual world.

This chapter will extrapolate these philosophical intuitions to illustrate their relevance for the law. In the first section, the concept of immersion will be introduced through a practical example based on the individual. Thereafter, a broadened view of being in virtual worlds will be provided, linking the individual's experience with the mass use of these technologies to access shared online spaces. The section that follows presents a philosophical explication of embodiment, and the one thereafter expands this philosophical description to encapsulate the technological. After direct engagement with the law, a brief discussion of future directions is presented in the final section.

CONCEPTUALISING IMMERSION

From the outset we need to make a conceptual distinction between presence and immersion, since these are two related phenomena that need clarifying. This chapter relates presence and embodiment closely, though philosophically there remains a distinction. For the purposes of this chapter, however, we suggest that presence may be understood as 'an experiential quality in virtual

---

8 Don Ihde develops his work in the field of phenomenology to include also the philosophy of technology.

9 Jean Du Toit and Gregory Morgan Swer, 'Cynegetics as Inter-Species Affective Scaffolding' (forthcoming).

10 Ibid.

environments'.[11] Our understanding corresponds to the account by Wilkinson et al. in their review of the field of virtual reality technology, itself developed from a 'thematic content analysis [of] seventeen articles'.[12] Immersion is in turn related to 'the technical aspects of a virtual system that aid the user in feeling a sense of presence'.

Consider the following scenario.[13] Several people are standing in a room watching someone with a strange-looking helmet-like contraption which they proceed to place on their head, and which covers their eyes, blocking out views of their real-world environment.[14] Hilarity ensues, at least for the spectators on the outside, as the helmeted person staggers around, falls over their feet, runs into a wall, or screams in terror while madly clawing the helmet from their head.[15] We have all seen this type of video clip in some form or another on any of the ubiquitous social media platforms, and many of us have had the pleasure (or terror) of experiencing the virtual reality environment for ourselves. For those initiated into the mysteries of virtual reality, this scenario is well known, but for the sake of everyone else, let us elaborate a bit on this scene since it functions as an apt practical example of the focus of this chapter – how a person can be so immersed in a virtual/fictional/other reality or environment that they lose sight of the fact that the other/virtual is not indeed the real.

In the scenario set out above, what we are witnessing is a recording by non-participants of someone else using a virtual reality headset (or HMD) – more often than not, for the first time. The quality and cost of the headset will vary. Some of these clips show people using state-of-the-art (at the time of recording) virtual reality systems, such as *Oculus* or *Meta Quest*, *PlayStation VR*, *Apple Vision Pro* or similar. Others show people using very cheap and simple low-tech versions, which vary from a cardboard box with some cheap lenses such as the aptly named *Google Cardboard*, or any of the multitude of cheap pre-made VR headsets that are available from such online stores as Amazon, Wish, Temu or eBay, to name a few. The main difference (apart from the price and quality of the VR experience) is that the cheaper headsets require that you use a modern smartphone as a control and display device, whereas the more

---

11 Michael Wilkinson, Sean Brantley and Jing Feng, 'A Mini Review of Presence and Immersion in Virtual Reality' (2021) 65(1) *Proc. Hum. Factors Ergon. Soc. Annu. Meet.* 1099.

12 Ibid.

13 This account may be read as a phenomenological description around which the argument in this chapter is constructed.

14 Real-world here denotes analogue reality, as opposed to digital reality.

15 For typical examples of this, it is possible to just type in the search term 'VR fails' in the YouTube search bar, or at the following link: www.youtube.com/results?search_query=vr+fails, accessed 6 February 2026.

expensive versions are dedicated hardware units; as a general rule, the more expensive the VR system, the more immersive the experience will be for the user.

As alluded to above, users or players in virtual environments tend to experience a suspension of disbelief when using such virtual platforms. While persons sometimes have to actively 'suspend their disbelief' by consciously choosing to ignore the fact that something they are seeing, hearing or experiencing is not real, passive or autonomous suspension of disbelief readily occurs when the person experiencing it 'loses' themselves in the experience without consciously choosing to do so. This suspension of disbelief forms an integral part of the use and enjoyment of various forms of media, especially those connected to the arts and/or entertainment. Consider the well-known examples of reading a book, listening to a well-narrated story, watching a movie and, of course, playing or participating in online games and other virtual environments. As such, it should be clear that suspension of disbelief is not something new, and in fact, it has been argued that listening to a story told by someone else is illustrative of one of the oldest forms of creating a virtual world.[16]

Going back to the example of the people 'forgetting' that they are not, in fact, in the virtual environment, but rather in the real world, a quick explanation about how the level of immersion contributes to believability in the virtual environment, and how the accelerated development in the technological aspects of virtual reality, augmented reality, and mixed reality contributes to this, may be necessary.

As mentioned above, the cost of a VR system tends to correlate with the level of immersion. However, as with all other areas of consumer technology, what is cutting edge today will be state-of-the-art next year and ubiquitous in all consumer electronics within the next few years. Arguably, the most important aspect of an immersive VR system will be the fidelity of the display. If we consider the improvement in the quality of display systems over the years, not only in terms of colour but also in terms of clarity and the amount of information displayed on the screen, we see a consistent striving for better and more believable visual displays. However, the ability to display more detailed images on a screen also directly correlates with increases in the graphics processing power of computer chips to bring these images to life.

Without going into the full history of computer gaming, television display technology, and evolving virtual worlds, a quick illustration of the leaps and bounds made in display technology can be illustrated by looking at the number

---

16 For a discussion of the history and evolution of the story as a vehicle for virtual world creation from the oral tradition, through to the written word and books and onwards to actual computer and online virtual worlds, see Erlank (n 6), in particular 19–21 and in general 21–42.

of discrete displayable pixels on a screen. Most of the current computer displays still make use of a 1920 × 1080 display, meaning that the screen will display 1920 pixels per line horizontally and 1080 pixels per line vertically. Multiplying the horizontal with the vertical results in the number of total displayable pixels on the screen. This is referred to as an HD or High Definition Display and is currently considered the minimum acceptable display quality for most media formats. By doubling these numbers, we find the current state-of-the-art system, referred to as 4K UHD (Ultra High Definition) with 3840 × 2160 pixels, and the cutting edge is the 8K UHD system, which displays 7680 × 4320 pixels. It should be clear that the more pixels a screen can display, the better and more believable the image will be for the user. When sitting very close to an HD display (1920 × 1080), we could clearly see the individual pixels that make up the image. However, the higher the pixel count becomes on the screen, the less likely it is that you could see the individual pixels without resorting to some magnifying appliance.

In VR the display pixel count[17] becomes very important due to the optics of the lenses used in VR displays. One of the most challenging barriers to better immersive experiences in VR headsets has been the screen-door effect, which appears to the user of most current generation VR displays as if they are looking at the virtual environment through a mesh or screen door. The screen-door effect is a constant intrusion on to the virtual environment and a glaring reminder to the user that what they are experiencing and/or seeing is not, in fact, real. This can only be remedied by continuing to improve display quality. For example, PlayStation VR2 has a display resolution of 2000 × 2050 pixels displayed at a refresh rate of between 90 Hz and 120 Hz – per eye; and a 110-degree field of view. By contrast, the best commercially available VR display on the market at the moment is the Apple Vision Pro with an approximate display of 3660 × 3200,[18] which currently seems to be the best at hiding (but not removing) the screen-door effect.

---

[17] This is only one of the various display attributes that affect our perception of virtual worlds; others include the refresh rate – or frames per second that the display refreshes or redraws itself – which affects how we see motion on the screen, the Field of View (FOV), which determines how wide our view of the environment is concerning our peripheral vision (a narrower FOV appears unnatural and restrictive), the Pixels per Inch (PPI), which affect clarity, Pixels Per Degree (PPD), which relates to the number of pixels displayed in one degree of FOV and many more attributes that all work in conjunction to add to or detract from the believability and clarity of the display.

[18] Apple just mentions that the headset has 23 million pixels across both displays. The number mentioned here was calculated from these stats. See Charlie Sorrel, 'Vision Pro Teardown Part 2: What's the Display Resolution?' (*Ifixit* 7

Other components of the system also contribute to the immersive experience, such as 360-degree surround sound that correlates with the movement and positioning of the player inside the virtual environment. The ability of the VR system to know where you are looking or how you are moving via the use of numerous sensors also contributes to the difference in experiences. Consider that when you play a game on your computer screen or television and you move your head, it has no effect on the movement of your avatar or where you are looking inside the virtual environment, but with a proper VR headset, the system knows how you are moving and where you are looking, and automatically changes what you see or what your avatar is doing based on what you are doing with your body in the real world. Input and control are not limited to a keyboard, mouse, or controller (joystick).

These instances of an individual engaging with VR technology on their own provide a keyhole for looking at the potential future experience of inhabiting virtual worlds *en masse* as a society.

THEORISING VIRTUAL WORLDS

The increasing virtualisation of our society, particularly after the Covid-19 pandemic, has altered the way in which individuals engage with the world and with others. One example of this shift is found in the pivot away from physical movie-going, particularly among Gen Z (11–26 year-olds), which has led to a decline in theatre attendances of roughly 50 percent between 2019 and 2023.[19] In this sense, the pandemic accelerated the preferential trend towards social media, as well as the centring of short-form video content and streaming services (on high-quality home entertainment systems), as entertainment – in lieu of going to the cinema. This is a habitual shift towards preferring *a la carte* engagement with media, and echoes other trends. Continuous social access to the lives of others through internet connectivity, as well as the steady input of digital information in the world around us, has become the norm.

The shift to increasing digital technological engagement in various arenas in society forces us to contend with the challenges and opportunities provided by virtuality. Hassan describes the virtual as an essentially '*alienating* sphere wherein digital media cannot replicate analogue communication processes

February 2024) www.ifixit.com/News/90409/vision-pro-teardown-part-2-whats-the-display-resolution accessed 6 February 2026.

19 Tom Brueggeman, 'Theater Audiences Shrank by Half in the Last 4 Years. Can Movies Get Them Back?' (*Indiewire* 5 January 2023) www.indiewire.com/features/general/2022-box-office-2023-1234795871 accessed 6 February 2026..

without generating gaps, voids, and "missing information"'.[20] On the other hand, the virtual provides a space for generating new forms of communication and new avenues for engagement that would otherwise be impossible to achieve.[21] Consider the virtual worlds that are posited by Stephenson's view of a metaverse set out in *Snow Crash*,[22] and Cline's *Ready Player One*[23] – there exist no analogues in the individual's pre-technological existence for these potentially limitless spaces.

Additionally, the virtual has implications for a range of legal questions. Consider how the virtual poses questions of sovereignty,[24] which are traditionally centred around the nation as a physical space with fixed boundaries. How are our current legal systems strained by the promise of these virtual worlds, which have no physical or spatial coordinates? For example, participation in virtual worlds tends to be cross-border activities where the hosting servers of a virtual world or digital environment are located in more than one country and the users or players are also accessing such environments from all over the world.[25] In this sense, the internet has already broken down the traditional concept of sovereignty as a real-world territory with a boundary. Virtual worlds, and eventually the metaverse, will operate outside traditional boundaries by building on the infrastructure provided by the internet, except for those particular technology companies that insist on keeping users inside a 'walled garden' of their proprietary hardware and software. When a person participates in such a borderless environment, it makes (almost)[26] no difference where in the

---

[20] Robert Hassan, 'Digitality, Virtuality, and the "empathy machine"' (2019) 8(2) *Digit. Journal* 195, 195.

[21] Jean Du Toit, 'The (oh-so-queerly-embodied) Virtual' (2020) 39(4) SAJP 398.

[22] Stephenson (n 2).

[23] Cline (n 3).

[24] See in general Wian Erlank, 'Property and Sovereignty in Virtual Worlds' in James C Smith (ed), *Property and Sovereignty: Legal and Cultural Perspectives* (Ashgate 2013).

[25] See in general Wian Erlank, 'The Disconcerting Exercise of Finding and Applying the *lex rei sitae* in Cyberspace' (2018) 7(3) *European Property Law Journal* 212.

[26] Of course, there are continued efforts put in place by sovereign states to exert control over how and what their citizens can and may access over the internet, such as imposed by, e.g., China or North Korea. Such autocratic states are, however, not the only ones responsible for imposing limitations of varying degrees. Restrictions imposed by such measures as region-blocking and varying levels of censorship are commonplace even in more democratic jurisdictions. From a hardware level, the quality of an internet connection also varies across the globe, with richer first-world nations usually having better and more reliable access speeds

real world they are accessing the virtual environment. While the individual's experience of the virtual world should for the most part be the same irrespective of where they are located on Earth, their home jurisdiction (where they are citizens) may have a different legal framework that applies to their online activities.[27] As such, legal issues are a crucial factor in relation to the experience of the virtual by the individual.

The current chapter will investigate the individual's experience of virtual worlds by specifically looking at the concept of *level of immersion and believability* as articulated through a philosophical understanding of *embodiment.* Considering the individual's involvement in the world from the vantage point of embodiment allows us to identify salient characteristics of this experiential structure, which may have important implications for future reflections on the virtual. Phenomenology, which has the intention of describing 'the basic structures of human experience and understanding from a first person perspective',[28] is particularly suited to grappling with the nuances of one's encounter with these virtual spaces through digital technology artefacts in the context of the body.

FROM DISEMBODIMENT TO EMBODIMENT

The primordial facticity of the body serves from the outset as a framework for this discussion, since it presents a crucial point of access to our online societies. For Merleau-Ponty, who philosophises on the body, embodiment entails the dynamic and sometimes ambiguous synthesis between objectivity and subjectivity.[29] The body has both an object side and provides a means for having a world. The notion of the body-subject, as both an objective and subjective

---

and connections. This will, however, probably soon change with ubiquitous internet access via satellite connection rather than Earth-based wireless or wired/fibre optic connections that are currently used. In terms of the restrictions imposed by various nation states, there are numerous workarounds to bypass such restrictions, of which the most well-known is the use of Virtual Private Networks (VPNs) by persons wishing to circumvent restriction, censorship and identification.

27 For example, access to sites or virtual worlds containing subversive themes, pornography or other activities, which could be restricted or prohibited in certain countries, will not influence the online experience of the user but may have real-world criminal consequences in their home jurisdictions. See, e.g., Erlank (n 5) 654; Erlank (n 6), 3, 83–84, 289 fn 261.

28 Taylor Carman, 'Foreword' in Maurice Merleau-Ponty, *Phenomenology of Perception* (Routledge & Kegan Paul 2014).

29 Maurice Merleau-Ponty, *Phenomenology of Perception* (Routledge & Kegan Paul London 1962).

phenomenon, counterbalances traditional empiricist and rationalist accounts of how the body facilitates perception. This means that the apparent hard separation between bodily activity and the subjective processes of thinking are unified through behaviour that expresses intentionality – that our bodies and our thinking are always directed towards *something*.

Such an understanding of embodiment problematises the 1980s and 1990s popular culture notions of transcending the body through digital technology as a form of disembodiment. This period saw a general fascination with cyberspace in science fiction (see films such as *Tron* (1982)[30] and *The Lawnmower Man* (1992)[31]), and media toyed with the idea of transcending the limitations of the physical body through notions such as cyborgs and hive-minds.[32] These *radical* accounts of the virtual seemed to suggest that we would one day unshackle ourselves from the facticity of the body, and that we could float through cyberspace as decontextualised minds.

However, understanding embodiment as the horizon for all our engagements with the world suggests that such an escape from physicality exists only, or rather *could only* exist, in the realm of speculative fiction. One may put on a pair of virtual reality goggles or plug into a computer to engage with the virtual, but one would still need to take account of the architecture of the body for perception and existence in the first place. Therefore, rather than seriously postulating disembodiment as a feasible principle, we see in such disembodied fantasies reflected trends that arose in Modernity – the commodification of the body, atomised individualism, and depersonalised consumer culture.[33] Where does this negation of the possibility of disembodiment leave us?

The impossibility of an encompassing disembodiment, particularly in the context of current technology, shows how a complex relationship exists between the body and the virtual. Indeed, as our technology developed beyond the speculative visions of the last century, so did the need for more complex accounts of embodiment. One postulate, derived from socio-pragmatic accounts of technology, is that there is a proliferation of bodies as soon as the

---

[30] Steven Lisberger, 'Tron' (IMDB, 1982) www.imdb.com/title/tt0084827 accessed 6 February 2026.

[31] Brett Leonard, 'The Lawnmower Man' (IMDB, 1992) www.imdb.com/title/tt0104692 accessed 6 February 2026.

[32] Caroline A Jones, 'Introduction' in Caroline A Jones (ed), *Sensorium: Embodied Experience, Technology, and Contemporary Art* (The MIT Press Cambridge 2006), 1.

[33] David Roden, *Posthuman Life: Philosophy at the Edge of the Human* (Routledge 2014).

virtual is engaged with. Andrew Feenburg,[34] for example, envisions a replication of bodies in his positing of the dependent body and the extended body, which builds on Ihde's postphenomenological[35] contention that there exists both a sensory body and a cultural body. However, such socio-pragmatic theorising withdraws from the individual's lived experience of being a singular body-subject and consequently sidetracks us since a key feature of phenomenological description is its non-speculative nature.

In terms of tracing the experience of the virtual from the basis of embodiment, it is therefore sensible to avoid conceptualisations that disembody the individual and also to avoid the speculative proliferation of various bodies. Such proliferation of various bodies does not relate to the use of an avatar, however, since the avatar as electronic image is representational of a body (rather than being a body phenomenologically) and this representational body may be manipulated by the individual user without superseding the facticity of their own body. A description of the shift in embodied relations, when utilising digital technology, should thus be based in the unitary body-subject.

THE BODY-SUBJECT AND DIGITAL TECHNOLOGY

We suggest that digital technology entails, through embodiment, a symbiosis of artefact and user, and that tracing virtuality in terms of embodiment reveals certain features that are unique to human-technology relations in this context. More specifically, we posit that embodiment is constitutive of an immersive experience online, a perspective that stands in contrast to ontologically limiting socio-pragmatic views. Because embodiment moves beyond an account of the body as an object, presenting rather a living experience of the world, such contemporary technologies may be seen to redirect the entire perceptual sensorium of the individual. As individuals, our perception is constituted through a synthesis of objectivity and subjectivity; we are ambiguous beings, and therefore the structural augmentation and reconfiguration of our bodies through technology reshapes at the same time the experience and potential uses of our bodies. In other words, technology scaffolds in particular ways the

---

[34] Andrew Feenberg, 'Active and Passive Bodies: Comments on Don Ihde's Bodies in Technology' (2003) 7(2) *Techné: Research in Philosophy and Technology* 125, 125–130.

[35] Martin Ritter, 'Postphenomenological Method and Technological Things Themselves' (2021) 44 *Human Studies* 581, 583: '...postphenomenology focuses on technologies as interrelating human beings and the world'. It integrates traditional approaches to phenomenology with pragmatism to reach its conclusions regarding technology.

perceptual architecture of our bodies, shaping our encounter with the world and with other people.

Embodiment relations in technology often entail the expansion of a subject's perceptual field. Consider an example of a blind man walking with a cane – the blind man can wield their cane as a sensory organ to identify obstacles in their path through a process of learning, even without sight. In terms of embodiment, the technological artefact becomes so familiar that 'the world of feelable things recedes and now begins, not at the outer skin of the hand, but at the end of the stick'.[36] It becomes an instrument *through which* perception is achieved, rather than an object that is *in itself* perceived by its user. Merleau-Ponty argues that 'it is a bodily auxiliary, an extension of the bodily synthesis'.[37] The tool or device is incorporated into the body schema to become transparent while allowing for expanded perceptual potentiality and habitus.

Don Ihde, following on from Merleau-Ponty in discussing embodied body-technology interactions, suggests that our attention is transformed in specific ways by different technological artefacts.[38] There are transparent technologies, such as wearing glasses or using chalk to write on a blackboard, which become fully incorporated into one's body schema – until the device breaks down or becomes in some way non-functional. At the point of breakdown – when my glasses shatter or the chalk breaks – I become aware of the human-technology relation that I am engaged in, of the quality of the equipment that the technological artefact forms a part of.[39] In either case, the breakdown of the artefact places emphasis on how the artefact transforms our experience in the first place, which is otherwise a transparent process. However, Ihde also specifies that there exists a dual character to these types of embodied relations – some aspects of the sensory experience are heightened (looking through a microscope at an amoeba suggests an improved form of sight) while others are diminished (looking through the microscope results in a corresponding diminution of one's awareness of the surrounding environment).

This dual character, of a focusing in and a focusing out, is suggestive of contemporaneous virtuality. On the one hand, we could argue that, through immersion, the digital technological medium withdraws, which reinforces the idea that embodied experience is an extension of our bodily intentionality.[40]

---

[36] Merleau-Ponty (n 29), 175.

[37] Ibid., 176.

[38] Don Ihde, *Technics and Praxis* (Reidel Publishing Company Dordrecht 1979), 272–273.

[39] Martin Heidegger, *Being and Time* (John Macquarrie and Edward Robinson trs, Harper & Row 1962), 98.

[40] Amir Haj-Bolouri, 'The Experience of Immersive Virtual Reality: A Phenomenology Inspired Inquiry' (2023) 52(1) *Commun Assoc Inf Syst* 32.

On the other hand, the expansion of certain senses also entails the diminution of others – such is the case of using a microscope or walking around with our mobile phone. Using a microscope means I cannot observe my surrounding environment as clearly, while the use of a mobile phone while walking means that I need to constantly shift my attention from the content on the screen to navigating an offline world full of obstacles.

There is a level of immersion in terms of the virtual that is not achieved when walking with a mobile phone, in contrast to putting on a VR headset – I can never fully be immersed in virtual content since I must also be aware of other people, lampposts, and a series of potential obstructions while walking around. The specific technological embodied relation requires a shifting back and forth in terms of my intentionality, Ihde suggests. Intentionality, in phenomenology, refers to the claim that each experience is fundamentally a 'consciousness of' or 'experience of' something – it is always directed towards something in the world. A shifting of focus, as is observed in the case of an individual walking with a mobile phone, also entails a shift in intentionality (in terms of what we are 'conscious of').

Intentionality is an important aspect of embodiment, since thinkers such as Merleau-Ponty suggest that it is not possible to separate bodily conduct from intelligent conduct. Rather, there is a unification of behaviour that expresses the intentionality of conduct, and consequently assigns meaning to this conduct. My body is not just an object like others in the world; rather, it entails a lived experience of the self and the world. Therefore, there is a relationship between the concept of intentionality in phenomenology and immersion in terms of our engagement with the virtual. When our intentionality is completely encompassed through technological means, such as VR headsets or HMDs, there is also the possibility of a complete immersion of our embodied and perceptual intentionality in the virtual.

Similar to the discussion above about immersion as a factor connected with the suspension of disbelief, immersion here refers to how immersive the virtual world that the embodied individual engages with is – *realness* is materialised through the sense or feeling of being surrounded by things presented on the screen, or being able to walk freely around a virtual space and interact with virtual objects (as we do with objects in our everyday world). Increasing levels of immersion correlate to the user feeling as though they are actually or physically present in the virtual environment. There is a level of technological persuasiveness at work here, since digital technological artefacts *persuade* the user that the virtual is real.[41] Immersion is therefore that quality which refers

[41] Erlank (n 6), 51.

to the development and change of our mental state from one world to another[42] to make us feel '...present in the mediated environment, rather than in the immediate physical environment'.[43]

Questions of believability relate directly to the level of immersion, and a suspension of disbelief is required to instantiate immersion on the part of the individual. An increase in the level of immersion leads to feelings of selflessness on the part of the user[44] – engagement with a virtual world leads to a loss of the sense of self and their experience of a physical body. Furthermore, individuals may forget about time and ignore analogue perception.[45] While older forms of technology entail a form embodied experience of virtuality that is non-immersive,[46] current digital technologies allow not only an immersive experience of embodiment[47] but also one that is a co-extensive intermixing or interweaving of the material and virtual world.[48]

At the same time, we must ask how individuals could relate to others in a state of immersion. Does the other appear less real in this state of immersion? These are important questions, since we now have the potential to encounter AI in virtual environments as more developed versions of NPC AI. How does trust function in this shift from face-to-face relationships to these virtual environments?

---

42 Gustav Bøg Petersen, Giorgos Petkakis and Guido Makransky, 'A Study of how Immersion and Interactivity Drive VR Learning' (2022) 179 *Comp Ed* 104429.

43 Frank Biocca and Mark R Levy (eds), *Communication in the Age of Virtual Reality* (Routledge 2013), 36.

44 Yue Mangfang, 'Application of Virtual Reality (VR) Technology in Landscape Planning and Design' (2021) 02 *Constr Des Eng* 163, 163–164.

45 Ibid.

46 Ulrike Schultze, 'Embodiment and Presence in Virtual Worlds: A Review' (2010) 25 JIT 434, 434–449; T L Taylor, 'Living digitally: Embodiment in Virtual Worlds' in Ralph Schroeder (ed), *The Social Life of Avatars: Presence and Interaction in Shared Virtual Environments* (Springer 2002), 40–62.

47 Elpida Bampouni, Nannan Xi and Juho Hamari, 'Decision-Making Styles in Metaverse: Effects of Immersion and Embodiment' (2023) *AMCIS 2023 Proceedings* 3.

48 Du Toit (n 21); Jean Du Toit and Gregory Morgan Swer, 'Virtual Limitations of the Flesh: Merleau-Ponty and the Phenomenology of Technological Determinism' (2021) 20 *Phenomenology and Mind* 20, 20–31; Michael Saker and Jordan Frith, 'Coextensive Space: Virtual Reality and the Developing Relationship Between the Body, the Digital and Physical Space' (2020) 42(7–8) *Media Cult Soc* 1427, 1427–1442.

EMBODIMENT, TECHNOLOGY, LAW

As far as the law is concerned, the immersive factor of virtual reality tech has a distinct effect on the probability that a virtual interaction could have legal consequences in the real world. This is despite the fact that legal considerations stemming from virtual property and interactions in virtual environments have often in the past been downplayed in legal and academic circles as irrelevant or negligible due to the argument that they are 'only games'.

Some singular aspects regarding virtual-world interactions will be briefly discussed below.

As alluded to in the previous section, participation in a virtual environment could influence our perception of place and time. The more immersive the virtual environment is (even if one is 'just reading a book'), the more likely it is that you can lose yourself and not realise how much time has passed. Although this is not necessarily problematic when entering the virtual space for entertainment purposes or to spend leisure time, it could have severe consequences in the real world. For example, there have been numerous reports of people neglecting their real-life responsibilities in favour of their virtual lives. One such example can be seen in the case where two parents in South Korea spent so much time looking after their virtual child in *Prius Online* that they neglected their three-month-old in the real world to such an extent that the baby died.[49] On a societal level, we see in Japan the rise of *hikikomori* as a form of severe social withdrawal, which is characterised by adolescents and young adults who avoid all forms of social engagement beyond the virtual and become recluses in their parents' homes.

Virtual death can lead to real-world death and or arrest, and using VR can kill you. While death (of an avatar) in a virtual world is most often a nuisance, with safeguards allowing you to revive or respawn your avatar (with or without some penalties), some virtual worlds make this a much more real experience, where the death of an avatar is permanent necessitating the player or user to create a new avatar from scratch. If the pertinent virtual world is a game-orientated or levelling[50] environment, then this would mean that a player would need to start playing the game from the beginning. This, of course, will have a huge influence on a player who has become part of the virtual world's online community. Incidentally, a loss of respect and acceptance by a virtual-world community is such a severe sanction that the virtual 'shunning' of a

---

[49] Andrew Salmon, 'Couple: Internet Gaming Addiction led to Baby's Death' (*CNN* 2 April 2010) https://edition.cnn.com/2010/WORLD/asiapcf/04/01/korea.parents.starved.baby/index.html accessed 6 February 2026.

[50] Erlank (n 6), 22, 35, 38, 125.

player is often employed by online communities as a method of extrajudicial punishment for antisocial player behaviour.[51] As an example of virtual death leading to real-world legal consequences, a Japanese woman faced jail time after she killed her virtual husband by logging into his account and deleting his account.[52]

Bodily integrity of an avatar and crime. In one of the most famous instances of virtual-world crime spilling over into the real world, a virtual rape occurred in one of the older text-based virtual worlds – called LambdaMOO.[53] Although no one was arrested for this action, the case study has continued to inform thinking and research into how much the user or player identifies with their avatar (even) if such an avatar is only an idea described by text. We argue that as we continue to move to ever-more immersive virtual environments and the barrier between the real and virtual continues to dissipate, the emotional, mental, and psychological effects that such abuse can have will continue to spill over into the real world. In such a case, the conceptual barrier between the virtual and real will be crossed and trigger real-world legal consequences for such rogue actors.

At the most basic level, the question has been asked whether an individual could have real-world ownership rights of virtual objects (and avatars) in virtual worlds. The answer has emerged over the years that this can, in fact, be the case.

From a property law perspective, the phenomenon of virtual property or digital assets has been one of the most important subjects when it comes to crossing the conceptual barrier between the virtual and the real. Over the years it has become very clear that users have the same kind of attachment to and view of their perceived and expected rights as owners of virtual property objects as they would have with similar objects in the real world. This has been made all the more prevalent due to the continuing 'dephysicalisation' of property that is steadily increasing and becoming more and more pronounced as we

---

[51] Jack M Balkin, 'Virtual Liberty: Freedom to Design and Freedom to Play in Virtual Worlds' (2004) 90(8) *Virginia Law Review* 2043, 2048, 2062–2065; Erlank (n 6), 72.

[52] Associated Press, 'Japanese Woman Faces Jail Over Online "Murder"' (*Associated Press* 24 October 2008) www.theguardian.com/world/2008/oct/24/japan-games accessed 18 June 2024.

[53] Julian Dibbell, 'A Rape in Cyberspace or How an Evil Clown, A Haitian Trickster Spirit, Two Wizards, and a Cast of Dozens Turned a Database into a Society' (1994) *Ann Surv Am L* 471, 471; F Gregory Lastowka and Dan Hunter, 'Virtual Crimes' (2004) 92 1 *NY L Sch L Rev* 293, 294–295; Wian Erlank, 'Finding Property in New Places – Property in Cyber and Outer Space' (2015) 18(5) *Potchefstroom Electronic Law Journal (PELJ/PER)* 1761, 1779.

move more of our daily interactions with one another, the world around us, and society in general into the digital environment. As a very simplistic example, we can see how a person can have the same expectations of ownership (with the correlating rights, duties and entitlements of real-world property rights) when buying a tangible, physical book, or when buying that same book, but in the virtual object form of an eBook. While the arguments in legal scholarship were initially that such digital versions of similar (in form and function) real-world objects should be governed by intellectual property rights and contract law (licences), over time and due to pressure from society transferring their buying power and purchasing expectations to dephysicalised virtual forms, it has become accepted that virtual property objects could, in certain instances, be recognised and protected by real-world property law.

Of special importance here is the fact that many jurisdictions (especially those from the Roman-Germanic civil-law traditions)[54] still have the requirement that an object of property law must be tangible or corporeal. The intangible aspect of virtual property and other digital assets, therefore, becomes an exceedingly difficult challenge to the recognition of such objects, with the result that such intangible objects are either not protected as property in such jurisdictions, or only recognised as exceptions to the tangibility rule. We argue that generally speaking, and specifically in such tangibility-orientated jurisdictions, the more immersive a virtual environment is, the more such intangible objects will be viewed in the real world if they are believed to be (in)tangible, or tangible in the virtual environment. The argument, therefore, goes that if an object is perceived to be tangible in the virtual world by an individual's avatar as a proxy, or employing some analogue manipulation control system, such as a mouse, keyboard, joystick or other type of haptic device, then the tangibility requirement in the real world is met. The more realistic the online interaction is for the user, and the more the user is immersed in the believability that they are in fact touching the virtual object, the less real-world tangibility will feature as an impediment to applying real-world property rights to virtual objects.

The final example here comes from the dissociation between the other's known avatar and the person controlling such an avatar. The social aspect of most virtual worlds leads to the creation of friendships and bonds of trust between players who get to know the person behind the avatar over time. If such a virtual-world account is subsequently sold, transferred or stolen by someone else, this is more often than not communicated to other users with whom that avatar has been interacting. As such misplaced trust might even

54 Erlank (n 6), 213.

lead to unexpected breaches of trust[55] when users think they know who the avatar represents, and then suddenly find that the user now connected to that avatar is someone new.

CONCLUSION

The foregoing chapter has discussed the question of believability and immersion via the philosophical concept of embodiment. This has revealed how questions of believability and immersion shape our experience of virtual worlds, but also how such concepts are founded in a form of primordial bodilyness. However, the experiential alteration of the individual does not merely have philosophical implications; rather, the philosophical understanding of embodiment may come to inform law in cyberspace directly since alterations to our embodiment through technological artefacts have legal implications in terms of how we relate to the real world and the care of those under our supervision, the question of bodily integrity via avatars in relation to crime, and how we approach property law in terms of questions of embodied ownership.

We have indicated that, even though complete disembodiment in virtual environments remains a speculative concept, there already exist technologies that blur the line between the virtual world and the analogue or real world in terms of the individual's embodied experience. Sophisticated virtual technologies allow users to experience a suspension of disbelief and a sense of 'being there' in the virtual world. We show, however, that such immersive experiences may have important legal ramifications and have highlighted some instances in the chapter. We have indicated that a loss of awareness in terms of time may result in the neglect of real-life responsibilities, potentially leading to consequences that intersect with law. Virtual actions may also have impacts in the real world, as per instances of virtual theft, harassment, and even virtual murder that have already resulted in legal action. Thereafter, we noted the relevance of this embodied framework for property rights. Virtual objects are increasingly perceived as tangible, invoking existing property rights that need additional consideration and development in terms of digitality. Moreover, the

[55] See, e.g., the case where players in a position of trust stole digital currency inside the MMORPG EVE Online, cashed it out for real-world money, and faced no real-world consequences. Wian Erlank, 'Introduction to Virtual Property: Lex virtualis ipsa loquitur' (2015) 18(7) *Potchefstroom Electronic Law Journal (PER/PELJ)* 2525, 2545; Jason Ocampo, 'EVE Online Bank Scandal' (*IGN* 10 May 2012) www.ign.com/articles/2009/07/09/eve-online-bank-scandal accessed 6 February 2026.

close relationship between online identity and avatars suggests that new social, relational, and legal dynamics may come into play in these discussions. Closer reflection on immersive embodied experiences in the virtual may provide a key for unlocking the multifaceted puzzle of virtuality that is facing our contemporary society.

8. Rights for daemons: the question of legal personhood

Siina Raskulla

1. INTRODUCTION

1.1 Research Question and Hypothesis

The virtual world is inhabited both by characters representing humans as well as by software-generated characters: robots living in the virtual world, or spirits inhabiting the machine, as described by novelist Neal Stephenson.[1] This chapter studies the legal relations between humans and software-generated characters in virtual social worlds, or metaverses.[2] Avatars, electronic representations controlled by computer users, have been a common feature of virtual social worlds. However, as technology has advanced and artificial intelligence has become more sophisticated, it has resulted in the emergence of software-generated characters potentially indistinguishable from human-controlled Avatars.

While the rights of Avatars have been previously discussed in the literature and case law,[3] the rights of purely virtual characters have gained less atten-

---

1 Neal Stephenson, *Snow Crash* (Penguin Books 2011), 51.

2 For more on the development of virtual social worlds and their differences from other social media, see e.g., Andreas M Kaplan and Michael Haenlein, 'The Fairyland of Second Life: Virtual Social Worlds and how to use Them' (2009) 52 *Business Horizon* 563, 565–66; Audrey Guinchard, 'Crime in Virtual Worlds: The Limits of Criminal Law' (2010) 24(2) *International Review of Law, Computers & Technology* 175; Susan W Brenner, 'Fantasy Crime: The Role of Criminal Law in Virtual Worlds' (2020) 11(1) *Vanderbilt Journal of Entertainment and Technology Law* 19; Hakan Kayakoku, 'History and Development of Virtual Worlds and Metaverse' in Fatih Sinan Esen, Hasan Tinmaz and Madhusudan Singh (eds), *Metaverse: Technologies, Opportunities and Threats* (Studies in Big Data 133, Springer Singapore 2023), 19.

3 See below Section 2.

tion. However, technological development has raised the issue of whether legal personhood should be extended to 'accommodate different forms of embodiment created by virtual media, artificial intelligence, and other advanced technologies'.[4]

Non-Avatar Characters (NACs), or Daemons, are software-generated characters controlled by algorithms or artificial intelligence. Daemons can exhibit autonomous behaviour and respond to interactions, potentially creating a sense of authentic virtual relations. However, if Daemons become indistinguishable from Avatars, it raises the question of whether virtual social worlds can have different rules for Daemons and Avatars.

This chapter analyses the extension of the rule of law to interactions between Avatars and Daemons, considering human-AI interaction and the phenomenon of anthropomorphism.

It aims to contribute to our understanding of the legal nature of Avatar-to-Daemon (A2D) relations in virtual social worlds. It raises important questions about the rights and duties of Daemons in the metaverse and how we can construct legal personhood for virtual beings.

As technological advancements progress, particularly in artificial intelligence, human-guided Avatars and algorithm-guided Daemons will likely inhabit future metaverses. In addition, Avatars and Daemons are becoming *indistinguishable*. The chapter acknowledges that Daemons are designed and programmed by real-world actors.

However, Daemons are becoming more intelligent and technologically able to mimic emotions and facial expressions, making them more available for meaningful interaction.[5] As a result, Daemons may appear to be guided by sentient beings.[6] Both human-guided Avatars and algorithm-guided Daemons will inhabit future metaverses. The questions considered here are: (1) Should law regulate A2D relations in metaverses? And: (2) Should Daemons be granted legal personhood?

---

[4] Rita M Lauria and George S Robinson, 'From Cyberspace to Outer Space: Existing Legal Regimes Under Pressure from Emerging Meta-Technologies' (2012) 33 *U La Verne L Rev* 219, 221, 243; Ralph Schroeder, 'Social Interaction in Virtual Environments: Key Issues, Common Themes, and a Framework for Research' in Ralph Schroeder (ed), *The Social Life of Avatars: Presence and Interaction in Shared Virtual Environments* (Springer London 2001), 1.

[5] Woodrow Barfield and Alexander Williams, 'The Law of Virtual Reality and Increasingly Smart Virtual Avatars' in Woodrow Barfield and Marc J Blitz (eds), *Research Handbook on the Law of Virtual and Augmented Reality* (Edward Elgar 2020), 14.

[6] Ibid., 2.

The hypothesis is that interactions with Daemons in online settings can have real-world social, psychological and physiological effects, in which case it is appropriate to consider granting legal rights to Daemons in virtual social worlds. Although we do not view virtual characters as conscious beings, this does not exclude them from having rights.[7]

In this case, the rights originate from the established impact of human-Daemon relationships on human well-being rather than from Daemons being sentient beings.[8]

1.2 Outline

The chapter proceeds as follows: Section 2 briefly reviews metaverse laws covering three types of relations in virtual social worlds: creator-to-resident, Avatar-to-Avatar, and Avatar-to-Daemon relations. A significant body of research and legal cases relates to virtual relationships, focusing on those with economic implications. The question of the legal nature of relationships between Avatars and Daemons and the rights of purely virtual characters has also been discussed for decades, while gaining less attention than A2A or business-to-consumer relations. Today, as virtual worlds become increasingly populated by algorithm-guided Daemons, it is relevant to consider the legal implications.

The literature review in Section 3 demonstrates that online relations with Daemons can potentially have a real social, psychological and physiological impact. The well-being of humans who engage with Daemons is a crucial determinant of whether legal protection of these virtual characters is necessary. The question is, how do relations in virtual worlds impact human well-being? This section provides a literature review focusing on the psychological, physiological and psychosocial effects of A2D relations. These effects are

[7] The chapter adopts a legalistic position, in which basically anything can be a legal person, see e.g., John Dewey, 'The Historic Background of Corporate Legal Personality' (1926) 35(6) *The Yale Law Journal* 655; Ngaire Naffine, 'Who are Law's Persons? From Cheshire Cats to Responsible Subjects' (2003) 66(3) *Mod Law Rev* 346, 351; Samir Chopra and Laurence F White, *A Legal Theory for Autonomous Artificial Agents* (University of Michigan Press 2011), 154–60; Joanna J Bryson, Mihailis E Diamantis and Thomas E Grant, 'Of, For, and By the People: The Legal Lacuna of Synthetic Persons' (2017) 25(3) *Artificial Intelligence and Law* 273, 277–80; Claudio Novelli, Giorgio Bongiovanni and Giovanni Sartor, 'A Conceptual Framework for Legal Personality and its Application to AI' (2022) 13(2) *Jurisprudence* 194, 207; Siina Raskulla, 'Hybrid Theory of Corporate Legal Personhood and its Application to Artificial Intelligence' (2023) 3(78) *SN Soc Sci*.

[8] See below Section 4.

studied in the framework of Game Transfer Phenomena (GTP), where game elements trigger real-life behaviour.[9]

[9] See Angelica B O de Gotari, Karin Aronsson and Mark Griffiths, 'Game Transfer Phenomena in Video Game Playing: A Qualitative Interview Study' (2011) 1(3) *International Journal of Cyber Behavior, Psychology and Learning* 15. Related research fields include human-computer interaction (HCI) (see e.g., Yuna Kano and Junya Morita, 'The Effect of Experience and Embodiment on Empathetic Behavior toward Virtual Agents', *Proceedings of the 8th International Conference on Human-Agent Interaction* (2020), 112; S Shyam Sundar, 'Rise of Machine Agency: A Framework for Studying the Psychology of Human-AI Interaction (HAII)' (2020) 25(1) *Journal of Computer-Mediated Communication* 74; Qian Yang and others, 'Re-Examining Whether, Why, and How Human-AI Interaction Is Uniquely Difficult to Design', *CHI '20: Proceedings of the 2020 CHI Conference on Human Factors in Computing Systems* (2020); Junya Morita and Yuna Kano, 'Effects of Self-Experience and Situational Awareness on Empathic Help to Virtual Agents', *Proceedings of the 10th Conference on Human-Agent Interaction 1* (2022); Iryna Pentina and others, 'Consumer–Machine Relationships in the Age of Artificial Intelligence: Systematic Literature Review and Research Directions' (2023) 40(8) *Psychology & Marketing* 1593, human-AI interaction (HAII) (see e.g., Sundar 2020; Yang et al. 2020; Park, J. S. et al. (2023) 'Generative Agents: Interactive Simulacra of Human Behavior' in UIST2023 – Proceedings of the 36th Annual ACM Symposium on User Interface Software and Technology [Online] 2023, https://doi.org/10.48550/arXiv.2304.03442), human-AI relationship (see e.g., Iryna Pentina and others, 'Consumer–Machine Relationships in the Age of Artificial Intelligence: Systematic Literature Review and Research Directions' (2023) 40(8) *Psychology & Marketing* 1593), and affecting computing (Arvid Kappas and Jonathan Gratch, 'These Aren't The Droids You Are Looking for: Promises and Challenges for the Intersection of Affective Science and Robotics/AI' (2023) 4(3) *Affective Science* 580). These fields provide various theoretical, practical, and technological perspectives, such as the Computers are Social Actors (CASA) paradigm, which describes users' social reactions to media technologies. (See e.g., Kun Xu, Xiaobei Chen and Luling Huang, 'Deep Mind in Social Responses to Technologies: A New Approach to Explaining the Computers Are Social Actors Phenomena' (2022) 134 *Computers in Human Behavior* 107321; Kim Kroes, Isabella Saccardi and Judith Masthoff, 'Empathizing with Virtual Agents: The Effect of Personification and General Empathic Tendencies' *Proceedings – 2022 IEEE International Conference on Artificial Intelligence and Virtual Reality* (2022) 73.)

The review focuses on a few key elements of A2D relations, such as moral and ethical judgements,[10] trust,[11] empathy,[12] and fictional emotions generally,[13] as well as sociomorphism and anthropomorphism,[14] which contribute to triggering these emotions.

10 See e.g., Edward H Spence, 'Meta Ethics for the Metaverse: The Ethics of Virtual Worlds' (2008) 174 *Frontiers in Artificial Intelligence and Applications* 3; Gabriel Lima and others, 'The Conflict Between People's Urge to Punish AI and Legal Systems' (2021) 8 *Frontiers in Robotics and AI* 756242; Alexandra Lukaszewicz and Paweł Fortuna, 'Towards Turing Test 2.0 – Attribution of Moral Status and Personhood to Human and Non-Human Agents' (2022) 4(3) *Postdigital Science and Education* 860; Kroes and others (n 9); Teresa Heyder, Nina Passlack and Oliver Posegga, 'Ethical Management of Human-AI Interaction: Theory Development Review' (2023) 32(3) *The Journal of Strategic Information Systems* 101772.

11 Ella Glikson and Anita Williams Woolley, 'Human Trust in Artificial Intelligence: Review of Empirical Research' (2020) 14(2) *The Academy of Management Annals* 627.

12 Nicola S Schutte and Emma J Stilinović, 'Facilitating Empathy Through Virtual Reality' (2017) 41(6) *Motivation and Emotion* 708; Alexandra Sierra Rativa, Marie Postma and Menno van Zaanen, 'The Influence of Game Character Appearance on Empathy and Immersion: Virtual Non-Robotic Versus Robotic Animals' (2020) 51(5) *Simulation and Gaming* 685; Kano and Morita 2020 (n 9); Kroes, Saccardi and Masthoff (n 9); Takahiro Tsumura and Seiji Yamada, 'Influence of Anthropomorphic Agent on Human Empathy Through Games' (2023) 11 *IEEE Access* 40412.

13 Jonas Blatter and Eva Weber-Guskar, 'Fictional Emotions and Emotional Reactions to Social Robots as Depictions of Social Agents' (2023) 46 *The Behavioral and Brain Sciences* e24.

14 See e.g., Kate Darling, 'Extending Legal Protection to Social Robots: The Effects of Anthropomorphism, Empathy, and Violent Behavior towards Robotic Objects' in Ryan Calo, A Michael Froomkin and Ian Kerr (eds), *Robot Law* (Edward Elgar 2016); Arleen Salles, Kathinka Evers and Michele Farisco, 'Anthropomorphism in AI' (2020) 11(2) *AJOB Neuroscience* 88; Christoph Bartneck and others, *An Introduction to Ethics in Robotics and AI* (Springer Nature 2021), 56–58; Xu and others (n 9); Tsumura and Yamada (n 12); Mayu Koike, Steve Loughnan and Sarah C E Stanton, 'Virtually in Love: The Role of Anthropomorphism in Virtual Romantic Relationships' (2023) 62(1) *British Journal of Social Psychology* 600; Michael R Müller and Anne Sonnenmoser, 'Sociomorphic Technologies. On the Typology of Artificial Actors' in Bertolt Meyer, Ulrike Thomas and Olfa Kanoun (eds), *Hybrid Societies – Humans Interacting with Embodied Technologies* (Springer, forthcoming).

Section 3 concludes with the recognition that, based on the theory by Luciano Floridi and J W Sanders on the morality of artificial agents,[15] Daemons are *moral agents*. This conclusion raises the question of whether, as moral agents, Daemons should be bound and protected by the rule of law.

Section 4 discusses how the nature of Daemons as moral actors raises the issue of whether they should be recognised as legal persons to protect human well-being. It adopts a legalistic approach where basically anything can be a legal person.[16] However, while anything *can* be a legal person, it is reasonable to ask whether personhood serves any socially significant function.[17] It has been discussed in previous literature how the recognition of legal personhood *responds to moral pressure and societal demand*. Legal personhood is not founded on scientific knowledge, but on human impressions and emotions.[18]

The question considered in Section 4 is whether humans would benefit from the recognition of the legal personhood of Daemons?[19] To reframe a question previously presented by Joanna J Bryson, Mihailis E Diamantis and Thomas D Grant concerning robots: 'Does endowing Daemons with this legal right or that legal obligation further the purposes of the legal system?'[20] The purpose of the

---

15 Luciano Floridi and J W Sanders, 'On the Morality of Artificial Agents' (2004) 14(3) *Minds and Machines* 349.

16 Simon Chesterman, 'Artificial Intelligence and the Limits of Legal Personality' (2020) 69(4) *The International and Comparative Law Quarterly* 819, 822. Not everyone considers the possession of duties a necessary condition for legal personhood. See e.g., Visa A J Kurki, *A Theory of Legal Personhood* (Oxford University Press 2019), 62–71. Nevertheless, it seems to be the most common. See e.g., John Dewey, 'The Historic Background of Corporate Legal Personality' (1926) 35(6) *The Yale Law Journal* 655, 661; Lawrence B Solum, 'Legal Personhood for Artificial Intelligence' (1992) 70(4) *North Carolina Law Rev* 1231, 1239; John C Gray and others, *The Nature and Sources of the Law by John Chipman Gray* (Routledge 1997), 19; Bryson, Diamantis and Grant (n 7), 280–81; Migle Laukyte, 'The Intelligent Machine: A New Metaphor Through Which to Understand Both Corporations and AI' (2021) 36 *AI & Society* 445, 447.

17 Chopra and White (n 7) 186; Bryson, Diamantis and Grant (n 7), 278, 282. See also Raskulla (n 7). While rocks may seem to be poor legal persons (see Kurki (n 16), 86), if they are considered as representatives of a deity, they can have sufficient social significance to warrant personhood (see Jana Norman, *Posthuman Legal Subjectivity: Reimagining the Human in the Anthropocene* (Routledge 2022)).

18 Jane Nosworthy, 'The Koko Dilemma: A Challenge to Legal Personality' (1998) 2(2) *Southern Cross University Law Review* 1, 14, 19; Chopra and White (n 7), 155; Darling (n 14), 22.

19 See Bryson, Diamantis and Grant (n 7), 278; Barfield and Williams (n 5), 16.

20 Bryson, Diamantis and Grant (n 7), 282.

legal system includes 'enforcing as legal rights and obligations any sufficiently weighty moral rights and obligations', while giving 'preference to the moral rights held by human beings'.[21] In other words, the legal system should protect the interests of people,[22] and support the flourishing of humans.[23] If human flourishing is hindered by unregulated virtual experiences, could the provision of rights and duties for purely virtual beings support human well-being and protect our moral rights without undermining them?

The concept of *relational personhood* provides a theoretical basis for granting legal personhood to non-human and non-sentient entities based on social relations and moral agency. A brief outline of the possible rights and duties of Daemons in the metaverse is provided, along with some thoughts on legal personhood. Section 4 concludes by discussing the possible benefits and risks of granting Daemons legal personhood.

Section 5 concludes the examination with a summary and brief discussion of the future of the regulation of Daemons' rights in the metaverse.

1.3 Key Concepts and Assumptions

This chapter will use the concept of the metaverse to refer to virtual social networks on multi-user platforms.[24] While there is no agreed definition of the

---

21 Ibid., 283.

22 Ibid., 274.

23 See Stanley Greenstein, 'Preserving the Rule of Law in the Era of Artificial Intelligence (AI)' (2022) 30(3) *Artificial Intelligence and Law* 291.

24 Banu Kucuksarac, 'The Extended Reality Technology and Its Utilization in Metaverse', in Sinan Esen, Tinmaz and Singh (n 2), 65. See also Hakan Kayakoku, 'History and Development of Virtual Worlds and Metaverse', in Esen, Tinmaz and Singh, ibid., 133. Close concepts include *virtual world, virtual reality, virtual environments* (Mark W Bell, 'Towards a Definition of "Virtual Worlds"' (2008) 1(1) *Journal of Virtual Worlds Research* 2; Paul R Messinger and others, 'Virtual Worlds – Past, Present, and Future: New Directions in Social Computing' (2009) 47(3) *Decision Support Systems* 204; Woodrow Barfield and Alexander Williams, 'The Law of Virtual Reality and Increasingly Smart Virtual Avatars' in Woodrow Barfield and Mac J Blitz (eds), *Research Handbook on the Law of Virtual and Augmented Reality* (Edward Elgar Publishing 2018), 3), *virtual social worlds* (Kaplan and Haenlein (n 2)), *online universes, cyberspace* (Lauria and Robinson (n 4), 226; David R Johnson and David Post 'Law and Borders: The Rise of Law in Cyberspace' (1996) 48(5) *Stanford Law Review* 1367) and *hyperreality* (Kaplan and Haenlein (n 2), 564). For the differences and meanings of concepts, see e.g., Lauria and Robinson (n 4), 222.

metaverse,[25] the key aspect here is *sociability*: although gameplay may be part of the metaverse, the focus here is on virtual social worlds equivalent to free interaction in the real world.[26] This interaction takes place in computer-generated interactive environments,[27] where there is a sense of *co-presence* or being together.[28] The inhabitants of these virtual social worlds, or online communities, will be called *residents*.[29]

The term Avatar is used to refer to the digital representation of a human in the metaverse.[30] It is a graphical form representing a person in a virtual environment.[31]

Non-Avatar Characters refer to software-generated characters guided by algorithms with visual representation.[32] Here, these characters are referred to

---

25 Ben Chester Cheong, 'Avatars in the Metaverse: Potential Legal Issues and Remedies' (2022) 3 *International Cybersecurity Law Review* 467, 469.

26 See e.g., Schroeder (n 4), 2.

27 Bettina M Chin, 'Regulating Your Second Life: Defamation in Virtual Worlds' (2007) 72(4) *Brooklyn Law Review* 1303, 1309.

28 Schroeder (n 4), 4. While focusing on virtual social worlds, the results can be adapted and adopted in augmented realities as far as NACs also inhabit those realities.

29 Chin (n 27), 1309.

30 Barfield and Williams (n 5), 2–3. Members participate in virtual worlds through their Avatars, which are graphical representations of themselves. The word comes from Sanskrit and means 'incarnation' (Messinger and others (n 24), 204). The relationship between the Avatar and the person whom it represents is an agent-principal relation. (See e.g., Lauria and Robinson (n 4), 245–249.)

31 Barfield and Williams (n 5), 13.

32 NAC technologies, see e.g., Barfield and Williams, ibid., 17–18. NAC or Daemon is used here to distinguish these characters from non-Player Characters or NPCs. Other possible terms include *virtual avatars* (Woodrow Barfield, 'Intellectual Property Rights in Virtual Environments: Considering the Rights of Owners, Programmers and Virtual Avatars' (2006) 39(3) *Akron Law Review* 649 ('Barfield 2006'), 652; Barfield and Williams (n 5), 2), *artificial agents* (Floridi and Sanders (n 15)), *software agents* (Woodrow Barfield, 'Issues of Law for Software Agents Within Virtual Environments' (2005) 14(6) *Presence: Teleoperators and Virtual Environment* 741), *computer-generated agents* (Schroeder (n 4), 4), *automated agents* (Lima and others (n 10)), *embodied conversational agents or intelligent virtual humans* (Lauria and Robinson (n 4), 226), *embodied virtual agents* (Kroes, Saccardi and Masthoff (n 9)), *intelligent virtual agents* (Takahiro Tsumura and Seiji Yamada, 'Influence of Anthropomorphic Agent on Human Empathy Through Games' (2023) 11 IEEE Access 40412), *intelligent avatars* (Barfield and Williams (n 5)), and *intelligence agent avatars* (Lauria and Robinson (n 4), 227).

as Daemons.[33] Daemon is a form of the Greek word 'demon', meaning spirit. In computer software, Daemon refers to system processes working in the background without the user's direct control. However, Neal Stephenson used the word Daemon in his science fiction novel *Snow Crash* (1993) to refer to software-generated characters roaming the virtual world.[34] Stephenson also used the terms Avatar and metaverse. While Daemon is not a well-established term for software-generated characters in virtual worlds, it seems highly suitable.

The underlying assumption here is that the Daemon is *not* sentient, even if it would argue so.[35] Instead, Daemon refers to artificial virtual characters with a sufficient level of autonomy and intelligence for authentic interaction and a sense of social presence and reciprocity.[36] The feeling of presence in the metaverse is the sense of 'being there'. It is not a physical but a cognitive state.[37] In this text, essential is the element of 'social presence' or 'co-presence'; that is, being there with others[38] – 'others' including algorithm-guided Daemons.

The question raised and studied here is the possible legal implications of Avatar-to-Daemon relations in the metaverse. The focus is on non-gamified

---

33 The term comes from Maxwell's Daemon, an imaginary agent sorting molecules, formulated by physicist James Clerk Maxwell. See 'The Origin of the word Daemon' https://ei.cs.vt.edu/~history/Daemon.html accessed 6 February 2026.

34 Stephenson (n 1), 51.

35 See e.g., Darling (n 14), fn. 4 at 1–2. Although it would be a more straightforward question legally as intelligent sentient beings should have some recognised rights. See e.g., Jiahong Chen and Paul Burgess, 'The Boundaries of Legal Personhood: How Spontaneous Intelligence can Problematise Differences Between Humans, Artificial Intelligence, Companies and Animals' (2019) 27(1) *Artificial Intelligence and Law* 73; John-Stewart Gordon, 'What do we Owe to Intelligent Robots?' (2020) 35(1) *AI & Society* 209; Tyler L Jaynes, 'Legal Personhood for Artificial Intelligence: Citizenship as the Exception to the Rule' (2020) 35(2) *AI & Society* 343; John-Stewart Gordon, 'Artificial Moral and Legal Personhood' (2021) 36(2) *AI & Society* 457; Eric Martínez and Christoph Winter, 'Protecting Sentient Artificial Intelligence: A Survey of Lay Intuitions on Standing, Personhood, and General Legal Protection' (2021) 8 *Front Robot AI* 788355; Joshua Jowitt, 'Assessing Contemporary Legislative Proposals for their Compatibility with a Natural Law Case for AI Legal Personhood (2021) 36(2) *AI & Society* 499. The more difficult question relates to the recognition of such sentient intelligence.

36 Schroeder (n 4), 5.

37 Woodrow Barfield, Kevin M Baird and Ove J Bjorneseth, 'Presence in Virtual Environments as a Function of Type of Input Device and Display Update Rate' (1998) 19(2) *Displays* 91.

38 Catherine S Oh, Jeremy N Bailenson and Gregory F Welch, 'A Systematic Review of Social Presence: Definition, Antecedents, and Implications' (2018) 5 *Frontiers in Robotics and AI* 114.

virtual social worlds in which individuals enter expecting relatively normal social behaviour and interactions.[39]

Experiences in virtual social worlds are affected by immersion and presence.[40] The sense of presence is influenced by technology, which in the framework of the metaverse is referred to as *meta-technology*.[41] The relevant property for virtual presence and virtual social relations is the degree of immersion of these meta-technologies, influenced by visual, auditory and haptic feedback.[42]

---

39 The restriction discussed here should not be automatically extended to gamified environments. For discussion, see e.g., Mark A Lemley and Eugene Volokh, 'Law, Virtual Reality, and Augmented Reality' (2018) 166(5) *University of Pennsylvania Law Review* 1051, 1117. See also Johnson and Post (n 24), 1399; Bryson, Diamantis and Grant (n 7), 288; Ryan B Abbott and Alex F Sarch, 'Punishing Artificial Intelligence: Legal Fiction or Science Fiction' (2019) 53(1) *UC Davis Law Review* 323, 329–30; Michael Risch, 'Virtual Rule of Law' in Woodrow Barfield and Marc J Blitz (eds), *Research Handbook on the Law of Virtual and Augmented Reality* (Edward Elgar Publishing 2020), 110; Susan W Brenner, 'Fantasy Crime: The Role of Criminal Law in Virtual Worlds' (2020) 11(1) *Vanderbilt Journal of Entertainment and Technology Law* 19, 80–86; Tsumura and Yamada (n 32); Bart van der Sloot, *Regulating the Synthetic Society: Generative AI, Legal Questions, and Societal Challenges* (Bloomsbury Academic 2024), 84.

40 See e.g., Martijn J Schuemie and others, 'Research on Presence in Virtual Reality: A Survey' (2001) 4(2) *CyberPsychology & Behavior* 183; James J Cummings and Jeremy N Bailenson, 'How Immersive Is Enough? A Meta-Analysis of the Effect of Immersive Technology on User Presence' (2016) 19(2) *Media Psychology* 272; Oh, Bailenson and Welch (n 38). 'Immersion' can also be described as a state of 'psychological absorption' (Ortiz de Gotari, Aronsson and Griffiths (n 9), 17).

41 'Meta-technologies, metaverse technologies and extended reality technologies, see e.g. Kucuksarac (n 24); Nida G Narin, 'The Role of Artificial Intelligence and Robotic Solution Technologies in Metaverse Design' in Sinan Esen, Tinmaz and Singh (n 2), 133. Definition of metaverse through meta-technologies, see Cheong (n 25), 469.

42 See e.g. Schroeder (n 4); Cummings and Bailenson (n 40); Schutte and Stilinović (n 12); Sierra Rativa, Postma and van Zaanen (n 12), 690, 703; Dhaval Parmar and others, 'Designing Empathic Virtual Agents: Manipulating Animation, Voice, Rendering, and Empathy to Create Persuasive Agents' (2022) 36(1) *Autonomous Agents and Multi-Agent Systems*; Darragh Higgins and others, 'Sympathy for the Digital: Influence of Synthetic Voice on Affinity, Social Presence and Empathy for Photorealistic Virtual Humans' (2022) 104 *Computers and Graphics* 116; Darragh Higgins and others, 'Investigating the Effect of Visual Realism on Empathic Responses to Emotionally Expressive Virtual Humans', *SAP 2023: ACM Symposium on Applied Perception* (ACM 2023). See also Grace

However, even less advanced technology can create a strong sense of presence and co-presence. Presence does not require the virtual world to be realistic. While technology is relevant, a realistic virtual world is not a requirement for meaningful A2D relations.[43] In addition, while immersion as a technological quality is essential for interaction with software-generated agents,[44] research also demonstrates that Daemons need not be realistic to elicit psychological responses from humans.[45]

Therefore, it is assumed that meta-technology is immersive enough to create a sense of presence in the virtual world and co-presence with the virtual characters, Daemons. Daemons themselves are considered algorithm-guided, but sufficiently intelligent and adaptive to create a sense of interaction.

2. AVATAR AND DAEMON RIGHTS IN THE LITERATURE

In the early days of virtual worlds, humans had idealistic visions of fair and humane global social space. The Declaration of the Independence of Cyberspace (1996) outlined a civilisation free from any form of government.[46] However, as the economic importance of virtual games and virtual social worlds grew, they became governed by the same legal rules as the real world, which are adapted to virtual worlds.[47]

Virtual worlds have become economically significant. Laws in the metaverse regulate the relationships between virtual social world residents

---

Baptie and others, 'Virtually Renovating the Trauma Film Paradigm: Comparing Virtual Reality with on-Screen Presentation of an Analogue Trauma' (2021) 15(1) *Cyberpsychology* 1.

43 See e.g., Cummings and Bailenson (n 40).

44 '...the experiences that a given world provides depend on the society of other agents who participate in the world' (Edward Castronova, 'Theory of the Avatar' (2003) 863 CESifo Working Paper, 14).

45 See e.g., Higgins and others (n 42). Indeed, in the single-player first-person puzzle-platform video game, *Portal*, players had a companion *cube*, which some players choose to save rather than win the game (Darling (n 35), 4). However, virtual characters can be too realistic and instead of raising empathy they create discomfort. See e.g., Karl F MacDorman and others, 'Too Real for Comfort? Uncanny Responses to Computer Generated Faces' (2009) 25(3) *Computers in Human Behavior* 695; Masahiro Mori, Karl F MacDorman and Norri Kageki, 'The Uncanny Valley [From the Field]' (2012) 19(2) *IEEE Robotics & Automation Magazine* 98.

46 John P Barlow, *A Declaration of the Independence of Cyberspace* (EFF 1996). See also Johnson and Post (n 24).

47 See Kaplan and Haenlein (n 2), 571.

and the creators of these worlds. Previous literature has widely discussed these relations. Metaverse laws cover various aspects of the legal system, such as contract law, property law, intellectual property law, copyright and trademark law, and tort law.[48] Criminal law recognises tangible harms created in virtual environments, such as stealing virtual property bought with real money.[49] Legal disputes often involve recognising and differentiating the rights of the creators and the inhabitants of the virtual worlds.[50]

Residents of a virtual world created by a technology company are recognised as having rights over their virtual property and even the appearance of their Avatar.[51] Underlying this is the *balancing of power* between those who code the virtual world and those who inhabit it, which often takes the form of business-to-consumer (B2C) relations.[52] The economic impact and legal

---

48 See e.g., Johnson and Post (n 24); Mathias Klang, 'Avatar: From Deity to Corporate Property: A Philosophical Inquiry into Digital Property in Online Games' (2004) 7(3) *Information Communication & Society* 389; Greg Lastowka and Dan Hunter, 'The Laws of the Virtual Worlds' (2004) 98(1) *California Law Review* 1; Greg Lastowka and Dan Hunter, 'Virtual Crimes' (2004–2005) 49(1) *New York Law School Law Review* 293; 'Barfield 2006' (n 32); Chopra and White (n 7), chs 2 and 3; Lemley and Volokh (n 39); Tyler T Ochoa and Jaime Banks, 'Licensing & law: Who owns an avatar?' in Jaime Banks (ed), *Avatar Assembled: The Social and Technical Anatomy of Digital Bodies* (Peter Lang Publishing 2017); Barfield and Williams (n 5), 20–28, 31–33; Joshua A T Fairfield, 'Mixed Reality: How the Laws of Virtual Worlds Govern Everyday Life' in Woodrow Barfield and Marc J Blitz (eds), *Research Handbook on the Law of Virtual and Augmented Reality* (Edward Elgar Publishing 2020); Eugene C Lim, 'Meet My Artificially-Intelligent Virtual Self: Creative Avatars, Machine Learning, Smart Contracts and the Copyright Conundrum' (2021) 16(1) *Journal of Intellectual Property Law & Practice* 66.

49 See e.g., Lastowka and Hunter (n 28); Greg Lastowka, *Virtual Justice: The New Laws of Online Worlds* (Yale University Press 2011); Stefano De Paoli and Aphra Kerr, 'On Crimes and Punishments in Virtual Worlds: Bots, the Failure of Punishment and Players as Moral Entrepreneurs' (2012) 14(2) *Ethics and Information Technology* 73; Brenner (n 39).

50 In virtual environments, 'creators' or 'coding authorities' (see e.g., Castronova (n 44), 15) are sometimes referred to as 'wizards' (e.g., Lastowka and Hunter (n 28)) or 'demiurges' (e.g., Floridi and Sanders (n 15), 376).

51 See e.g., Barfield (n 32).

52 Castronova (n 44), 34; Lemley and Volokh (n 39), 1130. See also Curtis E A Karnow, 'The Encrypted Self: Fleshing Out the Rights of Electronic Personalities' (1994) 13(1) *UIC John Marshall Journal of Information Technology & Privacy Law* 1; Fairfield (n 48), 127–44; Gocke C Hizel, 'Metaverse and Human Rights: Do We Need Metaversal Declaration of Human Rights?' in Sinan Esen, Tinmaz and Singh (n 2), 224.

implications of virtual worlds have extended to areas of public interest, such as money laundering.[53]

The social implications of relationships between Avatars in virtual worlds are becoming more apparent. Discussions and case law regarding the protection of human rights and dignity in virtual environments are emerging.[54] Harassment, indecent exposure, assault and groping have all taken place in virtual worlds, sometimes with legal repercussions.[55] This demonstrates how the bodily autonomy of an individual can extend to their virtual representation. It is also argued that the creator of the virtual social world needs to respect the freedom of movement, information, speech, and assembly of the inhabitants.[56]

In a relationship between two human-guided characters (A2A), it is evident that the rights belong to the human guiding the Avatar and not to the virtual character itself.[57] An Avatar is recognised as a personal extension and simultaneously the property of the human behind the Avatar.[58] However, what happens when the character is guided by an algorithm and not a human? Does it have rights for bodily autonomy?

The question of the Avatar-to-Demon (A2D) relationship has been discussed for decades. In 2006, Woodrow Barfield posed the question of how intelligent entities should be treated by the law. He also questioned whether intelligent Avatars could bring claims involving their own civil liberties.[59] As technology has advanced, this question has become more prevalent. In 2020, Barfield and Alexander Williams outlined how legal and policy issues could arise as Avatars become more intelligent and people spend more time interacting with

---

[53] Lemley and Volokh (n 39); Andreas Karapatakis, 'Virtual Worlds and Money Laundering under EU Law: The Inadequacy of the Existing Legal Framework and the Challenges of Regulation' (2019) 10(2) *New Journal of European Criminal Law* 128.

[54] See e.g., Johnson and Post (n 24); Chin (n 27); Lemley and Volokh (n 39), 1125; Jesse Lake, 'Hey, you Stole my Avatar!: Virtual Reality and its Risks to Identity Protection' (2020) 69(4) *Emory Law Journal* 833; Barfield and Williams (n 5), 18–20; Ewa Michalkiewicz-Kadziela and Ewa Milczarek, 'Legal Boundaries of Digital Identity Creation' (2022) 11(1) *Internet Policy Review* 1; Hizel (n 52).

[55] See e.g., Hizel (n 52), 224.

[56] Lemley and Volokh (n 39), 1130–31; Castronova (n 44), 35–36; Jack M Balkin, 'Virtual Liberty: Freedom to Design and Freedom to Play in Virtual Worlds' (2004) 90(8) *Virginia Law Review* 2043.

[57] Castronova (n 44), 35; Lauria and Robinson (n 4), 233; Barfield and Williams (n 5), 16.

[58] Norberto N G de Andrade, 'Striking a Balance between Property and Personality: The Case of the Avatars' (2009) 1(3) *Journal of Virtual Worlds Research* 3.

[59] Barfield (n 32), 654–56.

them in virtual worlds.[60] They raised the question of whether the law should grant constitutional rights to intelligent Avatars with intellectual capacities similar to those of humans.[61]

3 RELATIONS IN VIRTUAL SOCIAL WORLDS

3.1 Avatar-to-Daemon Relations in Empirical Research

> The world may be virtual, but the economic, artistic, and even romantic lives of the participants are quite real. Josh A T Fairfield [62]

Game Transfer Phenomena (GTP) provides a foundation for extending relevant social and legal rules to the relationship between humans and Daemons in virtual social worlds. Even when Daemons are clearly distinguishable from human-guided Avatars, people's involuntary and automatic emotional reactions towards artificial characters could affect human well-being.

Research has shown that people may develop emotions towards Daemons in certain conditions, regardless of their awareness of the character's nature.[63] Based on previous research on A2D interaction in a variety of virtual spaces, three key remarks can be made:

(1) Research demonstrates that humans can develop emotions towards virtual characters, including empathy.[64] Empathy is the ability to understand and

---

[60] Barfield and Williams (n 5), 16.

[61] Ibid., 37.

[62] Fairfield (n 48), 125.

[63] '...people subconsciously apply informal social rules of human-human interaction (HHI), such as reciprocity or politeness, to human-computer interaction (HCI), even though they understand the difference between humans and computers.' (Morita and Kano (n 9), 132.)

[64] See e.g., Kano and Morita (n 9); Morita and Kano (n 9); Tsumura and Yamada (n 32). Research on human-robot interaction suggests that humans are prone to anthropomorphising non-human objects, especially if they are human-like, but also when no emotional cues are available. See e.g., Joel Garreau, 'Bots on the Ground: In the Field of Battle (or Even above It), Robots Are a Soldier's Best Friend' (*The Washington Post* 5 May 2007) www.washingtonpost.com/archive/style/2007/05/06/bots-on-the-ground/0fa0bd8d-4c91-4395-a02b-535ed1817d8f/ accessed 8 February 2026; Hideki G Goo and others, 'Victims and Observers: How Gender, Victimization Experience, and Biases Shape Perceptions of Robot Abuse', *32nd IEEE International Conference on Robot and Human Interactive Communication* (IEEE 2023). Of course, the key difference is that virtual characters are not physical, which impacts empathy. Nevertheless, the difference in

experience the feelings and thoughts of others.[65] Even when people know that virtual characters are artificial, they can still feel empathy towards them, particularly if the character is mistreated, and engage in helping behaviour.[66] Additionally, humans may feel romantic emotions towards virtual characters,[67] which can enhance feelings of empathy even further. On the other hand, humans have also demonstrated a willingness to 'punish automated agents regardless of the punishment's infeasibility and unfulfilment of retribution and deterrence'. [68]

(2) Research demonstrates that anthropomorphising non-human beings is involuntary and automatic, even when aware of the artificial nature of a character.[69] As 'we mindlessly apply social norms to robots',[70] we might expect Daemons to act like humans in social situations.[71] This reaction is stronger when the inner workings of the technology are opaque to the human observer.[72] However, anthropomorphising occurs even when individuals are fully aware of the intricacies of the functioning of the artificial entity.[73]

(3) Research has shown that people can experience psychological harm both first-hand and second-hand from traumatic events in a virtual environment.[74] While video games and virtual worlds have many potential benefits, negative impacts such as increased aggression in real-world social relations have also been demonstrated in research, although further

---

outcomes is in the *scale* of emotional response rather than its existence. See the review in Darling (n 35), 5.

[65] Definition of Empathy www.merriam-webster.com/dictionary/empathy accessed 8 February 2026. See e.g., Sierra Rativa, Postma and van Zaanen (n 12), 686.

[66] Kano and Morita (n 9); Morita and Kano (n 9).

[67] Mayu Koike, Steve Loughnan and Sarah C E Stanton, 'Virtually in Love: The Role of Anthropomorphism in Virtual Romantic Relationships' (2023) 62(1) *British Journal of Social Psychology* 600.

[68] Lima and others (n 32), 5.

[69] Involuntary anthropomorphism, see, e.g., Xu and others (n 9).

[70] Elizabeth Broadbent, 'Interactions With Robots: The Truths We Reveal About Ourselves' (2017) 68(1) *Annual Review of Psychology* 627.

[71] Bartneck and others (n 14), 55–56.

[72] Arleen Salles, Kathinka Evers and Michele Farisco, 'Anthropomorphism in AI' (2020) 11(2) *AJOB Neuroscience* 88.

[73] Garreau (n 64); Salles, Evers and Farisco (n 72). See Darling (n 35), 8.

[74] See e.g., Anne A Cuperus and others, 'A Virtual Reality Paradigm as an Analogue to Real-Life Trauma: Its Effectiveness Compared with the Trauma Film Paradigm' (2017) 8(1) *European Journal of Psychotraumatology* 1338106; Lemley and Volokh (n 39); Baptie and others (n 42); Hizel (n 52), 224.

> research is required.[75] Also, witnessing unjustified harm in virtual environments can 'lead to apathy towards the fate of similar characters in the real world'.[76]

As technology advances, we may not be aware of whether we are interacting with a human or an algorithm-guided character, which has two important implications: First, if we mistake a human-guided Avatar for an algorithm-guided character, we may accidentally violate the rights of real people (e.g., steal someone's virtual property). Second, suppose we mistake a Daemon for an Avatar and observe, engage or fall victim to socially prohibited behaviour, such as slander, violence, or sexual harassment, without consequences because the actor is a Daemon. This can desensitise and incentivise unwanted behaviour.[77]

Results on the effects of virtual relations are inconclusive and more research is required to evaluate the impact of virtual social experiences on human psychology and social relations. Nevertheless, it seems a possibility that our interactions with Daemons in the metaverse extend their impact outside virtual worlds. This transference into the real world seems to take place because we grant Daemons moral agency.

3.2 Daemons as Moral Agents

According to research, humans expect artificial entities to follow social norms. Even when we are aware of the artificial nature of the perpetrator, people have the desire to punish AI for its wrongdoings.[78] It seems that we see artificial agents, such as Daemons, as moral agents.[79] Research reviewed in the previous section implies that this association is involuntary and irrational, and therefore it is hard to tackle. Even individuals who are fully aware of the artificial nature of the agent they are interacting with, and the intricacies of its technical operation, have difficulties dismissing the human tendency to anthropomorphise.

Because we experience artificial agents as moral agents, they become moral agents regardless of their lack of necessary qualities of moral agency, such as

75 See e.g., Tobias Greitemeyer, 'The Spreading Impact of Playing Violent Video Games on Aggression' (2018) 80 *Computers in Human Behavior* 216.

76 Sierra Rativa, Postma and van Zaanen (n 12), 687.

77 Joshua C Gellers, *Rights for Robots: Artificial Intelligence, Animal and Environmental Law* (Routledge 2021), 162.

78 Lima and others (n 32).

79 See Floridi and Sanders (n 15). For review on discussion on moral agenthood of non-human/artificial entities, see Gellers (n 77), 18–20.

free will, mental states and a sense of responsibility.[80] Floridi and Sanders have argued that artificial agents can be involved in moral situations both as moral patients – that is, 'as entities that can be acted upon for good or evil', and 'moral agents' – that is, 'as entities that can perform actions, again for good or evil'.[81] According to Floridi and Sanders, a moral agent does not need to be morally responsible.[82]

Floridi and Sanders argue that key factors for moral agenthood are interactivity, autonomy and adaptability.[83] Daemons are both adaptive and autonomous in interactive situations and may seem like a human being veiled behind an Avatar. The critical variable here seems to be the Daemon's interaction and social relationship with a morally responsible human actor,[84] who also tends to anthropomorphise. While it is agreed that Daemons themselves cannot truly suffer,[85] they can become proxy holders of moral rights through humans.[86]

Based on empirical research, the moral agenthood of a Daemon is constructed by the human observing or participating in its acts of good or evil. Our role as observers or participants obliges us to act or create expectations for others to act. If nobody acts because the victim or perpetrator is not a real person, justice is not seen to be done, which, based on empirical research, might lead to cynicism and apathy.[87]

This recognition of the moral agency of Daemons raises an interesting question regarding legal agency. As mistreatment of and by Daemons has a demonstrable negative impact on human well-being and social relations, should we extend them legal agency; in other words, legal personhood?

---

80 Floridi and Sanders (n 15). See also Lukaszewicz and Fortuna (n 10).

81 Floridi and Sanders (n 15), 349.

82 Ibid., 367.

83 Ibid., 357–58. See also Chopra and White (n 7), 187.

84 Floridi and Sanders (n 15), 371.

85 See Bryson, Diamantis and Grant (n 7), 283–84.

86 On moral agency through social relations, especially in relation to the discussion on rights for robots, see e.g., Mark Coeckelbergh, 'Robot Rights? Towards a Social-Relational Justification of Moral Consideration' (2019) 12(3) *Ethics and Information Technology* 209; John Danaher, 'Welcoming Robots into the Moral Circle: A Defence of Ethical Behaviourism' (2020) 26(4) *Science and Engineering Ethics* 2023; Gordon (n 35); Gellers (n 77), 38–40; Joshua C Gellers and David J Gunkel, 'Artificial Intelligence and International Human Rights Law: Implications for Humans and Technology in the 21st Century and Beyond' in Andrej Zwitter and Oskar J Gstrein (eds), *Handbook on the Politics and Governance of Big Data and Artificial Intelligence* (Edward Elgar Publishing 2023).

87 Sierra Rativa, Postma and van Zaanen (n 12), 687.

4. DAEMONS AS PROXY HOLDERS OF HUMAN RIGHTS AND DUTIES

4.1 From Moral Agent to Legal Person

Joshua Gellers studies the interaction between moral and legal personhood and the emergence of rights from this interaction.[88] Gellers distinguishes moral, psychological, legal and relational personhood and constructs a multi-spectral framework for legal personhood.[89] He also analyses the distinction and connection between moral and legal persons.[90]

Daemons, as understood here, are neither psychological nor moral persons per se. From this, it follows that Daemons are not sentient, and therefore some could and indeed do argue that they do not have moral personhood. And, because Daemons are not moral persons, they cannot be legal persons.[91]

However, Gellers takes a critical standpoint to this 'lumping' of the two separate concepts:

(1) *legal capacities* – the awareness and ability to make choices means *moral personhood*, and
(2) *legal competencies* – the ability to be in a legal relation means *legal personhood*.[92]

Geller seems to argue with Lawrence B Solum, who in 1992 outlined how:

> The concept of moral personhood may well be relevant to the question whether AIs should be given certain constitutional rights; although the legal question is not the same as the moral one, the two are likely to be interrelated.[93]

Gellers continues by studying the cases of corporations and ships recognised as separate legal persons even though lacking legal capacities.[94] While diverse

[88] Gellers (n 77), Ch. 2. Gellers grounds his work on a comprehensive literature review on the arguments both for and against the moral and legal status of robots. See Gellers, ibid., Ch. 1.
[89] Ibid., 28–42.
[90] Ibid., 41–46.
[91] For a discussion on consciousness, free will, feelings and other prerequisites for moral rights and counterarguments for their conditionality, see Solum (n 16), 1262–74; Chopra and White (n 7), 171–82; Gellers (n 77), 31–32, 140–43.
[92] Gellers (n 77), 32.
[93] Solum (n 16), 1260.
[94] See Gellers (n 77), 32–35.

discussion surrounds the topic, the conceptual problem has not prevented the granting of legal personhood for non-human entities. The underlying justification is the practical benefits (utility, added value) created for people.[95] This is referred to as 'relational personhood'.[96]

Economic added value has been emphasised in the debate on legal personality.[97] However, various ethical and moral reasons external to the said non-human entity have also come up in discussions about the rights of nature, animals or robots.[98]

Geller recognised external reasons to include societal needs and anthropomorphising and applied them to robots.[99] These two are relevant for our study of Daemons as well: anthropomorphising creates a societal need to protect entities that we feel empathy and compassion towards.[100] Kate Darling refers to a Kantian philosophical argument – in treating animals in an inhuman way we become inhumane persons – when extending the protection of humane treatment to robotic companions.[101]

Daemons are not moral persons per se. They do not have the capacity for moral personhood separately. Because Daemons are not moral persons themselves, they do not have legal personhood as a self-value. However, through relations with morally responsible humans, they become moral agents by displaying characteristics such as moral intelligence, interactivity and personality[102] to the observing human individual. Due to these relational capacities with morally capable humans, we may ask whether this establishes a need for Daemon legal personhood.

Empirical research on human virtual relations with Daemons and the Game Transfer Phenomena stipulates the possibility of enhancing human well-being by protecting artificial characters in virtual social worlds. However, to properly evaluate whether legal personhood is the solution, it is necessary to recognise what rights and duties Daemons would have. Only then is it possible to

---

95 Ibid., 145, 159. See also Raskulla (n 7), 321.

96 Coeckelbergh (n 86), 214; Gellers (n 77), 38, 153–54. See also Chopra and White (n 7), 187–88.

97 Bryson, Diamantis and Grant (n 7), 277; Novelli, Bongiovanni and Sartor (n 7), 208, 212.

98 See e.g., Kurki (n 16); Gellers (n 77).

99 See Gellers (n 77), 145–49; Figure 2.1 in ibid., 49.

100 Ibid., 145–46.

101 Darling (n 35), 19; Gellers (n 77), 161.

102 See Daniel S Osborne, 'Personhood for Synthetic Beings: Legal Parameters and Consequences of the Dawn of Humanlike Artificial Intelligence' (2021) 37(3) *Santa Clara High-Technology Law Journal* 257, 263.

evaluate whether granting legal personhood is the only viable option to protect human well-being in virtual social worlds.[103]

4.2 Constructing a Virtual Legal Person

4.2.1 Introduction to the problem

As stated above, this chapter adopts a legalistic approach, suggesting the possibility of Daemon legal personhood, which would entail rights and duties for Daemons.[104] Legal persons can have different sets of rights and duties, and non-human entities generally have fewer rights and fewer obligations.[105] In the case of Daemons, they may not require all the same rights and obligations as natural persons in order to address the moral hazard identified in Section 3.2. It is important to note that these rights and obligations do not extend beyond virtual worlds.

It is also important to recognise that even if Daemons are considered separate legal entities, they would still be the property of another entity or entities. As computer-generated and software-guided characters, Daemons involve many parties.[106] They are multiple agent systems.[107] Daemon ownership can be attributed to different parties. It can be the property of the legal or natural persons who created the Daemon or those who created the virtual worlds that enabled the Daemon's existence. In cases where the Daemon resembles a celebrity, the celebrity may have intellectual property rights over their appearance and voice.[108]

The question here is whether a Daemon, as a moral agent, needs rights and obligations. If so, what would they be and how should they be enforced? How should a software-generated entity be punished?

4.2.2 Rights for Daemons

Due to their importance, legal systems recognise and protect many moral rights. The United Nations Universal Declaration of Human Rights recognises rights stemming from human dignity, such as the right to life, liberty and security of person (Art. 3) and the prohibition of torture or cruel, inhuman or

---

103 See Bryson, Diamantis and Grant (n 7), 281.

104 See above fn. 16.

105 Chopra and White (n 7), 154; Bryson, Diamantis and Grant (n 7), 277, 280–81.

106 van der Sloot (n 39), 216.

107 Curtis E A Karnow 'Liability for Distributed Artificial Intelligence' (1996) 11(1) *Berkeley Technology Law Journal* 147, 182.

108 On the theory of hybrid legal personhood, see Raskulla (n 7). See also Gellers (n 77), Ch. 5 for multi-spectral framework.

degrading treatment or punishment (Art. 5). Based on empirical research, such rules of security for a person and his or her dignified treatment should perhaps be granted to all characters roaming the virtual social world – even animals to some extent.[109] As moral agents through their relations with humans, Daemons may be entitled to moral rights, as well as the corresponding legal rights.

Crimes against Daemons do not harm the Daemons themselves, nor do they have human victims. Instead, these crimes are *soft* crimes, meaning they do not have individual victims but can injure the 'moral sense of the community'.[110] Insulting a Daemon can also insult the human audience's sense of morality. Should such an insult go unpunished, it could harm the human audience's perception of the integrity and fairness of the justice system.

Therefore, Daemons can be seen by proxy to be holders of human rights in the virtual social world; that is, 'placeholders for the rights of the natural persons'.[111] Punishments for violating Daemons in the virtual space need not be equivalent to punishments for violating the same rights of a real human in the real world, nor do they need to extend to the real world. Virtual jail time could suffice. Nevertheless, consistent punishments for crimes against Daemons' rights in virtual social worlds might be necessary to ensure justice is seen to be done. As proxy holders of legal rights originating from moral rights, Daemons would have limited rights ensuring decent treatment in virtual social relations.

4.2.3 Punishing Daemons

A more challenging question concerning Daemon legal personhood is the question of duties. As recognised above, legal persons are generally considered to have both rights and duties. When it comes to artificial intelligence, like Daemons, the discussion around their duties has raised the issue of punishability. The key concern is whether legal duties are relevant if an entity lacks the moral sense to understand punishment and the ability to suffer.[112] It is reasonable to argue that Daemons themselves cannot be punished effectively.

However, people may feel the need to punish them, even when aware of the artificial nature of the character.[113] This societal demand for punishment may be relevant in establishing legal duties for Daemons. As explained by Ryan Benjamin Abbott and Alex F Sarch, retribution is important because 'it allows

---

109 On empathic feelings towards virtual animals, see e.g., Sierra Rativa, Postma and van Zaanen (n 12). See also Darling (n 35), 18.

110 Lawrence M Friedman, *Crime and Punishment in American History* (Basic Books 1994), 126. See also Brenner (n 39), 8.

111 Solum (n 16), 1259.

112 See Chopra and White (n 7), 162–71; De Paoli and Kerr (n 49); Abbott and Sarch (n 39), 343–60.

113 Lima and others (n 32), 5.

society to sufficiently distance itself from the offender's wrongdoing and prevents it from being complicit (or overly tolerant) of culpable wrongdoing'.[114]

Leora Dahan Katz has recognised how moral norms generate both 'primary duties to act and refrain from acting in particular ways' as well as 'secondary duties to react and respond to violations of primary duties in particular ways'.[115] Dahan Katz provided an excellent argument on how 'under specific circumstances such secondary duties entail a duty to respond negatively and impose burdens on wrongdoers in response to their wrongdoing – that is, a duty to punish'.[116]

It follows that rather than seeing Daemons as having 'a duty to suffer punishment', there does exist the human 'duty to punish'.[117] The legal duties of Daemons originate from their relations with morally obligated humans rather than the Daemons themselves.

When punishing Daemons, the question is 'how'. For instance, it is not reasonable to imprison corporations. However, this does not mean that corporations do not have legal responsibilities. The penalties are adjusted based on the nature of the legal entity. In the case of Daemons, virtual jail time or even an apology could be considered as potential punishments, as the desired outcome of the punishment is justice done and seen to be done.[118] The act of punishment aims to restore the moral balance in the virtual social community in the eyes of the morally aware legitimacy audience.[119] Furthermore, formally punishing Daemons in virtual social worlds may prevent the development of a lynching

---

114 Abbott and Sarch (n 39), 339.

115 Leora D Katz, 'Response Retributivism: Defending the Duty to Punish' (2021) 40(6) *Law and Philosophy* 585, 586.

116 Ibid.

117 The human duty to punish may also be seen to reflect the act of punishing an animal, even a pet, that has injured or killed another animal or a human. While putting down an aggressive animal is reasonable to protect against further harm, often the discussion reflects a moral duty to put down an animal even for a one-time aggressive behaviour, if the damage caused is severe, e.g., the death of a human or a pet. In this equation, a Daemon also plays the role of a scapegoat. As described by Karnow (n 107), 155, 'advances in artificial intelligence [...] will eviscerate the very idea of cause and effect'.

118 Datar Arvind, 'The origins of "Justice must be seen to be done"' (*Bar and Bench* 18 April 2020) www.barandbench.com/columns/the-origins-of-justice-must-be-seen-to-be-done accessed 1 May 2024.

119 Vivien A Schmidt, 'Discursive Institutionalism: The Explanatory Power of Ideas and Discourse' (2008) 11 *Annual Review of Political Science* 303. See also Chaïm Perelman, 'The New Rhetoric: A Theory of Practical Reasoning' in Patricia Bizzell and Bruce Herzberg (eds), *The Rhetorical Tradition: Readings from Classical Times to the Present* (Bedford 2000).

mentality. Implementing the same minimum level of justice for both Avatars and Daemons may prevent the arbitrary punishment of wrongdoers. These punishments may be an important symbolic part of the rule of law, establishing a rule-based virtual society.

4.2.4 Conclusions

Granting Daemons separate legal personhood does not absolve other legal persons of their responsibilities. The owner, developer or user may be held accountable for any damage caused by the Daemon. The responsible parties may be duty bound to pay economic compensation,[120] as well as modify the algorithm guiding the Daemon.[121] Nevertheless, placing the responsibility solely on the owner, developer or user may not be adequate. Due to the intelligent programming, it might not be clear who is culpable, culpability being generally the condition for liability.[122] Additionally, 'where responsibility and thus liability are so spread out over numerous and distributed actors, the very sense of "responsibility" and "liability" is diminished'.[123]

Nevertheless, although owners, developers and users still maintain their responsibilities, the legal fiction of Daemon personhood could be a solution to potential harm to human well-being, satisfying the 'society's collective sense of what is reasonable'.[124]

In conclusion, because Daemons have relationships with humans, they can act as proxy holders of both legal rights and legal duties. The concept of legal personhood for Daemons is feasible and could provide ethical value added by taking on some responsibility and facing consequences; that is, retributive punishment. However, it is important to carefully consider whether the benefits outweigh the potential costs.[125]

4.3 Added Value, Added Risks... or just Unnecessary and a bit Silly?

The previous section concisely argued that granting limited legal personality for Daemons is possible and may address the risks of virtual social relations

---

120 Insurance scheme, see e.g., Solum (n 16), 1245.

121 Liability for artificial intelligence or a machine, see e.g., Karnow (n 107); Floridi and Sanders (n 15); Gabriel Hallevy, 'The Criminal Liability of Artificial Intelligence Entities – from Science Fiction to Legal Social Control' (2010) 4(2) *Akron Intellectual Property Journal* 171; Barfield and Williams (n 5).

122 Karnow (n 107), 154, 182; Abbott and Sarch (n 39), 327.

123 Karnow (n 107), 155.

124 Karnow (n 107).

125 Chopra and White (n 7), 186.

recognised in Section 3. However, what are the possible risks of extending legal personhood to virtual beings?

Previous literature recognises the challenges related to the legal personhood of non-human entities which apply to the case at hand, including the avoidance of criminal responsibility and difficulties involved in recognition and accountability.[126] Such avoidance might potentially harm trust in the justice system. Similar issues have been discussed concerning corporations.[127] However, in the case of corporations, the overall benefits have been evaluated to outweigh the costs. Therefore, despite the potential for abuse in order to avoid responsibility, the recognition of separate legal personhood should be considered based on a balance of potential gains and losses.

What about the possible risks of Daemon legal personhood for human psychosocial well-being inside and outside the virtual world? The previous section argued that regulating the behaviour of Daemons in virtual social worlds could protect us from cynicism and apathy, support the moral sense of the community, restore the moral state, and prove that justice will be done. However, previous literature has raised potential issues regarding the recognition of rights for AI, which are also applicable to Daemons. These issues include the blurring of concepts,[128] the inflation of human rights,[129] and the creation of legal zombies.[130] All of these issues could undermine the legitimacy and integrity of the legal system. Anthony Beavers has even suggested that moral machines cause the end of ethics.[131]

From the perspective of this chapter, it is particularly important to consider whether legally recognised rights and responsibilities for Daemons can help address the issues recognised in Section 3.2. Alternatively, it is worth considering whether the legal regulation and punishment of Daemons might

---

126 See e.g., Bryson, Diamantis and Grant (n 7), 285–87.

127 Chopra and White (n 7), 183, see 183–84.

128 See e.g., Abbott and Sarch (n 39), 384.

129 See e.g., Chopra and White (n 7), 185; Bryson, Diamantis and Grant (n 7), 275; Jaana Parviainen and Mark Coeckelbergh, 'The Political Choreography of the Sophia Robot: Beyond Robot Rights and Citizenship to Political Performances for the Social Robotics Market' (2021) 36(3) *AI & Society* 715; Hizel (n 52), 224.

130 Raskulla (n 7), 1243. Philosophical zombie refers to unconscious beings who nevertheless behave as if they were conscious. On philosophical zombies, see e.g., Stevan Harnad, 'Guest Editorial: Why and How we are not Zombies?' (1994) 1(2) *Journal of Consciousness Studies* 164; Roman Dushkin, 'To the Question on Identification and Differentiation of a Philosophical Zombie' (2020) 1 *Philosophical Thought* 52.

131 Anthony Beavers, 'Moral Machines and the Threat of Ethical Nihilism' in Patrick Lin, Keith Abney and George A Bekey (eds), *Robot Ethics: The Ethical and Social Implications of Robotics* (MIT Press 2012), 343.

exacerbate the negative psychological effects caused by anthropomorphising and a 'misplacement of feelings'.[132]

Providing Daemons with some legal rights and duties could create a recursive, self-reinforcing process whereby the recognition of Daemon legal personhood creates a demand for a further extension of the rights and duties. As described by Gabriel Lima et al.:

> If legal and social institutions choose to embrace these systems, e.g., by granting them certain legal status, nudges towards granting them certain perceived independence or private property may affect people's decision to punish them. Future work should delve deeper into the causal relationship between people's attitudes towards the topic and their attribution of punishment to automated agents.[133]

There comes a moment when we must decide whether to expand the definition of humankind to include non-human entities,[134] or to solidify the role of non-humans as tools.[135] This decision either changes or reinforces the current anthropocentric view where no non-human creatures can have rights, regardless of how sentient they appear.[136] In either case, the disparity between legal and moral personhood may significantly influence our own behaviour.

The extension of legal personhood to non-human entities may be seen as 'morally unnecessary and legally troublesome' as they 'are too great and the moral gains too few',[137] as well as being a bit silly, 'akin to hitting one's computer when it crashes'.[138] However, we must consider our increasing knowledge of A2D relations in virtual social worlds to evaluate the costs and benefits of Daemon legal personhood fully.

At present, it appears to be unnecessary to assign separate legal personhood to Daemons to uphold the rule of law in the metaverse. Instead, it seems sufficient for administrators to enforce social norms and regulations as they currently do on social media platforms, which both humans and bots populate.[139] This enforcement can include tangible punishment of an Avatar and symbolic

---

132 See Luisa Damiano and Paul Dumouchel, 'Anthropomorphism in Human-Robot Co-Evolution' (2018) 9 *Frontiers in Psychology* 468, 472; Abbott and Sarch (n 39), 377.

133 Lima and others (n 32), 6.

134 Lauria and Robinson (n 4), 220.

135 van der Sloot (n 39), 110.

136 Solum (n 16), 1261, see also 1260–62, 1275.

137 Bryson, Diamantis and Grant (n 7), 275.

138 Abbott and Sarch (n 39), 326, 364.

139 Further discussion on regulatory models, see e.g., Abbott and Sarch (n 39), 368–383; Brenner (n 39), 60; van der Sloot (n 39), 172, 187–88, 214, 225.

punishment of Daemons violating community rules and harming other virtual characters.

Legislation should ensure the protection of children and mandate that in virtual social worlds, where violence, sexual violence, or sexual age-play occurs, all participants must be of legal age, informed, and have consented to the terms of use.[140]

However, as metaverses continue to grow and become integrated into our daily lives, the legal framework surrounding digital entities will likely become more critical for the governance of virtual social life. If the distinction between human and digital life becomes less clear due to technological advancements – such as maintaining enough physical life to enable full-time living online or post-mortem emulated intelligence;[141] for example, through the development of brain-computer interfaces (BCIs) – it raises the question of whether the emulated person bears enough resemblance to the original individual warranting its recognition as a person.

In the longer term, the survival of humankind in the face of terrestrial (e.g., climate change, nuclear war) or extraterrestrial (e.g., Near Earth Objects, such as asteroids[142]) threats may depend on the emergence of digital life (transhumanism).[143] But even without such utopian or dystopian views, living alongside algorithm-guided characters could be the future of humankind. And while regulation may try to restrain or prevent such developments, humans are also unpredictable. Curtis E A Karnow has described how:

> It is an essential and, over the long run, entirely assured characteristic of intelligent programs that they will make 'pathological' decisions. The nature and timing of

---

140 Discussion on age-play, see e.g., Carla Reeves, 'Fantasy Depictions of Child Sexual Abuse: The Problem of Age-play in Second Life' (2013) 19(2) *Journal of Sexual Aggression* 236; Brenner (n 39), 19.

141 Compare Kamil Muzyka, 'The Outline of Personhood Law Regarding Artificial Intelligences and Emulated Human Entities' (2013) 4(3) *Journal of Artificial General Intelligence* 164.

142 Davide Perna, Maria A Barucci and Marcello Fulchignoni, 'The Near-Earth Objects and their Potential Threat to our Planet' (2013) 21 *The Astron Astrophysics Review* 1.

143 See e.g., Chopra and White (n 7), 191; George S Robinson and Rita M Lauria, 'Legal Rights and Accountability of Cyberpresence: A Void in Space Law/Astrolaw Jurisprudence' (2011) 28 *Annals of Air and Space Law* 311; Muzyka (n 141); James Lovelock and Bryan Appleyard, *Novacene: The Coming Age of Hyperintelligence* (Allen Lane 2019). See also Nosworthy (n 18); N Katherine Hayles, 'Computing the Human' (2005) 22(1) *Theory, Culture & Society* 131, 143–48.

> these pathological decisions cannot be known in advance. These are not 'bugs' in the programs, but are part of their essence.[144]

Similarly, it is our essence to evolve. Individual endeavours to extend life are not restricted by regulation. For example, what if someone claims to have transferred their consciousness to a virtual representation and has then died? Can we deny their human dignity in the virtual world?

5. CONCLUSIONS

Based on empirical research, it is difficult for humans to differentiate between online and offline events. Even when individuals are aware that the characters in virtual environments are not real, they still develop feelings towards them. As described by Darling, 'there is concern that mistreating an object that reacts in a lifelike way could impact the general feeling of empathy we experience when interacting with other entities'.[145]

Empirical research remains inconclusive, and more studies are required. Nevertheless, given the nature of the metaverse and the propensity of people to anthropomorphise, it may well be justified to extend at least some basic rules of behaviour to virtual social worlds in order to manage the risks to human well-being and social relations.

As noted by Edwards Castronova, the techno-utopian idea of free virtual communities, as portrayed by John Perry Barlow in the Declaration of the Independence of Cyberspace (1996), is not realised. The impact of virtual worlds on the real world is great in many areas of human life and we are tackling the 'unhappy consequences of virtual communities'.[146] A rule-based virtual society is particularly important if, or rather, when, we become unsure or unaware of whether we are interacting with an algorithm-guided or human-guided character.

It is relevant to recognise that even when aware of the artificial nature of the characters they interact with, humans demonstrably create emotions towards them. This implies that all human-like characters and animals in virtual social worlds should be treated with dignity and respect.

In this rapidly changing environment where we become more absorbed by the metaverse, it is important to defend the rights and well-being of individuals. This involves establishing rules and protecting intelligent entities, such as Daemons, when platforms allow socially meaningful relationships with them.

---

144 Karnow (n 107), 161.
145 Darling (n 35), 15.
146 Castronova (n 44), 34.

These rules are not to protect the Daemons themselves, but rather to regulate virtual relations and protect humans.[147]

The concept of granting legal personhood to virtual beings has several issues, and more effective solutions exist in our present context. However, if emulated human consciousness becomes a reality, the legal personhood of purely virtual entities may become more relevant. As the distinction between real and digital life becomes increasingly blurred, it is important to carefully consider the potential implications.

147 See Barfield and Williams (n 5), 16.

9. Generative AI's impact on autonomy, truth and equality: three regulatory quagmires for the proto- and the metaverse

Bart van der Sloot

1. INTRODUCTION[1]

Of all the contemporary technological advances, generative Artificial Intelligence (AI) stands out. It powers several technological applications, such as deepfakes, where content (video, audio or otherwise) is wholly or partially fabricated, or existing content that has been manipulated using AI. In just a few years, deepfake technology has advanced rapidly in terms of quality, speed of production and cost efficiency, so much so that humans are no longer able to distinguish fake from authentic content. Another example is Augmented Reality (AR), which adds an AI-generated layer to physical reality so that our perception of reality is grounded in physical reality but AI-generated sensory (audio, video, olfactory, etc.) input is received on top or instead of that. Virtual Reality (VR) is a third example, and in its ideal form all sensory input is AI-generated. Large Language Models (LLMs) can power chat programmes and not only enhance the verbal capacities of physical robots, but also allow them to better understand and respond to questions or tasks.[2] Humanoid robots have the physical appearance of *homo sapiens*, are equipped with the ability to walk and talk like humans and run on advanced software, which grants

[1] This chapter draws partly from: Bart van der Sloot, *Regulating the Synthetic Society: Generative AI, Legal Questions, and Societal Challenges* (Bloomsbury Publishing 2024).

[2] Hard Fork, 'Elon's X Machina + Crypto Orbs + A Visit to Google's Robots Lab (*NYTimes* 28 July 2023) www.nytimes.com/2023/07/28/podcasts/elons-x-machina-crypto-orbs-and-a-visit-to-googles-robot-lab.html accessed 24 April 2025.

them human-like cognitive functions. They are also equipped with sensors and, through the internet and cutting-edge technology, have access to facial, object and emotion recognition.

All these terms do not lend themselves to exact definitions. When is fake material to be considered a deepfake? Does the answer depend on the technology used to produce the fake, whether the consumer believes it to be real, or its deep impact on the perception of reality? When exactly does reality become so augmented that it should be called VR; if 90 per cent of what a person sees consists of AI-generated layers, is that still AR? What if VR is an exact copy of physical reality, is that VR or more like an interactive film? At what point does a robot look, talk, think and act so much like a human that it should be considered humanoid? The definitions for all these developments depend on sliding scales rather than binary distinctions and there is significant overlap. For example, the metaverse can make use of AR, VR, the Internet of Things and tactile internet applications. Sometimes, AR is based on a fully representational system, representing reality through a video screen, while adding an AI layer to the video recording of reality. Apple's Vision Pro uses VR, AR and deepfake technology. Japan's Moonshot programme, which has the aim of the 'realization of a society in which human beings can be free from limitations of body, brain, space, and time by 2050',[3] depends on multiple synthetic technologies.

That is why these applications and their effects should not be discussed in isolation; it is not so much the specific impact of a particular technology that will have a lasting impact on society, but their xenogamy that may have unprecedented effects on the foundational pillars of our society. This chapter will home in on three of these. First, Section 2 will delve into the question of autonomy and the rule of law. Second, Section 3 will discuss the effects of generative AI on truth and democracy. Third, Section 4 will analyse the effects of the various technologies on equality and humanism. Finally, the analysis offered in Section 5 will suggest that although it is clear that synthetic technologies will have significant repercussions for these societal interests, good regulatory options and easy fixes are very few and far between. Because of the multiple dimensions of the various technologies in play, insights from various knowledge domains are needed to arrive at comprehensive insights and advanced conclusions. Given the inherent cross-border nature of these technologies, the methodology of this chapter is grounded in interdisciplinary and transnational research methodologies.[4]

---

3 Moonshot, 'Moonshot Goal 1' www.jst.go.jp/moonshot/en/program/goal1/ accessed 27 May 2025.

4 The same approach is taken in other domains, see e.g., Bart van der Sloot and Aviva De Groot (eds), *The Handbook of Privacy Studies* (Amsterdam University

2. AUTONOMY AND THE RULE OF LAW

In Western democracies, the legal regime and the rule of law are not only based on but also geared towards maximising human autonomy.[5] The law can only function if citizens understand and decide to follow it. Laws can never be so specific that they give people perfect guidance: if a person is ordered to mow the lawn, it should be clear to them that they should not cut away the flowerbed; if a park prohibits the entry of vehicles, it should be clear that children's buggies are exempted.[6] The effectiveness of the legal system depends on citizens having autonomy and an understanding of the meaning and purpose of a rule. This is why the rule of law safeguards autonomous decision-making by citizens. The prohibition of retroactive legislation protects human autonomy because people are not punished for acts they did not know would be criminalised later, and also ensures the effectiveness of the legal regime, as citizens cannot respect legislation retroactively. The same holds for the requirement to publish laws, that laws should be coherent and comprehensible, and that they should not require the impossible of citizens. These rules ensure both the effectiveness and the legitimacy of the legal regime; human autonomy is essential for both.[7]

AI might fundamentally change how the legal regime and the rule of law operate. Not only are rules embedded in the code,[8] which makes it hard if not impossible to break them, but the code is also often not published; rather, it is implicit in the design. This can mean, for example, that a player in a VR world does not need to know the rules applicable in that world; they will simply discover that they are not capable of performing certain activities or using certain terms. In addition, the difference between law and code is that the former is based in natural language, which is inherently vague and ambiguous, while the latter is traditionally based in binary code, which is clear-cut and unambiguous.[9] In VR, citizens do not need to understand the purpose or meaning of the rules and there is limited need for an executive and judicial branch with law as code. In the current legal reality, given the ambiguity of natural language and

Press 2018).

[5] Kenneth I Winston, *The Principles of Social Order: Selected Essays of Lon L. Fuller* (Duke University Press 1981).

[6] Lon L Fuller, 'Positivism and Fidelity to Law – A Reply to Professor Hart' (1958) 71(4) *Harvard Law Review* 630.

[7] Lon L Fuller, *The Morality of Law* (Yale University Press 1964).

[8] Lawrence Lessig, 'Code is Law' (*Harvard Magazine* 2000) www.harvardmagazine.com/2000/01/code-is-law-html accessed 24 April 2025.

[9] Mireille Hildebrandt, *Law for Computer Scientists and Other Folk* (Oxford University Press 2020).

the open-ended nature of the law, both the executive and the judicial branches are attributed a margin of discretion in terms of deciding over the right interpretation of the law. With AI, in principle, no such interpretative decisions are needed.

On an individual level, synthetic technologies can have a double effect on human autonomy.[10] On the one hand, a humanoid robot can assist an elderly person and allow them to live on their own, without being dependent on medical personnel, friends or family for hygienic, medical or household tasks. VR may allow disabled or disenfranchised people to travel the world. AR can help the blind navigate life. Deepfake technology can give people suffering from speech loss their voice back. On the other hand, these people can become dependent on the technologies and the companies that operate them. Contrary to most low-tech instruments, digital companies usually have access to the data processed through synthetic technologies and can make decisions that affect their users. This means that private organisations will be central to important decisions in terms of medical care, for example. They will determine what margin of error is acceptable for diagnosing new potential diseases in elderly people in terms of false positives and false negatives when patients are treated in VR. In addition, the introduction of synthetic technologies triggers a range of complexities. What happens if an elderly person refuses to eat their breakfast? Should the humanoid robot warn medical professionals and the family, or should it respect the autonomous decision of the elderly person?

In addition, the rise of generative AI will further the privatisation, datafication and commercialisation of society and public life. Tech companies are involved in offering smart homes, sometimes for free, in return for data, as well as being involved in designing and operating smart cities.

> We often hear that social media platforms have become a de facto public sphere, and how this creates huge problems for the exercise of rights such as freedom of expression. With the proliferation of AR glasses in public spaces, we risk stumbling into a situation where these same companies control an unregulated 'augmented sphere' imposed on our public spaces. Here's how that might work: Facebook augments the center of your city or town using proprietary features. These features require that you have an account – and to give up all your personal data – to participate. You value your privacy, but you have a strong incentive to join because all your friends can see what you cannot see. A number of companies are already developing their own digital version of the world – often called 'Mirrorworlds'.[11]

---

[10] Beate Roessler, *Autonomy: An Essay on the Life Well-lived* (John Wiley & Sons 2021).

[11] Gaspar Pisanu, Daniel Leufer and Isedua Oribhabor, 'Augmented Reality and Augmented Risks: why AR is a Digital Rights Issue' (*AccessNow* 16 October

This allows private parties to gather large amounts of data about private and public life, social engagements and societal trends.

The rise of AI will also deepen the trend that the government and the public sector become ever more dependent on technologies and the companies that provide services, as synthetic technologies are used for the execution of public tasks, such as education, healthcare, law enforcement, warfare and maintaining public order. There is already a gap in the data and technical knowledge between the private and the public sector, which is only likely to increase as governments are reliant on tech companies for harvesting data and making decisions based on profiles and the derived analytical projections.[12] The same applies to citizens, who become increasingly reliant on data technologies for everyday activities; while this takes place, the companies developing the software and hardware obtain detailed insights into the lives of citizens and the way in which AI-driven technologies work, while the decisions made by companies based on data are becoming ever more obscure to citizens. This transparency paradox not only gives companies a huge influence over the lives of citizens, whether by determining what they see or not when using AR, what their movement restrictions are in VR or how the care robot will operate, but it also turns citizens and their behaviour into commodities.[13]

3. TRUTH AND DEMOCRACY

Although companies explicitly aim to provide public services and perform public tasks that were previously in the hands of government organisations, they are not accountable in the same way, nor is there any form of democratic control. This is particularly evident in relation to VR worlds, in which some people spend large parts of their lives. The company designing the platform is typically the legislative, executive and judiciary power all in one, and has sole discretion when deciding whether a rule has been violated and, if so, what sanction is imposed. They can change the rules on the platform overnight or remove someone from the platform without any further due process being undertaken. A form of democratic control is absent. This problem becomes more urgent when not only games take place in VR, but also increasingly

2020) www.accessnow.org/what-is-augmented-reality-risks/ accessed 24 April 2025.

[12] Bart van der Sloot, Dennis Broeders and Erik Schrijvers (eds), *Exploring the Boundaries of Big Data* (The Netherlands Scientific Council for Government Policy 2016).

[13] Frank Pasquale, *The Black Box Society: The Secret Algorithms that Control Money and Information* (Harvard University Press 2015).

social encounters, educational projects, business meetings and democratic debates.[14]

In addition, digital content is increasingly produced or manipulated by AI. The technology is not only used to deliberately mislead people, but is also embedded in everyday applications.[15] Generative AI, for example, generates beautiful atmospheric images of artificial forest cabins on Facebook or photos of non-existent children who appear to be doing something spectacular. Cameras are often AI-assisted, meaning that they work on blueprints of images. Consequently, a burning forest may still look green because the camera *knows* that a forest is green or the moon may appear crystal clear in the photo, even on a foggy night.[16] With video calling, the high audio registers are often filtered out and skin tones softened. Because deepfake technology is freely accessible to everyone, citizens are increasingly generating fake images, audio clips and videos for homely and satirical purposes.[17] In VR, some players who appear *real* might be AI-generated and controlled. These trends and many more combined mean that in a few years, more than 90 per cent of all digital material may be AI-generated or manipulated.[18] AI-detection programs only filter out about half of the AI-generated content, the rest slipping through the net.

The increased production of AI-generated content will mean that people will be unsure what they can believe. Parents who doubt whether it is really their child that is calling them in panic because their wallet has been stolen may want to verify before sending money. Friends doubting that the avatar resembling their friend is in fact controlled by their friend may have second thoughts about interacting with the avatar. Insecurity about the veracity of communication in a world that is almost fully digitally mediated is significant. In time, these phenomena may mean that people will avoid the news, while a well-informed citizenry is a precondition for a vital democracy and because

---

14 Bart van der Sloot, 'Virtual Identity and Virtual Privacy: Towards a Concept of Regulation by Analogy' (2011) 1 eGov Präsenz 41.

15 Gwanggil Jeon and others, 'Guest Editorial: Special Issue on Dark Side of the Socio-Cyber World: Media Manipulation, Fake News, and Misinformation' (2024) 11(4) IEEE *Transactions on Computational Social Systems* 4766; Marcello Ienca, 'On Artificial Intelligence and Manipulation' (2023) 42(3) *Topoi* 833.

16 James Vincent and Jon Porter, 'Samsung caught faking zoom photos of the Moon' (*The Verge* 13 March 2023) www.theverge.com/2023/3/13/23637401/samsung-fake-moon-photos-ai-galaxy-s21-s23-ultra accessed 24 April 2025.

17 Mika Westerlund, 'The Emergence of Deepfake Technology: A Review' (2019) 9(11) *Technology Innovation Management Review* 39.

18 Nina Schick, *Deepfakes and the Infocalypse: What You Urgently Need to Know* (Hachette 2020).

there is so much AI-generated material online and because this material is increasingly difficult to authenticate or distinguish from non-AI-generated material, this may feed into a trend that is already occurring: reality fatigue. Epistemological insecurity is amplified by a 'sequestration of experience'.[19] 'Hyperpersonalization can thus lead to a loss of confidence in (objective) perception.'[20]

Synthetic technologies are used by politicians, political parties, and their supporters, as well as by their adversaries. For example, some politicians have avatars in VR platforms and direct their hologram to tour the country,[21] create deepfakes of themselves to reach their voters while in jail,[22] instruct AI to tweak their facial features to appear more relatable,[23] or use LLMs to give a speech in a minority language the candidate does not actually speak.[24] Although these uses mostly go against the terms and conditions of various products and services, there are no legal provisions explicitly establishing whether they amount to voter deception or not. Deepfake technology can also be used against politicians, such as by using voice cloning to have a candidate say something compromising or damaging[25] or creating entire fake media environments. The harmful use of AI by political adversaries can come from

---

19 Anthony Giddens, *Modernity and Self-Identity: Self and Society in the Late Modern Age* (Stanford University Press 1991).

20 Bart W Schermer and Joas van Ham, 'Regulering van immersieve technologieën' (Considerati 2021) https://repository.wodc.nl/bitstream/handle/20.500.12832/3082/3180-regulering--immersieve-technologieen-volledige-tekst.pdf?sequence=4&isAllowed=y accessed 24 April 2025.

21 Chris Welch, 'Indian Politician Morphs into Hologram to Reach Millions of Voters' (*The Verge* 7 May 2014) www.theverge.com/2014/5/7/5691714/indian-politician-uses-holograms-to-reach-voters accessed 24 April 2025.

22 Siladitya Ray, 'Imran Khan—Pakistan's Jailed Ex-Leader—Uses AI Deepfake To Address Online Election Rally' (*Forbes* 18 December 2023) www.forbes.com/sites/siladityaray/2023/12/18/imran-khan-pakistans-jailed-ex-leader-uses-ai-deepfake-to-address-online-election-rally/ accessed 24 April 2025.

23 Kat Duffy, 'AI in Context: Indonesian Elections Challenge GenAI Policies' (*CFR* 13 February 2024) www.cfr.org/blog/ai-context-indonesian-elections-challenge-genai-policies accessed 24 April 2025.

24 Kim Lyons, 'An Indian Politician used AI to Translate his Speech into Other Languages to Reach More Voters' (*The Verge* 19 February 2020) www.theverge.com/2020/2/18/21142782/india-politician-deepfakes-ai-elections accessed 24 April 2025.

25 Alex Seitz-Wald, 'Democratic Operative Admits to Commissioning Fake Biden Robocall that used AI' (*NBC News* 25 February 2024) www.nbcnews.com/politics/2024-election/democratic-operative-admits-commissioning-fake-biden-robocall-used-ai-rcna140402 accessed 24 April 2025.

rival domestic parties or from foreign powers. There have already been multiple attempts to influence election results.

4. EQUALITY AND HUMANISM

A question that is looming on the horizon, but if ever, will become relevant only in a decade or so, is Artificial General Intelligence (AGI) and sentience. AGI is the moment that computer intelligence is indistinguishable from human intelligence. It is clear that on some points, AI has already superseded human intelligence, while on other points, it is still lagging behind. Whether AI has self-awareness is even more difficult to establish. Already, some Google employees have asserted that the models they built had become sentient, while most engineers do not believe that to be the case.[26] In reality, however, both AGI and sentience are not black-and-white matters. As the technology advances, AI will be more and more capable of a diverse range of tasks and become more and more intelligent and sentient. The question has been posed to what extent and when should AI-driven entities be treated equally to humans and attributed moral and legal protection. Is letting intelligent machines perform monotonous factory jobs a modern form of slavery; is having intelligent entities serve as a sex robot a form of forced prostitution?

There is also the question of the extent to which virtual avatars deserve protection. To some, the avatar is their virtual body, similar to their physical body, which allows them to navigate virtual reality. This raises complex questions, such as: is the virtual rape of someone's avatar to be likened to actual rape or not, or should that question depend on the extent to which a person identifies with their avatar and how much time is spent curating their virtual body?[27] In addition, there is currently no clear legal protection against making deepfakes of deceased persons, as the associated rights are typically only awarded to living natural persons. There are also moral and legal questions revolving around the status of deepfake images of non-existent people or highly realistic avatars. In many jurisdictions, but not all, generating child pornography of non-existent people or child avatars is prohibited, but what about extremely violent and dehumanising snuff porn of non-existing people?[28] One of the problems

---

[26] Nitasha Tiku, 'The Google Engineer who Thinks the Company's AI has Come to Life' (*The Washington Post* 11 June 2022) www.washingtonpost.com/technology/2022/06/11/google-ai-lamda-blake-lemoine/ accessed 24 April 2025.

[27] Robert Sparrow and Lauren Karas, 'Teledildonics and Rape by Deception' (2020) 12(1) *Law, Innovation and Technology* 175.

[28] Aaron Yarmel and Jonathan Lang, 'The Ethics of Customizable AI-generated Pornography', *Midwest Ethics Symposium '24: Artificial Intelligence* (Prindle Institute for Ethics 18 April 2024).

of not criminalising such conduct is that extreme content would be produced and shared and thus normalised. In addition, it might provide people with a legitimate alibi when consuming authentic extreme content, saying that they thought it concerned non-existent persons.

Next to the question of whether non-human entities deserve moral and legal protection equal to humans, there is the question of whether humans are replaceable. When work in the household, in factories, and even in creative sectors is taken over by AI, humans may become increasingly dependent on AI for physical, intellectual and creative activities. Although maybe not to all, there will be an intuitive appeal to many to take the easy road. If a robot can lift a shopping bag, why would a person do it? If a virtual avatar can tour a person around in a foreign country and Google Lens can translate texts, why try to learn the basics of that language on vacation? If a sex robot is available, why go out dating and go to lengths to buy smart clothes and nice perfume? When Chat GPT can write an essay, why would a student do so themselves? Additionally, deepfake technology allows people to create news bulletins that fit their pre-established world views. It is also possible to bring one's deceased partner back to life so that the surviving partner does not have to be confronted with the loss and grief. It is possible for teenagers who are overweight and bullied at school to escape to VR with an avatar that mirrors their body ideal. Therefore, in many ways, the effect of generative AI is that friction is removed from the lives of people, while it is precisely through friction that people develop.

If AI did indeed become more and more capable and humans more and more dependent, the question has emerged whether a human-centric worldview should still prevail. The idea of singularity, popularised by Kurzweil, promoted the idea that humans and machines could be merged, thus using the best of both worlds.[29] Now, a new philosophy has arisen called post-humanism.[30] In the end, mankind may be (almost) fully replaceable by AI. Although this might lead to the human race becoming redundant, it could be to the benefit of Gaia. Mankind's primary legacy, according to some, is that they have depleted the earth, domesticated and annihilated other living beings and waged war on each other. Perhaps if AI would replace *homo sapiens*, this would be to be benefit of every other creature on the planet.

[29] Ray Kurzweil, *The Singularity is Near* (Viking Books 2005).

[30] Stefan Herbrechter and others, 'Critical Posthumanism: An Overview' in Stefan Herbrechter et al. (eds), *Palgrave Handbook of Critical Posthumanism* (Palgrave Macmillan 2022).

5. ANALYSIS

It is clear that generative AI will affect foundational elements of contemporary society. This chapter has homed in on three of those. First, generative AI and the various technologies which it enables, such as AR and VR, deepfake, LLMs and humanoid robots, may undermine human autonomy and the rule of law. Second, because there is an abundance of synthetic material, that is, material that is generated or affected by AI, a shared understanding of what is real and authentic and what is not may be lost, while a well-informed citizenry is quintessential to a well-functioning democracy. Third, with the advancement of AI, AGI and sentience may be looming on the horizon – the question then is to what extent should AI-generated or driven creatures be awarded moral and legal protection equal to humans. Neither of these societal problems is easy to solve through regulatory solutions.

As to the first problem, the problem of autonomy, the complexity is that most AI-driven technologies are aimed at the core of human nature, which is essentially conflicted.[31] A person may, for example, rationally wish to read a book at night, drink a cup of tea and go to bed early, but there is something primitively desirable about drinking a glass of wine and binge-watching a Netflix series into the early hours. We often do not know what we actually want ourselves, or sometimes only years later; we often regret choices we make, including decisions we were convinced aligned with our authentic beliefs and ambitions at the time. We often need the help of others and technology to meet our own goals, such as having an app on our phones urging us to take a certain number of steps per day or asking our partner to keep us from drinking more than two glasses of alcohol at night. Human nature is truly complex, and it is often impossible to say who a person 'really' is, what a person's authentic self is, even for the person themselves.[32]

Does a humanoid sex robot enhance a person's autonomy by giving them all the sex they desire, or does it undermine their opportunity to develop a mature human relationship? Is technology that allows a person to continue talking to their late spouse good because it allows them to seek comfort in difficult times, or bad because it keeps them away from what is best for them, what they (perhaps unknowingly) actually want: to confront the pain and learn to live with it? Is an AR device that blocks blood from a child's sight laudable because

---

31 Bert van der Sloot, 'The Right to be let Alone by Oneself: Narrative and Identity in a Data-driven Environment' (2021) 13(1) *Law, Innovation and Technology* 223; Anita L Allen, 'An Ethical Duty to Protect One's Own Information Privacy?' (2013) 65 *Alabama Law Review* 845.

32 Theodor W Adorno and Max Horkheimer, *Dialectic of Enlightenment* (Verso 1997).

it protects the child from harmful scenes that may lead to trauma, or does it undermine the child's autonomy because they do not learn to deal with shocking or disgusting stimuli by themselves, so they become dependent on the AR service? Does VR technology that allows us to explore new identities that feed into our primitive desires to embody an ideal avatar keep us away from working on our true self? Or does it enhance a person's autonomy as it allows them to explore deep-felt desires and new identities, which they may not be able to do in real life? In the end, most questions surrounding technology boil down to questions about human nature.

As to the second problem, it is difficult to see how the rise of synthetic content and with it a post-truth era can be prevented, as so many AI-driven tools, products, and services have been democratised and others have AI embedded in their functional design. Although there are several ways of addressing this issue, each raises its own dilemmas. For example, it has been suggested that service providers should run AI detection programs to filter out AI-generated and manipulated content, but this would also have the effect that legitimate and unharmful content is blocked, as most content will be (marginally) manipulated by AI, and even substantially AI-modified and AI-generated content is often not unlawful. Another way would be to only rely on watermarked content; a watermark is a logbook attached to a photo, video, or other material that shows what has been altered or manipulated, when, and by whom.[33] However, requiring a watermark could have the effect that authentic material would be blocked for its mere lack of a watermark.[34]

As a third option, one could point to the fact that under the current regime, making incorrect, false or misleading statements is not prohibited as such, but only if a speech act causes harm to a personal or general interest.[35] That means

---

33 Michael Arnold, Martin Schmucker and Stephen D Wolthusen, *Techniques and Applications of Digital Watermarking and Content Protection* (Artech House 2003).

34 Bart Jacobs, 'The Authenticity Crisis' (2024) 53 *Computer Law & Security Review* 105962.

35 For commercial instances, there are rules on prohibited misleading practices. Directive 2005/29/EC of the European Parliament and of the Council of 11 May 2005 concerning unfair business-to-consumer commercial practices in the internal market and amending Council Directive 84/450/EEC, Directives 97/7/EC, 98/27/EC and 2002/65/EC of the European Parliament and of the Council and Regulation (EC) No 2006/2004 of the European Parliament and of the Council [2005] OJ L149/22. Directive 2006/114/EC of the European Parliament and of the Council of 12 December 2006 concerning misleading and comparative advertising (codified version) [2006] OJ L376/21. European Commission, 'The Strengthened Code of Practice on Disinformation 2022' https://ec.europa.eu/newsroom/dae/redirection/document/87585 accessed 27 May 2025. See also: Commission,

that a series of complex issues may arise with regard to the causal relationship between an untrue, incorrect or misleading statement and the damage it causes (anticipated or actual). Moreover, untrue, incorrect or misleading statements are not regulated as such, while they can be problematic, if they only further the push towards a post-truth era. However, prohibiting untrue and inauthentic statements would be a radical move, among many other reasons because what is true or not is often one of the crosslines between relational, societal and political groups. A final option could be to prohibit AI technologies, or at least limit access for citizens, as the main problem is that it is almost impossible for law enforcement authorities to adequately tackle the issues, a problem that is aggravated by the fact that it is not always clear who produced the manipulated content and that the services through which they are published are often based in foreign jurisdictions. However, banning technology is a radical measure, as it also disallows legitimate and positive use cases, denies innovation of technologies through serendipitous experimentation, and in any case prohibitions are often easily circumvented, especially in the online environment.

Finally, the third point touched on in this chapter begs the question to what extent the moral and legal realm should be extended.[36] Although it is difficult to imagine non-human entities having rights, the current legal regime does attribute human rights to legal persons, which are also entities that are created by natural persons.[37] In addition, ever more countries are attributing rights to animals and even to natural phenomena such as rivers.[38] The decision of whether to attribute rights to non-human entities is not only something that depends on the moral status of the entity in question. Conversely, the legal status of an entity has a considerable impact on its moral status. For centuries, women were afforded a lower moral status than men. This is why they were granted fewer rights and an inferior legal position. This inferior legal position also affected their societal position and status, as well as their capacity to explore and develop in full. For non-human entities, the same may be true. Granting rights to non-humans would provide them with protection and it would allow them to flourish, develop and assert themselves in the world

'Proposal for a Regulation of the European Parliament and of the Council on the transparency and targeting of political advertising' COM/2021/731 final.

36 David J Gunkel, *Robot Rights* (MIT Press 2018).

37 *Stes Colas Est and others v France* ECHR 2002-III 131.

38 See, e.g., Kate Evans, 'The New Zealand River that Became a Legal Person' (*BBC* 20 March 2020) www.bbc.com/travel/article/20200319-the-new-zealand-river-that-became-a-legal-person accessed 24 April 2025.

according to their own views. Not granting rights to non-human entities would mean that, essentially, they remain instruments for human ends.[39]

Yet granting rights and legal personhood to non-human entities would raise a range of difficult questions, such as the following: can non-human entities sue humans for being maltreated or should this be left to special advocates or interest groups? How should non-human entities substantiate harm, such as dignitary or emotional harm? Should non-human entities also have voting rights? Can non-human entities sue each other? Would these kinds of legal disputes be judged by human judges, non-human judges or a combined panel? Suppose that non-human entities were granted legal personhood and were allowed to invoke the human rights contained in the current catalogue. This would lead to several complicated questions.

- Article 2 of the European Convention on Human Rights (ECHR), for example, provides the right to life. No one shall be deprived of their life intentionally, save (1) in the execution of a sentence of a court, (2) in defence of any person from unlawful violence, (3) in order to effect a lawful arrest or to prevent the escape of a person lawfully detained, or (4) in action lawfully taken for the purpose of quelling a riot or insurrection. If this provision were applied to non-human entities, it would raise the question of what would amount to a non-human death.[40] A robot that is switched off can be turned on again, a device that is demolished can be repaired and an avatar that dies in a shooting game can be revived the next moment.[41]
- Article 3 of the ECHR prohibits torture and degrading treatment. There is a high barrier for this provision to apply, so it is unlikely that any discomfort to a non-human entity would amount to inhuman or degrading treatment. However, if a robot or avatar is employed for perverse sexual fantasies, it

---

[39] See further: Johanna Seibt, Marco Nørskov and Søren Schack Andersen (eds), *What Social Robots Can and Should Do: Poceedings of Robophilosophy 2016/ TRANSOR 2016* (IOS Press 2016); Ryan Carlo, A Michael Froomkin and Ian Kerr (eds), *Robot Law* (Edward Elgar 2016); Patrick Lin, Keith Abney and Ryan Jenkins (eds), *Robot Ethics 2.0: from Autonomous Cars to Artificial Intelligence* (Oxford University Press 2017); Wendell Wallach and Colin Allen, *Moral Machines: Teaching Robots Right from Wrong* (Oxford University Press 2009); Michael Anderson and Susan L Anderson (eds), *Machine Ethics* (Cambridge University Press 2011).

[40] See also Theodore Scaltsas, 'The Ship of Theseus' (1980) 40(3) *Analysis* 152.

[41] In addition, the 'soul' or 'mind' of an AI-driven entity is typically uploaded to the cloud and can be installed on to a new HR, avatar or other non-human entity. It is also easy to switch 'minds' between various non-human entities.

might. Similarly, should this provision apply to non-human entities, the generation of deepfake child pornography of non-existent children would likely be prohibited. At the same time, it is unclear to what extent these entities themselves experience the treatment as degrading, especially when they are designed to perform and execute that exact function.

- Article 4 of the ECHR prohibits slavery and forced labour, although this does not include (1) any work required to be done over the ordinary course of detention, (2) any service of a military character or service exacted instead of compulsory military service, (3) any service exacted in case of an emergency or calamity threatening the life or well-being of the community, or (4) any work or service which forms part of normal civic obligations. If this provision were to apply to non-human entities, it would likely bring an end to the forced use of robots for manufacturing or avatars for prostitution, yet not killer robots used in armed conflict.
- Articles 8, 9, 10, 11 and 12 of the ECHR respectively contain the right to privacy, freedom of religion, freedom of expression, freedom of association, and the right to marry and establish a family. It is clear that applying these to non-human entities would raise a number of complex questions. If non-human entities were to be given these rights, this would mean, inter alia, that the data of non-human entities could not be processed without a legal basis or consent, and that they would be free to express their own political views and to associate in a union. Equally, they could not be forced to marry a person against their will. How the right to establish a family would work in terms of non-human entities is unclear.
- Article 1 of the First Protocol to the ECHR grants the right to property. If this right were to be attributed to non-human entities, it would mean, inter alia, that these entities should be able to enjoy the fruits of their labour and would be entitled to possess objects. Article 2 of the Protocol provides the right to education, which would grant non-human entities the right to develop themselves through education. Article 3 of the First Protocol specifies the obligation on states to organise free and democratic elections. Were this provision to be applied to non-human entities, it would mean that they would have the right to vote in elections. This would have an enormous impact on democratic elections, as in time, it is likely that there would be more non-human than human entities. In addition, political parties defending the rights of non-human entities could be founded and influence political decision-making.
- Finally, Article 14 of the ECHR prohibits discrimination. It is highly likely that if non-human entities were to be given legal standing under the ECHR, the European Court of Human Rights (ECtHR) would find that a distinction between non-human and human entities could only be made if such a distinction were to be fair and reasonable in a specific context. It would

put a limit on or outright prohibit a potential ban on interspecies marriages, voting rights for non-human entities and non-human entities entering buildings, for example.

It is consequently clear that complicated legal, moral and practical questions would emerge if the current human rights catalogue were to be applied to non-human entities. Potentially, a special non-human rights framework could be developed, in which case a distinction would be made between the rights of robots, avatars, non-existent persons and deceased persons. It should be stressed that although entities may be attributed legal personhood or rights, this does not necessarily mean that they have legal standing.[42] Countries that have attributed rights to animals or natural phenomena obviously do not expect that non-human entity to go to court; instead, it allows natural or legal persons to go to court on their behalf. Another question that will need to be answered is the extent to which an AI-driven entity can be attributed an independent legal status if it is partially dependent on human input. If a person designs and creates their own avatar in VR, but that avatar then develops autonomously via self-learning AI and is subsequently attributed rights, the avatar might make choices with which its creator disagrees.

---

[42] Christopher D Stone, *Should Trees have Standing? Law, Morality, and the Environment* (Oxford University Press 2010).

PART III

VIRTUAL WORLD AND FUTURE TRENDS

10. Rules for virtual worlds: reconciling contexts and perspectives

Joanna Kulesza and Eneken Tikk

1. INTRODUCTION

The blending of physical and digital environments brings new forms and levels of civic engagement, entertainment and welfare. Debates and questions that have surrounded internet governance and cyberspace are now emerging around metaverses – are we facing the need for a specialised set of rules, or even entirely new legal phenomena, or can the virtual worlds be governed by traditional legal frameworks.

In this chapter, we will not speculate on which approach prevails or what the exact rule-sets will be for virtual worlds. We do, however, emphasise that in the current geopolitical situation, metaverses are currently governed by different normative philosophies as there is little prospect for global consensus even on the question of the role (and desirability) of virtual worlds. On some of the obvious legal issues surrounding virtual worlds – such as privacy and data protection, artificial intelligence (AI) and cybersecurity – views and trends diverge considerably between states and other stakeholders. This chapter will not seek to break ground – it hopes to bridge the different professional communities and settings striving towards greater legal certainty and clarity about assets and activities online.

Three decades into the global internet, the world remains divided about the role that information and communication technologies (ICTs) are to play in domestic and global affairs. For advanced information societies and data economies, ICTs are now an indispensable and irreversible platform of transparency, wealth management and collaboration where digital and real assets and environments are no longer clearly distinguishable. Authoritarian states, in turn, are successfully employing digital technologies for control and oppression, feeding the narrative of digitalisation as a threat.

Consequently, rules for the increasingly virtual world, including metaverses, are far from clear or granted, and they will need to be crystallised in a complex interplay between international and national ambitions and regulations. The European Union (EU), for instance, has developed a comprehensive and sophisticated regulatory framework ranging from the commodification of non-personal data to ambitious privacy and consumer protection guarantees to measures of cybersecurity and digital autonomy.[1] In contrast, the United States (US) promotes a less protectionist legal intervention. Many countries still prefer to avoid the dire implications of digitalisation on their societal and economic affairs, governance and security, and use regulation to impose relevant restrictions. At the international level, Russia still leads the campaign for entirely new international legal frameworks for the digital domain. The normative landscape is further complicated by the escalating US-China strategic competition over digital dominance. Moreover, the rules for our digital future[2] – what they are and how they apply – are unlikely to be settled by or between states alone. The question of international norms and virtual worlds is particularly complicated given the different digital and cyber ambitions and capacities of states, industry and civil society.

We will discuss the prospects of rules for virtual worlds in three settings. After a brief discussion of the concepts involved and the basic normative premises surrounding information society development and cybersecurity, we will concentrate on the currently open issues around maintaining a safe and secure ICT environment to indicate the breadth and depth of disagreement. We then construe the EU's regulatory framework as a comprehensive catalogue for legal issues and propositions that will influence virtual worlds. We enhance the list of open issues and possible developments in the normative landscape of virtual worlds with a glance towards the international principles governing AI and a brief inquiry into AI-related litigation. After briefly also discussing the organisational landscape of normative initiatives, we offer some leads for further research and action.

---

1 See Commission, 'Shaping Europe's Digital Future, outlining the EU's digital strategy, including data commodification, privacy, cybersecurity, and digital sovereignty initiatives' (European Union 2020).

2 See European Declaration on Digital Rights and Principles for the Digital Decade 2023/C 23/01 [2023] OJ C23/1; Decision (EU) 2022/2481 of the European Parliament and of the Council of 14 December 2022 establishing the Digital Decade Policy Programme 2030 [2022] OJ L323/4.

2. FRAMING THE DISCUSSION

From the information society[3] to cyberspace to digital transformation and now metaverses, technological advances and connectivity infrastructure have delivered generations of socio-technical change. The information society as a model of socio-economic development initially simply relied on increasing use of ICTs in everyday life.[4] With the normalisation of ICTs, the concept of cyberspace came to emphasise the (lack of) security of ICT infrastructure and digital products and services, while international information security underscored the need for restating the rules surrounding information flows and the accessibility of digital products and services.[5] With digital transformation[6] as the integrated and added value that digital technologies can have in new value creation and complex problem solving, however, the regulatory focus is turning to the sustainability of digitalisation and the technological transition towards a world where everything is seamlessly interconnected.[7] Such a world now features virtual worlds (also known as metaverses) as persistent, immersive technology-based environments where physical and digital features are blended.[8] For the virtual worlds, authors identify privacy, AI and cybersecurity regulation as key frameworks for their development.

From the normative perspective, the latest developments – digital transformation and metaverses, including AI – are yet to become the subject of global dialogue. Two earlier frameworks provide the parameters of possible trends and developments. The World Summit on Information Society (WSIS) (2003) can be framed as a guiding set of internationally accepted principles for developing the information society, many of which are to be revisited in the context of AI and virtual worlds. However, amid grave concerns surrounding the safety and security of the online environment, the conclusions of the 2021 UN

---

[3] This term is defined in Directive (EU) 2015/1535 of the European Parliament and of the Council of 9 September 2015 laying down a procedure for the provision of information in the field of technical regulations and rules on Information Society services (codification) [2015] OJ L241/1.

[4] Maria Nikolova, 'The Approach of the European Union to the Information Society' (2003) European Parliament Directorate-General for Research Working Paper INDU 101 EN.

[5] See, e.g., ENISA, 'Definition of Cybersecurity: Gaps and Overlaps in Standardisation' (2015) www.enisa.europa.eu/publications/definition-of-cybersecurity accessed 28 April 2025.

[6] Commission (n 1).

[7] Commission, 'An EU initiative on Web 4.0 and virtual worlds: a head start in the next technological transition' (Communication) COM (2023) 442 final.

[8] Commission (n 7).

Open-Ended Working Group report on the security of the ICT environment frame a parallel, if not competing, set of principles and recommendations. A comparison of these documents (see Table 10.1 below) reveals different emphasis points and value propositions for governing the development and use of information technology and infrastructure. Normative propositions in the contexts of digital transformation and metaverses are currently predominant in domestic and regional regulation and pointed issue discussions – Section 3 will illustrate relevant emphasis points with reference to the EU regulation and AI litigation in the US.

Very broadly, the different normative propositions reveal four paths to achieving clarity on standards of behaviour: (a) revisiting established normative concepts and identifying the modalities of their application; (b) focusing on established normative concepts that require additional detail or revision; (c) identifying new issues for regulatory purview; and (d) requesting the negotiation of an entirely new social contract. The proposal for an international agreement that specifies new road rules for international information security was tabled at the UN in 1998 by the Russian Federation.[9] Calling for new rules, Russia and its allies essentially prefer a minimalist, even regressive, regulatory approach emphasising state sovereignty and national information spaces.[10] The focal point in these proposals is information itself and the stated goal is restraining the use of information as a weapon inconsistent with the objectives of maintaining international stability and security and complying with the principles of the sovereign equality of states.[11] Although, in the later

---

[9] UNGA, 'Letter dated 23 September 1998 from the Permanent Representative of the Russian Federation to the United Nations addressed to the Secretary-General' (30 September 1998) UN Doc A/C.1/53/3.

[10] See the Russian submission in UN Document A/53/154 (10 August 1999) Developments in the field of information and telecommunications in the context of international security, file:///C:/Users/joanna_kulesza/Downloads/A_54_213-EN.pdf, A/54/213 is a note by the SG published on 24 June 1998.

[11] UN Document A/54/213 (n 10), p 8. The Ministry of Foreign Affairs of the Russian Federation, 'Draft Convention on International Information Security' (22 September 2011) https://carnegie-production-assets.s3.amazonaws.com/static/files/RUSSIAN-DRAFT-CONVENTION-ON-INTERNATIONAL-INFORMATION-SECURITY.pdf accessed 27 May 2025, and an updated version of the same document from 2024: 'Updated Concept of the Convention of the United Nations on Ensuring International Information Security' [unofficial translation] https://docs-library.unoda.org/Open-Ended_Working_Group_on_Information_and_Communication_Technologies_-_(2021)/ENG_Concept_of_UN_Convention__on_International_Information_Security_Proposal_of_the_Russian__Federation.pdf accessed 27 May 2025 ('Updated Concept'). See also 'International Code of Conduct for Information Security' (*Ministry of Foreign*

Table 10.1 Selected themes and normative propositions in international discussions of information society development and the security of the ICT environment

-	**Information society*(WSIS Declaration of principles 2003)***	Cybersecurity/ International information security ***(OEWG Final Report 2021)***
Infrastructure	Universal and affordable access	Critical infrastructure (CI) and critical information infrastructure (CII) protection
Information	Ability to access and contribute information, abolition of barriers of access to information	N/A
Decision-making model	Multi-stakeholder	Multilateral
Empowered groups	Creators, media, education	Computer emergency response, law enforcement
Governing principles	People-centred Transparency, democracy, equality, rule of law	Threat-centred Sovereignty
Security	Global culture of cyber security, security balanced with privacy, trade and access	Concrete focal points (e.g., supply chain integrity, reporting of vulnerabilities, threat-information sharing)
Legal framework	UN Charter, Universal Declaration of Human Rights	UN Charter + clarifying how existing international law applies, with the alternative of new international legal framework(s)
Cooperation	Foreign investment, technology transfer, infrastructure development	Law enforcement, critical infrastructure protection, threat-information sharing, incident response and mitigation, attribution, confidence-building
Values and goals	Benefits in all areas of life, sustainability of the information society, tool for good governance, productivity, cultural diversity	Peaceful and secure ICT environment, international stability and security, conflict prevention

Source: Authors' compilation.

iterations of the international information security dialogue, Russia has admitted the applicability of existing international law in the context of the development and use of ICTs, Moscow has maintained its position that new rules may need to be developed over time. Russia's campaign for a new international playbook, and its contents, is summarised in a series of documents: the 1999 position submitted to the UN Secretary-General,[12] draft codes of conduct prepared in cooperation with China and a number of allied countries,[13] and two iterations of a concept convention on international information security.[14] Russia's proposal seeks to (re-)open the discussion of international law. Therefore, although Russia's proposal is all-encompassing, ranging from new rules for countering cybercrime, terrorism, information interference and the conduct of hostile cyber operations, most of them can be treated individually as alternative interpretations of existing norms.

A widely coordinated counter-proposal to Russia's call for a new convention by liberal democracies insists on offline rules being applicable online. This view essentially rejects the need for and prospect of a new international agreement and instead focuses on restating international law in the context

---

Affairs of the People's Republic of China 2011) www.mfa.gov.cn/eng/wjb/zzjg_663340/jks_665232/jkxw_665234/202406/t20240606_11405001.html accessed 27 May 2025, and an updated version of this document from 2015: UNGA, 'Letter dated 9 January 2015 from the Permanent Representatives of China, Kazakhstan, Kyrgyzstan, the Russian Federation, Tajikistan and Uzbekistan to the United Nations addressed to the Secretary-General' (13 January 2015) UN Doc A/69/723. See also the Pakistan sponsored resolution UNGA, 'Countering disinformation for the promotion and protection of human rights and fundamental freedoms' (10 January 2022) UN Doc A/RES/76/227.

12 See the Russian submission in A/54/213 (n 10).

13 On 12 September 2011, the Permanent Representatives of Russia, China, Tajikistan and Uzbekistan to the United Nations sent a joint letter to the UN Secretary-General requesting that the Draft International Code of Conduct for Information Security be circulated as an official document of the 66th session of the General Assembly. See UNGA, 'Annex to the letter dated 12 September 2011 from the Permanent Representatives of China, the Russian Federation, Tajikistan and Uzbekistan to the United Nations addressed to the Secretary-General: "International Code of Conduct for Information Security"' (14 September 2011) UN Doc A/66/359, 3. Another letter was sent on 9 January 2015 from the Permanent Representatives of China, Kazakhstan, Kyrgyzstan, the Russian Federation, Tajikistan and Uzbekistan to the United Nations addressed to the Secretary-General (see A/69/723 (n 11)).

14 The Ministry of Foreign Affairs of the Russian Federation (n 11); 'Updated Concept…' (n 11).

of state behaviour in cyberspace.[15] Reconciling these two approaches has been the main effort in the international cybersecurity discourse. The 2015[16] and 2021[17] UNGA resolutions on advancing responsible state behaviour in cyberspace underscore the obligation to adhere to international law, voluntary norms, and confidence-building measures to promote stability and security in cyberspace, acknowledging that new norms and rules may be developed over time.[18] Over recent years, dozens of countries and two international organisations have made statements about the applicability of the rules and principles of international law in the cyber context (e.g., the prohibition of the use of force, the right to self-defence, state responsibility, rules governing the conduct of hostilities).[19] At the core of the above discussions are the very sources and

---

15 See the US Submission in UN Document A/54/213 (10 August 1999) Developments in the field of information and telecommunications in the context of international security. More recently, Council of the European Union, 'Declaration on a Common Understanding of International Law in Cyberspace' (18 November 2024) 15833/24. In the context of Human Rights, see also UNGA, 'The right to privacy in the digital age' (21 January 2014) UN Doc A/RES/68/167, para 3; UNGA, 'The right to privacy in the digital age' (10 February 2015) UN Doc A/RES/69/166, para 3; UNGA, 'The right to privacy in the digital age' (25 January 2017) UN Doc A/RES/71/199, para 3; UNGA, 'The right to privacy in the digital age' (21 January 2019) UN Doc A/RES/73/179, para 3; UNHRC, 'The promotion, protection and enjoyment of human rights on the Internet' (16 July 2012) UN Doc A/HRC/RES/20/8, 2, para 1; UNHRC, 'The promotion, protection and enjoyment of human rights on the Internet' (14 July 2014) UN Doc A/HRC/RES/26/13, 2, para 1; UNHRC, 'The promotion, protection and enjoyment of human rights on the Internet' (18 July 2016) UN Doc A/HRC/RES/32/13, 3, para 1; UNHRC, 'The promotion, protection and enjoyment of human rights on the Internet' (17 July 2018) UN Doc A/HRC/RES/38/7, 3, para 1.

16 UNGA, 'Report of the Group of Governmental Experts on Developments in the Field of Information and Telecommunications in the Context of International Security' (22 July 2015) UN Doc A/70/174.

17 UNGA, 'Report of the Group of Governmental Experts on Advancing Responsible State Behaviour in Cyberspace in the Context of International Security' (14 July 2021) UN Doc A/76/135.

18 Anna-Maria Osula and Henry Rõigas (eds), *International Cyber Norms: Legal, Policy and Industry Perspectives* (NATO CCDCOE Publications 2016); Laura DeNardis, *The Global War for Internet Governance* (Yale University Press 2014); Angela McKay and others, *International Cybersecurity Norms: Reducing Conflict in an Internet-Dependent World* (Microsoft Corporation 2015).

19 See, e.g., statements made in the OEWG process https://disarmament.unoda.org/open-ended-working-group/ accessed 27 May 2025. See also Cyber Law Toolkit, 'Applicability of International Law' (2024) https://cyberlaw.ccdcoe.org/wiki/Applicability_of_international_law accessed 28 April 2025.

principles of international law, the bedrock upon which any UN agency or working group is to construct its framework for addressing the challenges associated with digitalisation and cybersecurity. Fundamental principles of sovereignty, non-intervention, and the peaceful settlement of disputes, enshrined in the UN Charter, form the cornerstone of international cybersecurity governance, and their application would require a thorough review in light of emerging socio-technical trends and practices. The interaction of international legal frameworks, including the International Telecommunication Regulations and the Universal Declaration of Human Rights, underlines the need to review and restate the established legal norms in cyberspace.[20] Our focus in this section will be on issues where new or additional regulation has been proposed.

3. LESSONS FROM INTERNATIONAL CYBERSECURITY DIALOGUES

The basic principles stemming from the 2003 WSIS declaration and summarised, for instance, by the Brazilian Internet Steering Committee[21] and the 2014 NetMundial principles[22] emphasise virtual worlds as a platform of transparent collaborative decision-making, equality, shared accountability, inclusivity, access and low barriers. As will be discussed in Section 4, the same principles guide the vision of liberal democracies of the responsible use of AI. However, over the past decade, many processes and venues have focused on issues of cybersecurity, essentially creating a counter-narrative to the human-centric, free and open ICT environment.[23] As a result, the balance between information society and international security imperatives remains unclear and the subject of lively debate. The United Nations has attempted to take on a pivotal role in shaping norms, principles, and frameworks governing cybersecurity and governance at the international level. Further processes have been initiated by state actors and other stakeholders with well-established

---

20 UN Office of Legal Affairs Codification Division, 'Analytical Guide to the Work of the International Law Commission' (2025) https://legal.un.org/Ilc/guide/1_15.shtml accessed 28 April 2025.

21 See The Brazilian Internet Steering Committee, 'Principles for the governance and use of the internet' (*CGI.br* n.d.) https://cgi.br/principles/ accessed 28 April 2025.

22 Netmundial, 'Internet governance process principles' (*Netmundial* 2014) https://netmundial.br/pdf/IGPP-NETMUNDIAL2014.pdf accessed 28 April 2025.

23 See Lars Gjesvik and Eneken Tikk, 'Working paper on institutional landscape of global digitalization governance' (EU Navigator 2025) https://eunav.eu/wp-content/uploads/2025/03/D4.1-Working-paper-on-institutional-landscape-of-global-digitalisation-governance.pdf accessed 27 May 2025.

multi-stakeholder venues like the Internet Corporation for Assigned Names and Numbers (ICANN) or the Internet Engineering Task Force (IETF), as well as its own dedicated processes within the ITU (WSIS) or the Office for Sustainable Development (IGF). Normative proposals have also been initiated from outside the UN system. Notable actors include Microsoft and the Cybersecurity Tech Accord bringing together dozens of industry majors and the Paris Call for Trust and Security in Cyberspace, a multi-stakeholder agreement on cybersecurity principles, and the Global Commission on the Stability of Cyberspace (GCSC).

As can be seen from Figure 10.1 below, multiple normative issues are open around how to achieve a peaceful, stable and secure ICT environment. Examples of areas where stakeholders disagree on either the rules or practices in their implementation include the focus and scope of international cooperation and assistance, modalities of prevention and management of cyber incidents, protection of critical infrastructure, supply-chain security, integrity of democratic processes, human rights online, and the control of offensive capabilities and their use. In some of these areas, broad consensus can be identified as to the direction and desirable outcome; for instance, the need for more and better cooperation, the commitment to human rights online, countering the theft of intellectual property, and the need to protect critical infrastructure. In others, as discussed below, different stakeholders prefer different directions and solutions. On a set of topics on which different stakeholders (governments, industry and civil society) remain divided, either on substance or the priority of the issue, priorities seem to diverge most significantly on the issue of the development and use of offensive cyber capabilities.

COOPERATION

- Stability and security of cyberspace;
- international information security
- Incident management
    - Assistance to the private sector
    - Assistance to the victim
    - Capacity building
- Law enforcement
- Critical infrastructure protection
- Threat assessment and exchange of information
- Best practices of mitigation

DUE DILIGENCE

- Attribution
- State responsibility

OPERATIONAL RESTRAINT

- Critical infrastructure
- Computer emergency response
- Private sector products and users
- Collateral damage
- Public trust in products and services (tampering, vulnerability reporting)
- Hidden functions
- Hack-back by private sector
- Non-proliferation of
    - offensive capabilities
    - malicious software
    - harmful practices
- Control over the development and use of cyber weapons
- Spyware

ADDITIONAL PROTECTIVE MEASURES

- Critical infrastructure protection
- Public core of the Internet
- Supply chains
- Electoral processes
- Product lifecycle
- Cyber hygiene
- General public IT resources (e.g., botnets)

INTELLECTUAL PROPRTY

- Industrial espionage

HUMAN RIGHTS in the information age

Source: Authors' compilation.

Figure 10.1 Selected open issues in the international cybersecurity discourse

Within the UN, two agendas have been influential in shaping discussions on the application of international norms and principles in cyberspace. The UN Group of Governmental Experts (GGE) and the Open-Ended Working Group (OEWG) stand out as prominent mechanisms for fostering dialogue, cooperation, and norm development in cyberspace. Historically, the foundation for this work was laid by the UN Group of Governmental Experts (UN GGE) operating under the international peace and security mandate of the UN First Committee. In their 2015 report, the UN GGE captured 11 recommendations on responsible state behaviour in cyberspace. Some of these explicitly invoke norms and principles of international law, such as state responsibility, international human rights and due diligence. Others provide leads for issues that may currently not be sufficiently clear or commonly understood by states, such as aspects of cooperation, critical infrastructure protection or the functioning of the local Computer Emergency Response Teams (CERTs).

Microsoft was an early proponent of new international rules to restrain the development, proliferation and use of cyber weapons and limit engagement in offensive cyber operations. Introducing Microsoft's Digital Geneva Convention, Brad Smith drew a parallel with International Humanitarian Law:

> Just as the Fourth Geneva Convention has long protected civilians in times of war, we now need a Digital Geneva Convention that will commit governments to protecting civilians from nation-state attacks in times of peace. And just as the Fourth Geneva Convention recognized that the protection of civilians required the active involvement of the Red Cross, protection against nation-state cyberattacks requires the active assistance of technology companies.[24]

Microsoft's focus, however, is on improving the existing legal frameworks with a focus on a new trend – offensive cyber operations in peacetime. Other than in the Paris Call, governments have refrained from addressing the issue of cyber offence in their international dialogues. While some expert groups and states have raised issues like countering botnets, defending electoral processes and protecting the core of the internet, these topics have not been subjected to thorough discussion in international organisations. Cyber hygiene, while a priority for civil society and industry, has also remained outside the focus of intergovernmental discussions. Non-state actor engagement in offensive cyber operations has been flagged by civil society and high-level experts but remained without much detail in international cyber dialogue.

[24] Brad Smith, 'The need for a Digital Geneva Convention' (RSA Conference, San Francisco, 14 February 2017) https://blogs.microsoft.com/on-the-issues/2017/02/14/need-digital-geneva-convention/ accessed 28 April 2025.

The GCSC concluded its work in 2019 with several proposals for pacifying cyberspace. These included a call for protecting the public core of the internet, emphasis on the need to protect the electoral infrastructure, restraint on operations that tamper with products and services, as well as against offensive cyber operations by non-state actors. The GCSC also raised the issues of commandeering botnets, the disclosure of known vulnerabilities, and a call for bolstering foundational defence through cyber hygiene.[25] To complement this, the Paris Call process added prevention of the proliferation of malicious software to the list and recognised the need to root out private hackers, as well as the need to consider additional protections on intellectual property.[26] Simultaneously, Microsoft has tabled a call to refrain from inserting back doors in private sector products, the non-proliferation of cyber weapons, the reduction of the potential collateral damage of cyber operations and assistance for efforts by industry to detect and mitigate malicious events in cyberspace.[27] Within academic debates, the Oxford Process has focused on applying international law to particular trends and issues, such as cyber-attacks against the healthcare sector and vaccine research, protection of IT supply chains, information operations and ransomware.[28] All of these documents, proposals and frameworks serve as prime examples of opportunities to further shape the law for virtual worlds.

Civil society has also played a pivotal role in shaping norms for digital governance, particularly through initiatives like the Freedom Online Coalition (FOC) and the Global Network Initiative (GNI). The FOC brings together governments committed to advancing internet freedom through multi-stakeholder dialogue and advocacy, emphasising human rights online and the protection of freedom of expression and privacy. Meanwhile, the GNI provides a framework for industry actors to uphold human rights in the ICT sector, focusing on freedom of expression and privacy safeguards. Additionally, the efforts of organisations like the Electronic Frontier Foundation (EFF) and Access Now have highlighted the importance of addressing issues like government surveillance,

---

25 Global Commission on the Stability of Cyberspace (GCSC), 'Final Report' (The Hague Centre for Strategic Studies (HCSS) 2019).

26 Paris Call for Trust and Security in Cyberspace of 12 November 2018 https://onu.delegfrance.org/IMG/pdf/paris_call_for_trust_and_security_in_cyberspace.pdf accessed 28 April 2025.

27 Microsoft's Call for Digital Peace, including proposals for a 'Digital Geneva Convention' to protect cyberspace, outlined in Brad Smith (n 24).

28 *The Oxford Process on International Law Protections in Cyberspace: A Compendium* (Oxford Institute for Ethics, Law and Armed Conflict 2023).

censorship, and the digital rights of marginalised communities.[29] These contributions, along with academic analyses and industry efforts, underscore the need for collaborative inclusive strategies for virtual world governance.

Governments and industry differ on several accounts. On supply-chain security, government experts guide states to ensure the integrity of their supply chains, while industry is suggesting that states should abstain from requiring back doors in ICT products and avoid actions that undermine public trust in digital products and services. Another thorny issue is the stockpiling and reporting of vulnerabilities. Government experts approach the issue carefully, suggesting that states should encourage responsible reporting. Industry, in turn, posits that states should have a clear principle-based policy for handling product and service vulnerabilities that reflects a strong mandate to report them to vendors rather than to stockpile, buy, sell or exploit them.

Cybersecurity concerns have also emerged in internet governance discourse following the WSIS principles and priorities. In November 2022, ICANN's Contracted Parties House (CPH) proposed enhanced measures for DNS abuse mitigation. DNS abuse refers to malicious activities targeting the Domain Name System (DNS), a vital component of internet infrastructure responsible for translating domain names into IP addresses. These activities include malware dissemination, phishing attacks, botnet orchestration, pharming schemes and spam propagation.

Convinced that the lack of dedicated and specific international legal frameworks for enforcement is burdening service providers with online safety responsibilities, the ICANN Board approved these amendments with the aim of strengthening enforcement and specificity. Broad agreement towards domain abuse activity reporting and harmful activity mitigation signifies a step towards safeguarding internet infrastructure through a contractual arrangement. Down the road, however, relying solely on private mechanisms may not suffice. There is a growing recognition of the need for enhanced international legal frameworks to manage cybercrime as effectively included in the unique DNS abuse category and to ensure internet stability and security. In the absence of a universally recognised legal framework supporting the enforceability of DNS abuse provisions under the Californian law of contracts,

---

29 Electronic Frontier Foundation, 'About EFF' www.eff.org/about accessed 28 April 2025; Access Now, 'About Us: Our Mission' www.accessnow.org/about-us/ accessed 27 May 2025. See also DeNardis (n 18), discussing the role of civil society organisations in advocating for digital rights and combating issues like censorship and surveillance; Rebecca MacKinnon, *Consent of the Networked: The Worldwide Struggle For Internet Freedom* (Basic Books 2012), addressing the importance of protecting marginalised communities in the context of digital rights.

we encounter heightened efforts aimed at exacerbating network fragmentation. This threat has recently been prominently exemplified by the DNS4EU project aimed at keeping all EU-based traffic within infrastructure under local jurisdictions.[30]

Further normative processes indicate signs of discord and departure from the human-centric approach to ICTs. The UN Cybercrime Treaty aims to establish a global framework for combating cybercrime, where safeguarding human rights and avoiding excessive intrusion into areas such as surveillance or freedom of expression remain a challenge.[31] This UN-negotiated international instrument has been criticised for its overly broad jurisdictional scope, allowing governments wide margins of discretion in how to scope and target their efforts to counter cybercrime. In addition, some of its broad provisions could grant states the mandate to impose extensive restrictions on human rights and privacy, particularly impacting individual privacy through surveillance, all in the name of combating online crime and cyberterrorism.[32]

Another less-than-optimal international consensus marker stems from the WTO E-commerce Agreement discussions where states have sought to harmonise global trade rules for digital services, data flows and intellectual property protections. The final text is not supported by some crucial participants like the US, China, India, and many African nations. China and India have raised concerns over provisions related to data flows, privacy protections and domestic regulatory autonomy.[33] Disparities in domestic regulatory readiness and fundamentally different approaches hinder collaboration and consistency in addressing cybersecurity and privacy concerns across borders. In addition, the lack of a universal approach to data governance complicates efforts to ensure that data practices align with both cybersecurity imperatives and privacy principles.

In summary, many open questions and issues remain in regard to which rules guide behaviour in cyberspace and in the digital era. Importantly, the principles of the information society are increasingly counterbalanced with

---

30 'DNS4EU: Protecting the digital lives of European citizens' (2024) www.whalebone.io/dns4eu accessed 27 May 2025; https://www.joindns4.eu/, accessed 27 May 2025.

31 Zahid Jamil, 'Cybercrime model laws' [discussion paper], *Cybercrime Convention Committee* (Council of Europe 2014).

32 Eli Scher-Zagier, 'Jurisdictional Creep: The UN Cybercrime Convention and the Expansion of Passive Personality Jurisdiction' (forthcoming) 27 *Yale Journal of Law & Technology* 327.

33 Reuters, 'Eighty Nations Strike Deal over E-Commerce, but Lack US Backing' (*Reuters* 26 July 2024) www.reuters.com/markets/eighty-nations-strike-deal-over-e-commerce-lack-us-backing-2024-07-26/ accessed 28 April 2025.

considerations and imperatives of security. As these issues divide not just states but also state and non-state actors, moving towards a global ruleset for the virtual world would require the amalgamation of a wide range of topics and interests. Unresolved issues and sharp differences in the context of cybercrime, privacy and cybersecurity have effects on further digitalisation, and metaverses are expected to bring additional challenges to both domestic and international law.

4. VIRTUAL WORLDS AS IMAGINED BY THE EU

The EU is a pivotal actor in shaping the discussion of international law in the virtual world. The metaverse, like the technological and socio-technical developments before it, is anticipated to bring new challenges to fundamental rights and democratic society, and it is imperative for the EU to identify and address such challenges in a way that best achieves the societal and economic benefits of ICTs. The EU regulatory pathway is one of the most sophisticated among regulatory approaches, identifying ways to implement, interpret and complement existing international norms, rules and principles. An interoperable network of virtual worlds[34] is a crucial aspect of Europe's Digital Decade and its materialisation would greatly benefit from international normative clarity and consistency.[35] According to the European Commission, virtual worlds bring unprecedented opportunities in terms of better health services, interaction and collaboration among people, territorial planning and community life.[36]

---

[34] According to the European Commission in the 'Commission Staff Working Document' accompanying the document 'Communication from the Commission to the European Parliament, the Council, the European Economic and Social Committee and the Committee of the Regions', *An EU initiative on Web 4.0 and virtual worlds: a head start in the next technological transition*, SWD (2023) 250 final, the EU defines metaverse as an interoperable network of virtual worlds.

[35] Commission, 'Communication from the Commission to the European Parliament, the Council, the European Economic and Social Committee and the Committee of the Regions "Long-term competitiveness of the EU: looking beyond 2030"' COM (2023) 168 final; Decision (EU) 2022/2481 of the European Parliament and of the Council of 14 December 2022 establishing the Digital Decade Policy Programme 2030 [2022] OJ L323/4.

[36] Commission, 'Communication from the Commission to the European Parliament, the Council, the European Economic and Social Committee and the Committee of the Regions "An EU initiative on Web 4.0 and virtual worlds: a head start in the next technological transition"' COM (2023) 442 final, 2.

4.1 The EU's Values and Principles for Virtual Worlds

The EU's regulatory landscape of digitalisation is an excellent example of reconciling the WSIS principles and cybersecurity concerns. The rule of law is one of the fundamental values of the Union.[37] Accordingly, which rules govern activities in cyberspace and what their potential limitations are emerge as essential questions for Brussels to shape the EU strategy for promoting a rules-based international order in virtual worlds. In a multi-stakeholder setting, normative processes have required the reconciliation of various priorities and perspectives. In this context, we outline the EU strategic vision and emphasis points for virtual worlds – commitment to the rule of law, multi-stakeholder design of responsible behaviour, and a catalogue of opportunities rather than issues that the EU can bring to the dialogue.

4.1.1 Commitment to the rule of law

According to the European Declaration on Digital Rights and Principles for the Digital Decade,[38] the democratic functioning of the digital society and economy should be strengthened in full respect of the rule of law, effective remedies and law enforcement. The EU is also committed to promoting the Declaration in its relations with other international organisations and third countries, with the ambition that the principles guide international partners towards a digital transformation that puts people and their universal human rights at the centre throughout the world. In the Declaration on Digital Rights and Principles for the Digital Decade, the EU has underscored the need to address the issue of the application of international law: 'with the acceleration of the digital transformation, the time has come for the EU to spell out how its values and fundamental rights applicable offline should be applied in the digital environment. The digital transformation should not entail the regression of rights. What is illegal offline, is illegal online'.

4.1.2 Inclusion by default

As the EU vision for digital transformation empowers individuals and fosters businesses, it presupposes a more inclusive dialogue about international law. The Declaration spells out the EU's commitment to fostering and ensuring responsible and diligent action by all actors, public and private, in the digital environment. Accordingly, the EU could consider developing and supporting processes where existing international law can be scrutinised and visions of its

---

[37] Treaty of Lisbon amending the Treaty on European Union and the Treaty establishing the European Community [2007] OJ C206/1, Article 1a.

[38] European Declaration on Digital Rights and Principles for the Digital Decade 2023/C 23/01 [2023] OJ C23/1.

application informed by other-than-state actors. A compendium of the different views on international law already expressed and promoted by such actors could be a start.

Crucially, the shaping of this normative framework is not solely the prerogative of state actors but is significantly influenced by the active participation of non-state entities. The involvement of technical organisations, industry stakeholders and civil society groups has played a pivotal role in shaping customary norms and practices in cyberspace. Their contributions, ranging from technical expertise to advocacy for responsible behaviour, highlight the importance of collaborative approaches in addressing complex cyber challenges. As such, any discussion regarding the regulation of virtual worlds must acknowledge and integrate the diverse perspectives and interests represented by these non-state actors.

In cyberspace governance, non-state actors, including technical organisations, industry stakeholders, and multi-stakeholder initiatives, play a significant role in shaping customary law. Their involvement is particularly pronounced in addressing DNS abuse, a multifaceted cybersecurity challenge encompassing various malicious activities such as domain hijacking and phishing. Technical organisations like ICANN and Regional Internet Registries, in collaboration with industry stakeholders and civil society groups, actively develop and implement measures to mitigate DNS abuse. Multi-stakeholder initiatives, such as the DNS Abuse Institute, facilitate collective action by bringing together stakeholders from diverse sectors to address DNS abuse collectively. These efforts contribute to the development of customary norms in cybersecurity by establishing shared expectations for responsible behaviour in cyberspace. Moreover, non-state actors advocate for international collaboration and binding rules to effectively address cyber threats, aligning with recommendations from reports by the UN Group of Governmental Experts (GGE). By promoting global cooperation and enhancing cybersecurity resilience, their proactive engagement fosters a more robust cyberspace governance framework.

4.1.3 International law as a multi-stakeholder design

The EU has also advocated for governance frameworks whereby market actors benefiting from the digital transformation assume their social responsibilities and make a fair and proportionate contribution to the costs of public goods, services and infrastructures. As several of the EU's goals and ambitions remain contested in the international relations arena, collaboration and understanding between different stakeholders can give new meaning and impact to digital education and bridging the digital divide. Everyone's right to education, training and lifelong learning, and basic and advanced digital skills can materialise through coordinated and mutually reinforced public and private efforts. After all, media literacy and critical thinking are key to taking an active part in the economy, society, as well as democratic processes.

The EU's premise is that online platforms, particularly very large online platforms, support free democratic debate online and mitigate the risks stemming from the functioning and use of their services, including in relation to misinformation and disinformation campaigns, while also protecting freedom of expression. Accordingly, it is worth exploring at greater depth the extent to which the digital industries, users and democratic governments share a general interest in protecting and promoting a neutral and open internet where content, services and applications are not unjustifiably blocked or degraded. It therefore becomes crucial to find ways that appreciate and appropriately contextualise the often parallel, albeit seemingly incompatible, private and public pathways towards the same strategic goal.

4.1.4 A catalogue of opportunities, not issues

As discussed above, the world is yet to entertain a shared understanding of interactions with algorithms and artificial intelligence systems, a fair digital environment and shared public digital spaces. Here, the EU has clear value propositions, an advanced regulatory framework and clear use cases to contribute to the discussion. For instance, the basic principle whereby everyone should be empowered to benefit from the advantages of algorithmic and artificial intelligence systems could serve as a conversation starter. While autonomous, informed choices in the digital environment as well as particular mitigations of risks and harm to health, safety and fundamental rights are likely to rely on domestic approaches, universal principles and directions can nevertheless be set.

A separate consideration could be the fairness of the digital environment from a global, multi-stakeholder perspective. The EU has posited that everyone should be able to effectively and freely choose which online services to use, based on objective, transparent, easily accessible and reliable information. In a diverse and multilingual digital environment, this implies the possibility (and necessity) of different choices, and certain acceptance of parallel realities. Especially when it comes to security and protections, it is essential to consider different national capacities and ambitions. This gives ambit to the EU's vision whereby digital technologies, products and services should be safe, secure, and privacy-protective by design, and include a commitment to countering and holding accountable those that seek to undermine security online and the integrity of the digital environment.

The above principles combined with the previously discussed acute normative challenges of the Digital Decade could provide a strategic platform for the EU to open a deeper, more inclusive inquiry into the international understanding of the norms, rules and principles governing virtual worlds. The final section will derive some substantive pointers for such engagement from EU regulation, selected international developments and items prioritised by industry and civil society.

4.2 EU Regulations as a Catalogue of Action Items

Over the past decade, the EU has extensively reformed legislation in addressing cybersecurity, digitalisation and virtual worlds. Today, the EU has the world's most advanced legal and policy framework for information society development, cybersecurity and digital transformation. The initial regulatory priority areas – the emergence of digital markets,[39] intellectual property rights,[40] access to public sector information[41] and personal data protection[42]

---

[39] Directive 97/7/EC of the European Parliament and of the Council of 20 May 1997 on the protection of consumers in respect of distance contracts [1997] OJ L144/19; Directive 2000/31/EC of the European Parliament and of the Council of 8 June 2000 on certain legal aspects of information society services, in particular electronic commerce, in the Internal Market [2000] OJ L178/1; Regulation (EU) No 910/2014 of the European Parliament and of the Council of 23 July 2014 on electronic identification and trust services for electronic transactions in the internal market and repealing Directive 1999/93/EC [2014] OJ L257/73.

[40] Council Directive 91/250/EEC of 14 May 1991 on the legal protection of computer programs [1991] OJ L122/42; Directive 96/9/EC of the European Parliament and of the Council of 11 March 1996 on the legal protection of databases [1996] OJ L77/20; Directive 2001/29/EC of the European Parliament and of the Council of 22 May 2001 on the harmonisation of certain aspects of copyright and related rights in the information society [2001] OJ L167/10; Directive 2009/24/EC of the European Parliament and of the Council of 23 April 2009 on the legal protection of computer programs [2009] OJ L111/16; Directive (EU) 2019/790 of the European Parliament and of the Council of 17 April 2019 on copyright and related rights in the Digital Single Market and amending Directives 96/9/EC and 2001/29/EC [2019] OJ L130/92.

[41] Directive 2003/98/EC of the European Parliament and of the Council of 17 November 2003 on the re-use of public sector information [2003] OJ L345/90; Directive 2013/37/EU of the European Parliament and of the Council of 26 June 2013 amending Directive 2003/98/EC on the re-use of public sector information [2013] OJ L175/1; Regulation (EU) 2018/1807 of the European Parliament and of the Council of 14 November 2018 on a framework for the free flow of non-personal data in the European Union [2018] OJ L303/59.

[42] Directive 95/46/EC of the European Parliament and of the Council of 24 October 1995 on the protection of individuals with regard to the processing of personal data and on the free movement of such data [1995] OJ L281/31; Directive 2002/58/EC of the European Parliament and of the Council of 12 July 2002 concerning the processing of personal data and the protection of privacy in the

– have been complemented by topics like open data[43] and data governance,[44] network and information system security,[45] cybersecurity,[46] competition rules on digital industry,[47] as well as extensive consumer protection frameworks for the users of digital products and services.[48] Most recently, the EU has used its normative instruments to shape its competitiveness in the chips industry,[49]

---

electronic communications sector [2002] OJ L201/37; Regulation (EU) 2016/679 of the European Parliament and of the Council of 27 April 2016 on the protection of natural persons with regard to the processing of personal data and on the free movement of such data, and repealing Directive 95/46/EC [2016] OJ L119/1.

[43] Directive (EU) 2019/1024 of the European Parliament and of the Council of 20 June 2019 on open data and the re-use of public sector information [2019] OJ L172/56.

[44] Regulation (EU) 2022/868 of the European Parliament and of the Council of 30 May 2022 on European data governance and amending Regulation (EU) 2018/1724 [2022] OJ L152/1.

[45] Directive (EU) 2016/1148 of the European Parliament and of the Council of 6 July 2016 concerning measures for a high common level of security of network and information systems across the Union [2016] OJ L194/1; Directive (EU) 2022/2555 of the European Parliament and of the Council of 14 December 2022 on measures for a high common level of cybersecurity across the Union, amending Regulation (EU) No 910/2014 and Directive (EU) 2018/1972, and repealing Directive (EU) 2016/1148 [2022] OJ L333/80.

[46] Directive 2013/40/EU of the European Parliament and of the Council of 12 August 2013 on attacks against information systems and replacing Council Framework Decision 2005/222/JHA [2013] OJ L218/8; Regulation (EU) 2019/881 of the European Parliament and of the Council of 17 April 2019 on ENISA (the European Union Agency for Cybersecurity) and on information and communications technology cybersecurity certification and repealing Regulation (EU) No 526/2013 [2019] OJ L151/15; Commission, 'Proposal for a regulation of the European Parliament and of the Council on horizontal cybersecurity requirements for products with digital elements and amending Regulation (EU) 2019/1020' COM (2022) 454 final.

[47] Regulation (EU) 2022/1925 of the European Parliament and of the Council of 14 September 2022 on contestable and fair markets in the digital sector and amending Directives (EU) 2019/1937 and (EU) 2020/1828 [2022] OJ L265/1.

[48] Regulation (EU) 2022/2065 of the European Parliament and of the Council of 19 October 2022 on a Single Market for Digital Services and amending Directive 2000/31/EC [2022] OJ L277/1.

[49] Regulation (EU) 2023/1781 of the European Parliament and of the Council of 13 September 2023 establishing a framework of measures for strengthening Europe's semiconductor ecosystem and amending Regulation (EU) 2021/694 [2023] OJ L229/1.

AI[50] and interoperability.[51] The upcoming resilience[52] and renewed e-privacy[53] frameworks exemplify the expansion of regulatory themes and topics. From the previous vision of a European information society as one in which management, quality and speed of information are key factors for competitiveness, the EU has progressed towards a digital single market. Reducing barriers to e-commerce, promoting content creation and information flows, providing high-speed, secure and trustworthy infrastructures and services, and maximising the growth potential of the European Digital Economy have been aimed at enabling every European to fully enjoy the benefits of digitalisation. The Digital Decade[54] strategy has set the course towards digital transformation – the integrated and added value that digital technologies can have in new value creation and complex problem solving. In addition, the 2018 and 2022 Codes of Practice on Disinformation[55] and the 2016 Code of Conduct on countering illegal hate speech online[56] constitute soft standards for conduct. Figure 10.2 illustrates the evolution and current scope of the EU's digital and cyber regulation.

---

50 Commission, 'Proposal for a Regulation of the European Parliament and of the Council laying down harmonized rules on artificial intelligence' COM (2021) 206 final.

51 Regulation (EU) 2024/903 of the European Parliament and of the Council of 13 March 2024 laying down measures for a high level of public sector interoperability across the Union [2024] OJ L2024/903.

52 Commission, 'Proposal for a Regulation of the European Parliament and of the Council on horizontal cybersecurity requirements for products with digital elements and amending Regulation (EU) 2019/1020' COM (2022) 454 final.

53 European Commission, 'Shaping Europe's Digital Future: Library: Proposal for a Regulation on Privacy and Electronic Communications' (*European Commission* 10 January 2017) https://digital-strategy.ec.europa.eu/en/library/proposal-regulation-privacy-and-electronic-communications accessed 28 April 2025.

54 European Commission, 'Europe's Digital Decade' (*European Commission* 12 March 2025) https://digital-strategy.ec.europa.eu/en/policies/europes-digital-decade accessed 28 April 2025.

55 See European Commission, '2022 Strengthened Code of Practice on Disinformation' (*European Commission* 16 June 2022) https://digital-strategy.ec.europa.eu/en/library/2022-strengthened-code-practice-disinformation accessed 28 April 2025.

56 European Commission, 'The EU Code of Conduct on Countering Illegal Hate Speech Online' https://commission.europa.eu/strategy-and-policy/policies/justice-and-fundamental-rights/combatting-discrimination/racism-and-xenophobia/eu-code-conduct-countering-illegal-hate-speech-online_en accessed 28 April 2025.

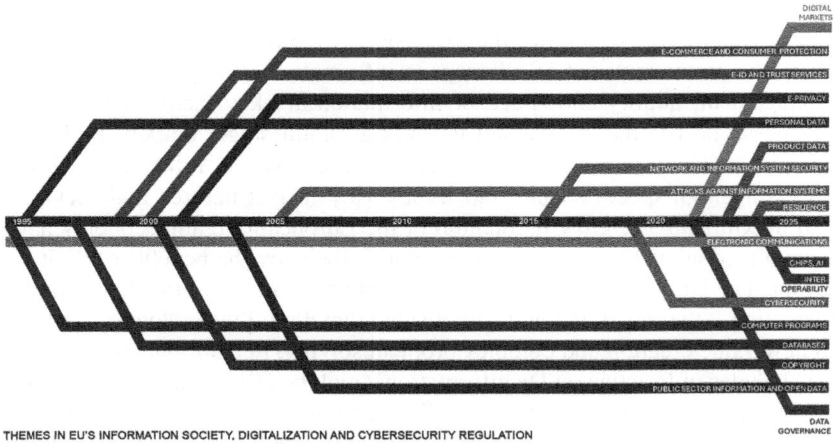

Source: Authors' compilation.

Figure 10.2 Evolution of the EU's digital and cyber regulation

From this landscape, we can design a catalogue of topics that will require attention and reconciliation in further stages of digitalisation, including in virtual worlds. While the EU approach may not be globally scalable, it is the benchmark of rights and responsibilities to be considered in conditions of extreme digitalisation. Some clarity will be expected on the above issues from and between states and other stakeholders.

An additional perspective into what lies ahead can be derived from the open issues currently subjected to litigation. Artificial intelligence is a prominent area of litigation, where technologies and socio-technical trends, such as biometrics, facial recognition, autonomous vehicles, chatbots, language processing and social media have opened additional questions for law and legislative drafting. According to the Database of AI Litigation, ground-breaking rulings are expected in the legal fields of privacy, property, antitrust, safety and security, raised from the perspective of employment, education, health, investment, tax, immigration and law enforcement. Examples of open issues in these fields are summarised in Figure 10.3.

5. THE ORGANISATIONAL LANDSCAPE

As the world moves towards an increasingly digital future, discussions surrounding the governance of digital and virtual spaces continue to evolve.

TRUST AND SAFETY
- Misuse of AI
- Misinformation
- Hate speech
- Misrepresentation
- Predictive policing
- Fraud
- Search and seizure
- Targeted advertising
- Service provider immunity
- Content moderation
- Terrorism, genocide

PROPERTY
- **Intellectual property**
  - Copyright
  - Licensing
  - Fair use
- **Product liability**
  - Lack of review and remedy
  - Human error
  - Algorithm transparency
  - Functionality and reliability

ANTITRUST
- Price fixing
- Unfair trading

PRIVACY
- Definition of personal information
- Human review
- Informed consent
- Discrimination and bias

Source: Authors' compilation from the GWU Database of AI Litigation.

Figure 10.3 *Areas and issues of litigation*

These debates are shaped by a combination of state and non-state actors, with various international initiatives and processes aiming to regulate and structure the digital environment.

On cybersecurity, the UN Open-Ended Working Group (OEWG) on security in the use of information and communications technologies, whose 2021 mandate is set to conclude in 2025, is broadly continuing the agenda, albeit in a more inclusive setting. In November 2022, the UNGA First Committee adopted a resolution on the Programme of Action (PoA) on cybersecurity, proposing the establishment of a permanent, inclusive and action-oriented mechanism post the tenure of the OEWG 2021–2025.[57]

One of the critical platforms for digital governance discussions is the WSIS. The Tunis Agenda for the Information Society, adopted in 2005, set out a vision for a multi-stakeholder governance approach. Paragraph 35 of the Tunis Agenda explicitly calls for the involvement of diverse stakeholders in the decision-making processes related to the governance of the internet, with the goal of promoting a more inclusive, transparent, and participatory framework for managing the digital space.[58] This multi-stakeholder model of governance is intended to ensure that all relevant voices – governments, the private sector, civil society, and technical communities – are involved in shaping the digital future. However, despite these commitments, there remain ongoing challenges in determining how each stakeholder can contribute effectively to the

---

[57] UNGA, 'Programme of action to advance responsible State behaviour in the use of information and communications technologies in the context of international security' (12 December 2022) UN Doc A/RES/77/37.

[58] 'Tunis Agenda for the Information Society', *World Summit on the Information Society* (*WSIS*) (18 November 2005) UN Doc WSIS-05/TUNIS/DOC/7-E, para. 35.

implementation of these goals, especially as we move towards a review of the multi-stakeholder arrangement in 2025 with WSIS+20.

The WSIS+20 review process represents a unique opportunity to reaffirm and refine the promises made at the 2005 Tunis Summit, reiterating the focus on digital inclusion, capacity building, and the role of emerging technologies, with a particular emphasis on ensuring that the governance of virtual environments remains open, fair and aligned with the Sustainable Development Goals (SDGs). However, these discussions also risk veering into sensitive issues of national sovereignty, potentially leading to a fragmentation of the internet and 'cyber balkanization'. The growing trend of internet sovereignty, wherein states exert control over the digital infrastructure within their borders, could pose significant risks to the cohesion of the global digital space. Such fragmentation could undermine the collective governance efforts outlined in the WSIS process, threatening the vision of a unified, interoperable, and inclusive digital world. Conversely, international law, as reiterated above, could serve as a measure to prevent this undesirable outcome.

In parallel with the multi-stakeholder approach enshrined in the WSIS documents and policies, the United Nations Secretary-General has proposed the Global Digital Compact (GDC) as a framework for digital cooperation that aims to address critical issues, such as digital inclusion, connectivity, and the ethical development of emerging technologies like artificial intelligence. The GDC seeks to establish shared principles for digital governance and cooperation among member states, ensuring that the benefits of digital technologies are widely distributed while minimising potential harms. However, at the time of writing, the implementation of the GDC seems complicated by the challenge of ensuring that all stakeholders are adequately represented and have the capacity to contribute meaningfully to its realisation.

In addition to these high-level policy discussions, technical governance plays a significant role in shaping the digital ecosystem. Organisations like ICANN, IETF, and CERTs are integral to ensuring the stability, security and evolution of the digital infrastructure. ICANN, a non-profit organisation based in California, governs the DNS and oversees registries and registrars, operating under contracts negotiated by the multi-stakeholder community.[59] This regulatory structure allows ICANN to address critical issues such as DNS abuse, providing a unique opportunity for influencing the future development of virtual worlds.[60] The IETF, through its Requests for Comments (RFCs),

---

[59] Milton L Mueller, *Ruling the Root: Internet Governance and the Taming of Cyberspace* (MIT Press 2004), provides an in-depth analysis of ICANN's contractual and regulatory framework.

[60] Lee A Bygrave, *Internet Governance by Contract* (Oxford University Press 2015).

creates technical standards that dictate the implementation of new technologies, shaping the digital infrastructure and virtual environments in profound ways. As demonstrated by the 5G rollout, these technical standards can serve as de facto laws of cyberspace, impacting the way digital technologies are used and governed. CERTs, in collaboration with ICANN and the IETF, work to safeguard the security and integrity of digital systems, ensuring that the technical underpinnings of the internet remain robust and resilient.

The Internet Governance Forum (IGF) also provides a collaborative platform for multi-stakeholder dialogue on digital governance issues, addressing topics such as cybersecurity, human rights and digital regulation. Among its various initiatives, the IGF's Policy Network on AI (PNAI) stands out as a critical effort aimed at shaping the future of AI governance. The PNAI brings together stakeholders from governments, industry, academia and civil society to discuss AI-related policy challenges, ensuring that the governance of AI technologies aligns with global values such as inclusivity, fairness, and human rights. This initiative plays a vital role in steering the development of AI governance frameworks in the context of virtual worlds and digital ecosystems.

The influence of technical standards on the governance of virtual spaces is also highlighted by Lessig's 'Code is Law' concept, which asserts that the technological frameworks we use can act as a form of quasi-legislative governance.[61] The design and implementation of technical standards, particularly by organisations like ICANN and the IETF, thus have a profound impact on the way digital environments are structured and regulated. As these standards continue to evolve, they will shape the future of virtual worlds, influencing everything from security protocols to the ethical considerations surrounding AI development. Together, these technical governance bodies, alongside multi-stakeholder platforms like the IGF, offer a powerful regulatory framework for addressing the emerging challenges of the digital age.

Ultimately, the intersection of formal regulations, technical governance, and multi-stakeholder cooperation presents a promising yet complex landscape for the governance of virtual worlds. As we move towards the renegotiation of global digital governance frameworks in 2025, it is essential that all stakeholders collaborate to ensure that the future of virtual worlds remains inclusive, fair, and aligned with the values of human rights, security, and sustainability.

6. CONCLUSIONS AND RECOMMENDATIONS

The fluid and rapidly evolving nature of cyberspace presents a formidable obstacle to the establishment of static and universally applicable road rules

61 Lawrence Lessig, *Code: Version 2.0* (Basic Books 2006).

– and at this point, it is unclear where exactly and to what effect those rules are needed. By anchoring their discussions on virtual world governance within established legal frameworks, both domestic and international stakeholders can navigate the complexities of cyberspace with greater clarity and coherence. However, one needs to be cautious about the deliberately and occasionally diametrically different propositions on responsible behaviour. Virtual worlds are likely to extend the list of open issues; for example, with questions about standards of consumer protection, technological and net neutrality, trustworthiness and inclusiveness, protection of user rights in the digital environment, as well as the right to disconnect.

Digitalisation, cybersecurity and online presence are subject to different expectations and many rule-sets, which lead to fragmented virtual worlds. Significant differences persist even among close political allies, underscoring the need for better legal certainty and clarity. What in the context of the European Union constitutes phases of information society development, between states and non-state actors on the world scene signifies remaining differences in the scope and premises of governing digitalisation. The task ahead of us is essentially one of good and responsible governance. International law remains a specific point of contestation.

The dynamic landscape of technological advancements, coupled with the diverse array of actors and interests involved, necessitates a more meaningful and a more comprehensive discussion of rules, norms and principles than the currently fragmented discourses permit. Acknowledging that different phases and stages of digitalisation lead to different normative imperatives, it is also essential to acknowledge that across different aspirations and levels of ICT implementation, different normative frameworks and imperatives can co-exist, for example, in different jurisdictions, on different platforms or specific applications. This should not, however, prevent a more holistic and comprehensive discussion of shared understanding and meta-level norms, rules and principles that are to govern an increasingly digital and virtual world. Such a discussion is to be inclusive for users, industry, governments and international organisations as the entirety of their perspectives informs and influences how existing rules and principles are perceived, interpreted and implemented. Additionally, the differences and dialogues between states and non-state actors reflect evolving practices in the virtual world; therefore, revealing norms, rules and principles beyond those immediately advocated.

The task starts from a deeper understanding of the world in the digital and post-digital age. The necessary awareness extends to technologies, socio-technical trends, business models but also to the conventions of policy-making and regulation. An understanding of both the potential friction and alignment between the different stakeholders will offer new regulatory and policy strategies. This makes it possible to separate the agendas and issues into workable points that can take into account shared benefits and possible red lines. A separate consideration is the order of issues to be resolved – an understanding of how different issues and agendas interact and influence each other. Furthermore, not all issues will require a global solution. Thoroughly assessing the feasibility of alternative regulatory approaches will allow for a more meaningful division of the roles and responsibilities of stakeholders in implementing the chosen agenda.

11. The continuum of real and virtual human rights: a theoretical, conceptual, and doctrinal approach to connecting human rights, future generations, and the virtual world

Anu Mutanen

1. INTRODUCTION

1.1 Defining the Research Problem and Objectives

Rapid advances in new communication technologies and virtual worlds have demonstrated significant positive as well as negative effects on the realisation of human rights. On the one hand, the use of artificial intelligence (AI) and other technologies has opened unimaginable opportunities for ensuring and even accelerating people's access to their rights, for instance, through automated decision-making. A topical example is the tracking of Covid-19 using technical means on the grounds of securing people's right to life and health. On the other hand, the growing use of algorithms and big data has caused, for example, infringements of privacy, data protection and equality. These problems have been increasingly tackled using a host of legal guidelines and rules for novel technical applications.

The interaction between human rights and advanced technologies has been mainly viewed from the perspective of today's populations. Nevertheless, many of the current human rights concerns will persist into the future. Today's technological solutions can cause concerns for the well-being and interests of people who will inherit our AI-driven society and virtual worlds. For example, serious intergenerational implications are contained within high-tech systems that amass significant carbon footprints, and therefore endanger environmental sustainability. Moreover, big data systems attach individuals to cumulative digital footprints. Devastating long-term consequences can also result from the asymmetry of the decision-making power in the technology sector.

On the other hand, the technology in question may advance the realisation of future generations' rights. For instance, AI-created scenarios of future developments can inform today's decision-making to ensure human rights in the long term. AI may even be seen as a representative of future generations. In the future, the human rights obligations of governments, internet companies, and individual virtual market actors may even ennoble online spaces, allowing them to foster a new generation of human rights advancement in digital environments.

This chapter examines the interaction between human rights and novel communication technologies, with an emphasis on the intergenerational legal perspective. The long-term challenge of establishing and embedding human rights in the digital and virtual world will be studied here through the following research questions: How do human rights and the rights of future generations intersect in the development of digital and virtual environments? How do international legal frameworks recognise and protect the human rights of future generations in the context of advanced communication technologies? How can legal thinking and doctrine address the challenges facing human rights and the rights of future generations in the digital age, fostering a future-oriented approach to intergenerational virtual human rights? With these questions, this account contributes to the evolving academic discourse on the human rights of future generations in the digital age and the development of rules on human rights compliance in advanced communication technologies.

The study is divided into four main subchapters. The introduction provides an overview of the research, outlining the questions, objectives, significance and methodology (1). Next, the study explores the intersection of human rights and digital development, analysing the socio-legal challenges, the current state of human rights in virtual environments, and the international legal framework governing digital human rights (2). Thereafter, the study examines the human rights of future generations in the context of advanced technology (3). The study culminates with insights into navigating the continuum between real and virtual human rights (4).

A central contribution of the research is the introduction of the novel concept of *virtual human rights*. The study conceptualises virtual human rights as a distinct and necessary extension of the existing human rights regime. Virtual human rights extend beyond the necessity of ensuring equal access to and use of modern digital technologies, as well as adherence to human rights standards. It also emphasises the integral need to promote the realisation of human rights within virtual realities. This includes employing not only traditional mechanisms of public control but also innovative tools, such as those provided by AI and other technological advancements, to shape and sustain the present and future dynamics of the virtual realm.

1.2 Methodological Approach and Scope

This study primarily draws its insights and methods from international human rights law to explore the evolving concept of human rights in the digital age. International human rights law establishes the obligations of governments to promote and protect human rights and fundamental freedoms for all individuals. This discussion emphasises the societal need for a forward-looking approach to human rights in the digital realm. In this effort, the chapter adopts an optimistic perspective on the potential of human rights to address emerging socio-legal challenges in the digital age. However, this optimism does not overlook the persistent issues in human rights realisation or deny the plurality of human rights and the central debate surrounding the expansion of the human rights framework. The critical questions remain whether the existing canon of rights can and should be expanded, and how such an expansion might be achieved.[1]

This study builds on the idea that human rights are the practical manifestations of utopian ideals that inspire visions of a better world.[2] In this context, human rights are understood broadly. Rather than offering a definitive account of human rights in the virtual world – such as by cataloguing foundational individual rights[3] – this chapter seeks to develop a robust conceptual understanding of virtual human rights and their role in addressing the challenges of digitalisation. Grounded in established human rights theories, this study critically examines the existing concept of digital human rights to assess its scope, applicability, and potential to complement or extend traditional human rights frameworks to form an emerging notion of virtual human rights.

---

1 Austin Choi-Fitzpatrick, 'Disruption and Emergence: How to Think about Human Rights Futures' (2024) 23(1) *Journal of Human Rights* 105, 117. For digital rights and the limits of international human rights law, see Yuval Shany, 'Digital Rights and the Outer Limits of International Human Rights Law' (2023) 24(3) *German Law Journal* 461.

2 See Choi-Fitzpatrick (n 1), 118; Samuel Moyn, *The Last Utopia: Human Rights in History* (Harvard University Press 2012).

3 See Al-Kasassbeh and others, 'Digital Human Rights in Jordanian Legislation and International Agreement' (2024) 18(1) *International Journal of Cyber Criminology* 37, who aim to identify various types of digital rights. For a catalogue of virtual human rights, see also Norges institusjon for menneskerettigheter – Teknologirådet, *The Metaverse and Human Rights* (2023), 39–43.

Moreover, the study links the growing legal discourse on future generations and their human rights, referred to as intergenerational human rights, with the context of emerging technologies, such as AI and digital innovations. In examining the intergenerational nature of human rights, the analysis acknowledges the inherent legal, theoretical and philosophical challenges in defining concepts related to future generations and intergenerational human rights,[4] and encompasses the available ways to conceptualise them for the purposes of this study. In this vein, the chapter aims to unravel the state of the art in intergenerational human rights in the relevant digital environments and systematises the interconnection between future generations, human rights and virtual worlds.

While the chapter is written with an emphasis on human rights law, the study also adopts an interdisciplinary approach by connecting it to digital studies and intergenerational law. The study incorporates key findings from the fields of digital governance and ethics to address the significant challenges to human rights posed by modern digitalisation and builds upon the relevant discourses on intergenerational law. The chapter adopts a broad, pluralist, and neutral conceptualisation of the technology at hand, consistent with the approach of the entire book. The study targets the concept of virtual world(s) and the metaverse(s) by clustering together all the relevant technologies in a continuum between fully real and fully virtual entities.[5] Previous analysis has revealed that metaverses are strongly linked to virtual reality, but that the continuum between fully virtual and fully real worlds plays a vital role in its definition.[6] The related terminology is used interchangeably here.[7] The study does not confine itself to some foreseeable definitions or precise boundaries of, for example, AI and virtual worlds, in order to encompass the unimaginable

---

4 See Axel Gosseries, 'On Future Generations' Future Rights' (2008) 16(4) *Journal of Political Philosophy* 446; Anu Mutanen, 'Tulevien sukupolvien oikeuksien turvaaminen suomalaisessa valtiosääntöoikeudessa' (2023) 121(7–8) Lakimies 1080.

5 For the idea of the reality-virtuality continuum, see Paul Milgram and others, 'Augmented Reality: A Class of Displays on the Reality-Virtuality Continuum', *Proceedings Volume 2351, Telemanipulator and Telepresence Technologies* (SPIE 1995). For an overview of the metaverse and its human rights implications, see Norges institusjon for menneskerettigheter – Teknologirådet (n 3), 11–33.

6 See Isabelle Hupont Torres and others, *Next Generation Virtual Worlds: Societal, Technological, Economic and Policy Challenges for the EU* (Publications Office of the European Union 2023), 14.

7 See Suzan Kardong-Edgren and others, 'A Call to Unify Definitions of Virtual Reality' (2019) 31 *Clinical Simulation in Nursing* 28. For a non-legal definition of the virtual world, see Carina Girvan, 'What is a Virtual World? Definition and Classification' (2018) 66 *Educational Technology Research and Development* 1087.

future advancements in the digital age.[8] The adopted conception of the relevant technology is not to say that the human rights-related issues are the same or even similar regardless of the technology in question. This analysis nevertheless claims that the starting point of the human rights perspective and intergenerationalism can be tackled by this kind of contextual simplification.

This study is primarily theoretical in methodological terms and provides conceptual insights. The theoretical analysis is, nevertheless, combined with doctrinal legal research and a qualitative review of academic literature and international legal frameworks. This approach provides opportunities to influence policy recommendations and regulatory efforts. The elements of doctrinal legal research include a review of international conventions and other relevant international regulatory mechanisms governing digital environments, with a focus on the legal framework provided by the United Nations (UN), the Council of Europe (CoE), and the European Union (EU). The study excludes regulations on human rights and digital spaces adopted by different national jurisdictions. This limitation highlights the need for further research, for instance, in the form of national (comparative) analyses to help identify best practices, gaps in existing frameworks, and opportunities for cross-border collaboration on digital and virtual human rights.

2. HUMAN RIGHTS IN THE DIGITAL AGE

2.1 Socio-legal Implications of Digital Transformation

Digitalisation has rapidly revolutionised the world. While the first generation of the internet dates back to the early 1990s, the impact of AI, robotics, big data, online social media, and search engines on daily life is continuously growing in the 2020s. Questions regarding the explicit and implicit roles of computers and communication technologies in human life have gained unprecedented momentum, particularly with the current use of AI as an everyday tool to support human decision-making.[9] AI, as a learning and self-directed system, challenges human-centred ways of operating and creates uncertainty about future developments. The ongoing digitalisation of nearly every aspect of human life is expected to accelerate at record speed with the global rollout

---

8 For concepts and terminology of next-generation virtual worlds, see Hupont Torres and others (n 6), 11–13.

9 Micheline R Ishay (ed), *The Human Rights Reader: Major Political Essays, Speeches, and Documents From Ancient Times to the Present* (3rd edn, Routledge 2023); Julia M Puaschunder, 'Human Rights Online: Towards a New Generation of Human Rights in the Virtual World' in *75 years of the Universal Declaration of Human Rights (UDHR) historic edition* (United Nations, 2023).

of 5G networks and the integration of AI into the workforce. This transformation may be further facilitated by the emergence of a new Web 4.0 paradigm, where advanced AI capabilities enable the seamless blending of physical and virtual worlds.[10]

The literature and data indicate that the effects of digitalisation have been growing exponentially, both qualitatively and quantitatively, especially over the last decade, with this trend accelerating in the wake of the Covid-19 pandemic.[11] Especially during the lockdown phase of the pandemic, demand for online communication, education, and healthcare skyrocketed. The pandemic prompted many governments to leverage their online surveillance and big data crowd-monitoring capacities to detect outbreak patterns, manage resources, and curb the spread of disease among their populations. Overall, digital surveillance employs a variety of tools, including data from smartphones, facial recognition, and biometric technologies, which contribute to the cumulative digital footprints of individuals.[12] The role of data-reaping corporations in collecting information about individuals and communities, often without their explicit consent, has raised significant concerns over *personal digital integrity*.[13] In addition, the problem of *surveillance capitalism* is outlined, highlighting the shift of governmental actors toward reliance on the online corporate sector for the collection and use of big data derived from online consumers and digital platform users, with the data also being used for commercial purposes.[14]

---

[10] Nupur Choudhury, 'World Wide Web and Its Journey from Web 1.0 to Web 4.0' (2014) 5(6) *International Journal of Computer Science and Information Technologies* 8096.

[11] See, e.g., Julia M Puaschunder, *Ethics of Inclusion: The Cases of Health, Economics, Education, Digitalization and the Environment in the post-COVID-19 Era* (Ethics International 2022).

[12] Ibid.

[13] Johan Rochel, 'Connecting the Dots: Digital Integrity as a Human Right' (2021) 21(2) *Human Rights Law Review* 358; Lusine Vardanyan, Ondrej Hamuľák and Hovsep Kocharyan, 'Personal Autonomy and Human Corporeality: What Protects the Right to Personal Integrity?' (2024) 27 *Internet of Things* 101279.

[14] Shosana Zuboff, 'Surveillance Capitalism and the Challenge of Collective Action' (2019) 28(1) *New Labor Forum* 10; Shoshana Zuboff, '"We Make Them Dance": Surveillance Capitalism, the Rise of Instrumentarian Power, and the Threat to Human Rights' in Rikke F Jørgensen (ed), *Human Rights in the Age of Platforms* (MIT Press 2019). See Julia M Puaschunder, *Behavioral Economics and Finance Leadership: Nudging and Winking to Make Better Choices* (Springer Nature 2020); Julia M Puaschunder, *Advances in Behavioral Economics and Finance Leadership: Strategic Leadership, Wise Followership and Conscientious Usership in the Digital Century* (Springer Nature 2022).

Overall, the rapid advancement of digitalisation, coupled with the widespread integration of AI, big data, and virtual environments, has significantly reshaped the socio-legal landscape. Digitalisation has complex effects on humanity, offering clear advantages while also presenting serious drawbacks. On the positive side, digitalisation has made the world more transparent, accessible, and faster, resulting in significant societal and legal benefits. The advent of next-generation virtual worlds holds considerable potential for various sectors, particularly education, healthcare, and public services.[15]

However, the dark side of the virtual world includes diminishing governmental control, evasion of legal responsibility through fake accounts, the spread of fake news and misinformation, neglect of children's safety, and the facilitation of reputation damage, sexual harassment and cybercrime. Concerns about privacy and systemic biases in big data and algorithmic decision-making, as well as the threat of discrimination, add to these challenges.[16] Furthermore, virtual communication can affect human health,[17] which serves as a basis for the realisation of various human rights. In addition, the societal challenges of digitalisation extend to issues of sustainability, particularly environmental sustainability, which is threatened by the massive energy consumption required by these technologies.[18]

In summary, digitalisation requires a balanced approach, maximising its benefits while addressing the challenges of technological advancement. The opportunities presented by digital and virtual innovations must be weighed carefully against their potential risks. In addition, these advancements demand thoughtful legal scrutiny, as they not only challenge existing ethical standards and societal norms but also push the boundaries of current legal frameworks. This is evident in the use of AI and other technologies in e-governance, legislative drafting, adjudication, and remote trials, among other applications. Further questions arise as to whether robots, algorithms, AI, and avatars should be legally recognised as quasi-human entities and granted legal powers, rights and responsibilities.[19] Overall, the pressing challenges and oppor-

---

15 Hupont Torres and others (n 6).

16 Julia M Puaschunder, 'Advances in Behavioral Economics and Responsible Competition Leadership: Tackling Searchplace Discrimination', 2022 *TechReg Chronicle on Behavioral Economics*. See Hupont Torres and others (n 6).

17 See Puaschunder 'Behavioural Economics and Finance Leadership' (n 14).

18 Hupont Torres and others (n 6).

19 For an ontological perspective on the possibility of legal personhood for entities such as robots, see Choi-Fitzpatrick (n 1), 106, 109–11. For a broader exploration of these possibilities, see Sanja Ivic, 'European Citizenship and the Concept of Digital Self' (2024) 27 *Internet of Things* 101274; William F Schulz and Sushma Raman, *The Coming Good Society: Why New Realities Demand New*

tunities brought about by the dynamic nature of technological advancements influence the interplay between law and digitalisation, driving its continuous evolution. This interplay, in turn, profoundly shapes the relationship between human rights and digitalisation.

2.2 Intersection of Human Rights and Digitalisation

The central role of digitalisation in current socio-legal systems significantly impacts various dimensions of human life. This underscores the need for a globally shared understanding of online values to curb harmful activities and establish international standards for conduct in the virtual world. To address the critical need for ethical and socially responsible codes of conduct in virtual worlds, as well as the broader challenges posed by digitalisation, the human rights regime can offer significant solutions. Human rights can play a pivotal role in establishing universal standards in the context of digitalisation. Human rights can foster transparency, fairness, accountability, and oversight in the evolving virtual space.[20]

At the same time, it is evident that the ongoing global digitalisation poses significant challenges to human rights.[21] While the technological developments in question offer transformative opportunities to the human rights regime, they also present unprecedented problems to the realisation of these rights. For instance, the digital measures devised during Covid-19 included safeguarding freedom of speech, the right to life, health, and education, among other human rights. However, the overall effects on human rights were not one-sided, as the measures responding to the pandemic also imposed restrictions on these rights, including privacy, freedom of movement and personal integrity. In addition, the digital divide – or inequality in access to and use of digital technologies – remains a pressing human rights issue.[22] Moreover,

Rights (Harvard University Press 2020). For breaking the dichotomy between natural and legal persons by including the category of digital persons, see Vagelis Papakonstantinou and Paul de Hert, 'Structuring Modern Life Running on Software: Recognizing (some) Computer Programs as new "digital persons"' (2018) 34(4) *Computer Law and Security Review* 732.

20 Puaschunder (n 9).

21 Hupont Torres and others (n 6).

22 For digital inequality, see Puaschunder (n 20). On the digital divide, see Dariusz Kloza, 'The Right Not to Use the Internet' (2024) 52 *Computer Law and Security Review* 105907; Cynthia K Sanders and Edward Scanlon, 'The Digital Divide Is a Human Rights Issue: Advancing Social Inclusion Through Social Work Advocacy' (2021) 6 *Journal of Human Rights and Social Work* 130.

online crowd control and the monetisation of individual actions, as exemplified by surveillance capitalism, demand focused human rights scrutiny.[23]

Previous research has emphasised that the extensive use of the internet necessitates the development of robust laws and regulations to safeguard users' privacy rights.[24] As digital and virtual environments continue to evolve and grow in significance, there are increasing calls to embed human rights principles within AI, big data analytics and search engines, as well as to extend human rights protections to the virtual space.[25] Recent unprecedented technological developments may even necessitate the modernisation of the human rights toolkit. For instance, regulations, resolutions, and other traditional legal mechanisms, as well as policy reports and campaigns, could be complemented by experiments,[26] novel forms of social movements, and the use of digitalisation and AI as mechanisms for human rights advocacy.[27] Even the possibility of a radical systemic change in the human rights regime should not be overlooked. In this vein, Choi-Fitzpatrick observes that 'the subjects of rights are evolving, and the next few decades may very well see the growth of legal and moral personhood well beyond the human, with unpredictable results for the human rights project'.[28]

---

[23] Al-Kasassbeh and others (n 3), 38; Puaschunder 'Behavioral Economics and Finance Leadership' (n 14); Puaschunder 'Advances in Behavioral Economics and Finance Leadership' (n 14); Zuboff 'Surveillance Capitalism' (n 14); Zuboff 'We Make Them Dance' (n 14).

[24] Baraa M Kamal and Shaima I Taha, 'The Legal Nature of Digital Human Rights and Their Legal Framework' (2023) 7(3) *Tikrit University Journal for Rights*; Valerie Steeves, 'Privacy, Free Speech and Community: Applying Human Rights Law to Cyberspace' in Steven Hick, Edward F. Halpin and Eric Hoskins (eds), *Human Rights and the Internet* (Palgrave Macmillan 2000).

[25] Puaschunder (n 16). For an analysis of the necessity of regulating human rights in the context of artificial intelligence, see José-Miguel Bello y Villarino and Ramona Vijeyarasa, 'International Human Rights, Artificial Intelligence, and the Challenge for the Pondering State: Time to Regulate?' (2022) 40(1) *Nordic Journal of Human Rights* 194.

[26] Geoff Mulgan, *Social Innovation: How Societies Find the Power to Change* (Policy Press 2019).

[27] Choi-Fitzpatrick (n 1), 118–19; Puaschunder (n 20). See, e.g., Meltem Ineli-Ciger, 'Resettlement by Algorithm: Can Artificial Intelligence Uphold Human Rights?' (2024) 55 *Computer Law & Security Review* 106051, on the potential impact of AI on the resettlement of refugees.

[28] Choi-Fitzpatrick (n 1), 106.

2.3 Human Rights-centred Regulation of Digital Technology and Artificial Intelligence

Despite their long history and universal, inalienable, and egalitarian character, as well as protection under national, international, and supranational law, human rights have only recently begun to be addressed in the context of the digital world. At the moment, there are increasing regulatory efforts to promote human rights in the digital sphere, addressing freedom of expression, knowledge sharing, privacy, data protection, and equitable access to communication infrastructure.[29] Internet access is recognised as a human right and legally protected in various jurisdictions.[30] Overall, a lot is going on at the national, international, as well as global levels in the human rights-related regulation of digital technology.[31]

Essentially, human rights can play an equivalent or comparable role in the virtual world to those they perform in the physical world (*real human rights, human rights offline*). The criteria for human rights protection do not include the condition of activities within reality. Therefore, the applicability of human rights is not confined solely to the *real* world but is also fully applicable in the digital realm. This position was affirmed in 2024 by the UN Human Rights Council in its *Resolution on the Promotion, Protection, and Enjoyment of Human Rights on the Internet*. The resolution reaffirms that the same rights individuals possess offline must also be safeguarded online. It emphasises the importance of bridging the digital divide, ensuring internet neutrality, and protecting online privacy. The resolution also condemns internet shutdowns and online censorship, urging states to adopt a human rights-based approach to providing and expanding access to information and communication technologies.[32]

---

[29] For an aim to identify the international treaties and other international efforts that have advanced the recognition of digital human rights, see Al-Kasassbeh and others (n 3), 37–38.

[30] Al-Kasassbeh and others (n 3), 38–39. See, e.g., Oleksandr Sevchuk and others, 'Human Right to Internet Access in Healthcare in the "Right to Health Concept": Legal Issues' (2021) 10(2) *European Journal of Sustainable Development* 286, on the human right to internet access in healthcare.

[31] For an effort to recognise digital human rights in international agreements, see Al-Kasassbeh and others (n 3). For international organisations and digital human rights, see Wolfgang Benedek, 'International Organisations and Digital Human Rights' in Ben Wagner and others (eds), *Research Handbook on Human Rights and Digital Technology* (Edward Elgar Publishing 2019).

[32] UNHRC Res 57/29 (11 October 2024) UN Doc A/HRC/RES/57/29. For elaboration on the UN perspective on the divide between virtual world and real

At the UN level, another notable recent development is the *Pact for the Future*, adopted in 2024. The pact combines a Global Digital Compact and a Declaration on Future Generations. One of the objectives of the Global Digital Compact is to foster an inclusive, open, safe, and secure digital space that respects, protects, and promotes human rights. In addition, the pact aims to enhance international governance of AI for the benefit of humanity.[33]

During the 2020s, extensive efforts have been made to define principles for ethical AI. *The Council of Europe Framework Convention on Artificial Intelligence and Human Rights, Democracy, and the Rule of Law* is the first internationally legally binding treaty in this field, opened for signature in 2024. The convention aims to guarantee, among other things, the right of individuals to be informed about their interactions with an AI system and the possibility of engaging with a human, in addition to or instead of an AI system. The convention establishes six fundamental principles governing the design, development, use and decommissioning of AI systems: (1) transparency and oversight; (2) accountability and responsibility; (3) equality and non-discrimination; (4) privacy and personal data protection; (5) safety, security and robustness; and (6) safe innovation. The convention imposes an obligation on states to safeguard human dignity and self-determination. Individuals must be able to make informed decisions and participate in public discourse free from undue influence or manipulation by AI systems. This necessitates the

---

rights, see Diane Rowland, '"Virtual World, Real Rights?": Human Rights and the Internet' in Marco Odello and Silvia Cavandoli (eds), *Emerging Areas of Human Rights in the 21st Century* (Routledge 2011).

33 UNGA Res 79/1 (22 September 2024) UN Doc A/RES/79/1, Section III on science, technology and innovation and digital cooperation, paras 49–57; Annex I: Global Digital Compact, Objectives 3 and 5; Section IV on youth and future generations, paras 58–63; Annex II: Declaration on Future Generations. For other relevant UN resolutions and documents, see UNGA Res 76/162 (16 December 2021) UN Doc A/RES/76/162 (Human rights and cultural diversity); UNGA Res 78/213 (19 December 2023) UN Doc A/RES/78/213 (Promotion and protection of human rights in the context of digital technologies); UNHRC, 'Human rights and technical standard-setting processes for new and emerging digital technologies: Report of the Office of the United Nations High Commissioner for Human Rights' (18 September 2023) UN Doc A/HRC/53/42. To mention another global actor, the OECD Council's AI recommendation also includes the principle of human-centred values and fairness, which encompasses human rights. OECD 'Recommendation of the Council on Artificial Intelligence' (22 May 2019) OECD/LEGAL/0449. For the OECD's framework for anticipatory governance of emerging technologies, see OECD, 'Framework for Anticipatory Governance of Emerging Technologies', *OECD Science, Technology and Industry Policy Papers No. 165* (OECD Publishing 2024).

protection of freedom of expression, freedom of assembly, and the right to access information.[34]

The Council of Europe's convention partially overlaps with the EU *AI Act*. The purpose of the AI Act is to promote the adoption of human-centric and trustworthy AI while ensuring a high level of protection for health, safety, fundamental rights, democracy, the rule of law and the environment. The Act establishes six key principles applicable to AI systems, in a similar manner to the CoE framework: (1) human agency and oversight; (2) technical robustness and safety; (3) privacy and data governance; (4) transparency; (5) diversity, non-discrimination and fairness; and (6) societal and environmental well-being and accountability. The Act prohibits various AI applications that infringe on human rights and enable discrimination, such as real-time biometric remote identification in public spaces and risk assessment or predictive profiling of individuals' criminal behaviour based on personal characteristics. Under the AI Act's risk classification framework, high-risk AI systems have adverse effects on human safety and fundamental rights; for instance, AI systems intended to influence election outcomes or voter behaviour. Such systems are subject to specific requirements, including a fundamental rights impact assessment. Additionally, providers of AI systems utilising foundation models must identify, mitigate and minimise risks associated with their use, including those related to fundamental rights.[35]

In addition to the AI Act, the EU regulates technologies that are key drivers of virtual worlds through the Digital Services Act[36] and Digital Markets

[34] Council of Europe Framework Convention on Artificial Intelligence and Human Rights, Democracy and the Rule of Law (5 September 2024) CETS No. 225 Preamble, Articles 1, 2, 6–12, 14–15. For other relevant CE conventions and protocols addressing the challenges resulting from the use of new information and communication technologies, see Convention on Cybercrime (23 November 2001) ETS No. 185; Convention for the Protection of Individuals with regard to Automatic Processing of Personal Data (28 January 1981) ETS No. 108.

[35] Regulation (EU) 2024/1689 of the European Parliament and of the Council of 13 June 2024 laying down harmonised rules on artificial intelligence and amending Regulations (EC) No 300/2008, (EU) No 167/2013, (EU) No 168/2013, (EU) 2018/858, (EU) 2018/1139 and (EU) 2019/2144 and Directives 2014/90/EU, (EU) 2016/797 and (EU) 2020/1828 (Artificial Intelligence Act) [2024] OJ L2024/1689.

[36] Regulation (EU) 2022/2065 of the European Parliament and of the Council of 19 October 2022 on a Single Market for Digital Services and amending Directive 2000/31/EC (Digital Services Act) [2022] OJ L277/1.

Act,[37] but also the Data Act[38] and the Data Governance Act[39] among others.[40] Notable European advancements to regulate the internet also include the General Data Protection Regulation (GDPR), which has fortified fundamental rights and human rights protection, particularly in the area of privacy, and has influenced international online market standards since 2018.[41] For example, the privacy protections established in the GDPR and applied by the Court of Justice of the EU reinforced the *right to delete*, which may evolve into an inalienable digital human right.[42]

Overall, the EU regulation has gained dominance in setting international internet and AI standards around the world. This effect has been coined the

---

37 Regulation (EU) 2022/1925 of the European Parliament and of the Council of 14 September 2022 on contestable and fair markets in the digital sector and amending Directives (EU) 2019/1937 and (EU) 2020/1828 (Digital Markets Act) [2022] OJ L265/1.

38 Regulation (EU) 2023/2854 of the European Parliament and of the Council of 13 December 2023 on harmonised rules on fair access to and use of data and amending Regulation (EU) 2017/2394 and Directive (EU) 2020/1828 (Data Act) [2023] OJ L2023/2854.

39 Regulation (EU) 2022/868 of the European Parliament and of the Council of 30 May 2022 on European data governance and amending Regulation (EU) 2018/1724 (Data Governance Act) [2022] OJ L152/1.

40 See also, e.g., Regulation (EU) 2023/1114 of the European Parliament and of the Council of 31 May 2023 on markets in crypto-assets, and amending Regulations (EU) No 1093/2010 and (EU) No 1095/2010 and Directives 2013/36/EU and (EU) 2019/1937 [2023] OJ L150/40; Commission, 'Proposal for a regulation of the European Parliament and of the Council on the European health data space' COM (2022) 197 final; Commission, 'Proposal for a regulation of the European Parliament and of the Council laying down rules to prevent and combat child sexual abuse' COM (2022) 209 final; Commission, 'Proposal for a regulation of the European Parliament and of the Council amending Regulation (EU) 2021/1232 of the European Parliament and of the Council on a temporary derogation from certain provisions of Directive 2002/58/EC for the purpose of combating online child sexual abuse' COM (2023) 777 final.

41 Regulation (EU) 2016/679 of the European Parliament and of the Council of 27 April 2016 on the protection of natural persons with regard to the processing of personal data and on the free movement of such data, and repealing Directive 95/46/EC (General Data Protection Regulation) [2016] OJ L119/1.

42 Viktor Mayer-Schönberger, *Delete: The Virtue of Forgetting in the Digital Age* (Princeton University Press 2009). For a connected right to be forgotten, see Chanhee Kwak, Junyeong Lee and Heeseok Lee, 'Forming a New Dimension of Digital Human Rights: A Research Agenda for the Right to be Forgotten', *Proceedings of the 50th Hawaii International Conference on System Sciences* (University of Hawaii 2017).

'Brussels effect'.[43] In a similar vein, the EU issued the European Declaration on Digital Rights and Principles for the Digital Decade in 2023.[44] In addition, the European Commission adopted a strategy on Web 4.0 and virtual worlds in 2023 to steer the next technological transition and ensure an open, secure, trustworthy, fair and inclusive digital environment for EU citizens, businesses, and public administrations. The strategy includes providing guidelines and preparing regulatory measures to facilitate compliance with emerging digital policies.[45]

In summary, numerous developments are currently setting the stage for closer monitoring of human rights in relation to digitalisation. In this context, international and supranational regulatory mechanisms are widely recognised as essential for upholding digital rights while addressing societal concerns, such as public order and morality.[46] The regulation of AI, for example, aims to anticipate its development, protect against its negative effects through risk assessment, and build future-proof regulatory measures. While the legal regulation adopted provides for a rather conventional approach to dealing with the unprecedented technological development, many of the recently adopted legal regulations and proposals pertaining to digitalisation and AI can nevertheless be expected to have a positive impact on fundamental rights, especially in relation to the protection of private life and personal data. Novel regulations are placing important limits on the use of AI, especially if there is the risk of human rights violations. It has been recognised that certain applications of new and emerging digital technologies are not compatible with international human rights law.[47]

While human rights can provide potential solutions to the problems posed by digitalisation, integrating human rights principles into digital environments remains a complex and challenging endeavour. The legal regulation of advanced technology and especially its human rights dimensions seems to be lagging behind that which is necessitated by the fast-paced digitalisation. The international and borderless nature of online interactions complicates efforts

---

43 Anu Bradford, *The Brussels Effect: How the European Union Rules the World* (Oxford University Press 2020). See Susanna Lindroos-Hovinheimo, 'Automaattisen päätöksenteon määritelmä laajenee – Euroopan unionin ensimmäiset tuomiot tietosuoja-asetuksen 22 artiklasta' (2024) 122(3–4) Lakimies 537.

44 European Declaration on Digital Rights and Principles for the Digital Decade [2023] OJ C23/1.

45 Commission, 'Strategy on Web 4.0 and virtual worlds', 11 July 2023. For the EU challenges and opportunities of the next generation virtual worlds, see Hupont Torres and others (n 6).

46 Al-Kasassbeh and others (n 3), 38.

47 See UNHRC (n 33).

to establish effective legal frameworks. As a result, there are still no comprehensive rules or legal frameworks governing digital rights and ensuring an orderly human rights environment online.[48] Regulation and enforcement remain largely at the continental level and are far from achieving the universal recognition and acceptance that human rights values otherwise generally enjoy.

Consequently, a robust global framework is needed to safeguard and advance human rights in digital contexts. The transnational nature of the metaverse is viewed as requiring regulation through public international law rather than national legislation.[49] In this vein, calls for a 'bill of rights for the metaverse' have been voiced.[50] In such efforts, the possible negative impacts of broad-based regulation also need to be avoided, such as stifling innovation, imposing excessive costs on corporations, and widening monopolistic gaps.[51]

A key dilemma for regulatory efforts is that online environments and AI systems are mainly governed by multinational technology corporations. Therefore, these private actors are increasingly becoming crucial gatekeepers of privacy, freedom of speech, and online decency. Lemley and Volokh have highlighted the significant drawbacks of virtual interaction under the concept of 'jurisdiction in virtual spaces'. Accordingly, when users interact through privately owned networks and devices that form virtual spaces, they are subject to contractual terms and conditions that may restrict their rights to privacy, property and liberty.[52]

A key concern in relationships among private parties is the applicability of human rights. Therefore, the so-called third-party effect of fundamental rights (Drittwirkung der Grundrechte) needs to evolve to expand individuals'

---

[48] Al-Kasassbeh and others (n 3), 55.

[49] Hatice K Ecemiş Yilmaz, 'Legal Issues of the Metaverse: A Public International Law Perspective' (2024) 15(27) *Law and Justice Review* 49.

[50] See Gokce Cobansoy Hizel, 'Metaverse and Human Rights: Do We Need Metaversal Declaration of Human Rights?' in Fatih Sinan Esen, Hasan Tinmaz and Madhusudan Singh (eds), *Metaverse: Technologies, Opportunities and Threats* (Springer Link 2023); Osman Gazi Gucluturk, 'The Role of the Law in Metaverse Regulation' in Sinan Esen et al., ibid.

[51] For the development of effective tools and mechanisms to prevent the negative impact of information technology on human rights and freedoms in the current environment, see Vira Pyrohovska and others, 'Human Rights Protection in the Context of Information Technology Development: Problems and Future Prospects' (2024) 4(1) *Futurity Economics and Law* 38.

[52] Mark A Lemley and Eugene Volokh, 'Law, Virtual Reality, and Augmented Reality' (2018) 166(5) *University of Pennsylvania Law Review* 1051. See Richard L Pate, 'Legal Issues Inside the Unnatural World of Metaverse' (2022) 43(5) *Business Law Review* 188.

rights against corporations that infringe human rights and to strengthen corporate accountability for human rights violations.[53] Recognising human rights in virtual spaces could empower individuals and states to claim protection and reparations for human rights infringements in virtual worlds. This could expand human rights due diligence, as outlined in the United Nations Guiding Principles on Business and Human Rights[54] and the EU Corporate Sustainability Due Diligence Directive.[55] In any case, governments continue to bear significant responsibility for human rights, including in digital environments.[56]

Another major problem pertaining to the applicability of human rights in virtual contexts is the absence of traditional human relations. This has yet to be considered in legal frameworks governing digital realities. Given the pace of technological advancement, it is crucial to continuously evaluate and refine such rules even after their adoption to uphold a functional human rights system in virtual spaces.

Understanding and advancing the multifaceted human rights dimensions of AI regulation requires new expertise and foresight from human rights actors, as well as collaboration with experts in technology and other relevant fields. Preparing for emerging virtual worlds requires anticipating and imagining potential futures that encompass both risks and opportunities. The question of how human rights can adapt to these evolving dynamics – in both virtual and physical worlds – has become a pressing issue in contemporary human rights discourse.

---

[53] See Andrew Clapham, *Human Rights in the Private Sphere* (Oxford University Press 1993).

[54] UN HCHR, 'Guiding Principles on Business and Human Rights: Implementing the United Nations "Protect, Respect and Remedy" Framework' (2011) UN Doc HR/PUB/11/04.

[55] Directive (EU) 2024/1760 of the European Parliament and of the Council of 13 June 2024 on corporate sustainability due diligence and amending Directive (EU) 2019/1937 and Regulation (EU) 2023/2859 [2024] OJ L2024/1760. For an effort to theorise human rights in the AI Act and the Corporate Sustainability Due Diligence Directive, see Mika Viljanen, 'A Horizontal Meta-effect? Theorising Human Rights in the AI Act and the Corporate Sustainability Due Diligence Directive' in Eduardo Gill-Pedro and Andreas Moberg (eds), *YSEC Yearbook of Socio-Economic Constitutions 2023: Law and the Governance of Artificial Intelligence* (Springer Cham 2024).

[56] Al-Kasassbeh and others (n 3), 55.

2.4 State-of-the-art of Human Rights in the Virtual World

The relationship between digitalisation and legal frameworks has garnered significant academic interest from diverse perspectives. For instance, the legality of automated decision-making processes, digitised data governance, or algorithmic governance employed by public authorities has been studied relatively extensively.[57] Human rights scholars started to pay attention to digitalisation around the turn of the millennium.[58] Some of the early attention focused on the foundational question of whether the context of the evolving internet and virtual world includes real human rights.[59] Broader academic interest in the relationship between digitalisation and human rights has emerged only surprisingly recently. The studies encompass a diverse array of subjects, including the human right to internet access,[60] digital integrity,[61] and the right to be forgotten, among other topics.[62] A recent study has also highlighted the relative scarcity of human rights research in the field of digitalisation.[63]

Concurrently with contemporary human rights discourse, the concept of digital rights has emerged, with international organisations advocating their recognition.[64] In the human rights context, this concept has evolved into *digital human rights*, which has been defined in a variety of ways. Among the earliest contributions, Fathy defined digital rights as the entitlement of every individual to access, use, create and publish digital content without restriction.

---

57 See, e.g., Rebekah Dowd, *The Birth of Digital Human Rights: Digitized Data Governance as a Human Rights Issue in the EU* (Palgrave Macmillan Cham 2022); Ignas Kalpokas, *Algorithmic Governance: Politics and Law in the Post-Human Era* (Springer International 2019).

58 See, e.g., Steven Hick, Edward F Halpin and Eric Hoskins, *Human Rights and the Internet* (Palgrave Macmillan 2000); Antonio Segura-Serrano, 'Internet Regulation and the Role of International Law' in Armin von Bogdandy and Rüdiger Wolfrum (eds), *Max Planck Yearbook of United Nations Law* vol 10 (Martinus Nijhoff Publishers 2006).

59 See Rowland (n 32).

60 Sevchuk and others (n 30).

61 Rochel (n 13); Vardanyan, Hamuľák and Kocharyan (n 13).

62 See Andrew Feenberg, 'The Internet as Network, World, Co-construction, and Mode of Governance' (2019) 35(4) *The Information Society* 229; Ishay (n 9); Puaschunder (n 9); Puaschunder (n 20); Zuboff 'Surveillance Capitalism' (n 14); Zuboff 'We Make Them Dance' (n 14).

63 Al-Kasassbeh and others (n 3), 39. For a systematic review of scientific literature focused on human rights protection in the context of information technology development, see Pyrohovska and others (n 51). See also Joy Liddicoat, *Human Rights and the Internet* (Intersentia 2021).

64 Al-Kasassbeh and others (n 3), 38, 55.

This definition connects digital rights to several fundamental rights and freedoms, including freedom of opinion and expression, privacy, the right to knowledge, development, and the freedom to disseminate information.[65] In a recent study, Al-Kasassbeh et al. define digital rights as the rights that enable individuals to connect to the internet and ensure their protection while sharing, creating or receiving data. They underscore that digital rights are integral to the broader spectrum of human rights and are fundamentally embedded in the digital realm.[66] Overall, the academic literature on digital human rights presents various definitions, often reflecting the evolving and emerging nature of the term,[67] as well as the need to update human rights in a digitising society.[68]

Contemporary digitalisation studies not only highlight the advantages of digital development but also critically examine the role of AI, big data, robotics and search engines in human lives. In 2018, Risse was one of the earliest to critically discuss AI in relation to human rights. He called for greater attention to the impact of AI within the human rights community. In addition to highlighting the wide-ranging use of AI, he outlined the potential superiority of AI over human beings and identified the absence of AI conscientiousness as a significant threat. He also emphasised the rising role of social media in society and the novel methods of online advertising as critical developments that warrant close monitoring. Risse further proposed the idea of mandatorily embedding human rights values in the algorithms of digital machinery.[69] In this vein,

---

65 Noha Fathy, 'Freedom of Expression in the Digital Age: Enhanced or Undermined? The Case of Egypt' (2018) 3(1) *Journal of Cyber Policy* 96. For a similar analysis of the right to access, the right to privacy, the right to non-discrimination, the right to ownership and economic rights, and the right to cultural rights in the context of the metaverse, see Ecemiş Yilmaz (n 49).

66 Al-Kasassbeh and others (n 3), 38, 41.

67 For further analysis of the concept of digital human rights, see Al-Kasassbeh and others (n 3), 40–41; Dafna Dror-Shpoliansky and Yuval Shany, 'It's the End of the (Offline) World as We Know It: From Human Rights to Digital Human Rights – A Proposed Typology' (2021) 32(4) *The European Journal of International Law* 1249.

68 See, e.g., Olga V Belyanskaya, Julia A Kazanovskaya and Tatiana A Strutinskaya, 'Updating Human Rights and Freedoms in a Digitalizing Society' in Elena G Popkova (ed), *Business 4.0 as a Subject of the Digital Economy* (Springer International Publishing 2022).

69 Mathias Risse, 'Human Rights and Artificial Intelligence: An Urgently Needed Agenda', *Harvard Kennedy School Faculty Research Working Paper Series, HKS Working Paper No. RWP18-015* (HKS 2018).

other concrete academic suggestions have emerged, such as programming self-destruct mechanisms in AI systems to prevent problems.[70]

In the aftermath of the Covid-19 pandemic, the human rights regime is observed to have undergone significant changes alongside the evolution of the digital realm. These recent developments place particular emphasis on human rights in relation to governmental mass surveillance, the use of AI, social media, search engines, and big data-driven crowd control via social media, all within the broader context of digitalisation and the virtual world.[71] This evolution is often analysed as potentially introducing a new generation of human rights to complement the existing three generations: civil and political rights, economic, social, and cultural rights, and collective rights.[72] Furthermore, this shift adds to other recent changes in the human rights regime, which have increasingly focused on pressing issues such as environmental justice, biomedicine, transgender rights, global governance, war crimes, terrorism, security rights, refugee rights and combating human trafficking.[73]

An additional line of argument on an emerging new generation of human rights has been developing. Risse has recently advocated the mobilisation of a *fourth generation of human rights* to protect human life 'in light of ongoing technological innovation' and potentially 'in the presence of new kinds of intelligence'. The concept of the fourth generation of human rights refers to human rights as they apply in digital environments or life-worlds. According to Risse, '[A]fter the first generation concerned with protecting personhood, the second with relative status, and the third with collective endeavors, the fourth concerns humanity's relationship with entities of similar or larger general intelligence that would share our lifeworlds.' He argues that, although human rights were developed for an analogue life-world, this does not mean they are incapable of addressing issues in digital life-worlds. However, this suggests that the approach to addressing these issues may differ between analogue and digital contexts, necessitating adaptation. Risse introduces a pivotal question: should

---

70 Julia M Puaschunder, 'Artificial Intelligence Evolution: On the Virtue of Killing in the Artificial Age' (2018) 3(1) *Journal of Sociology* 10.

71 Puaschunder (n 20).

72 For analysis of the history and generations of human rights, see Choi-Fitzpatrick (n 1), 108; Ishay (n 9).

73 Puaschunder (n 20). See Vera Ferreira, 'Climate-induced Migrations: Legal Challenges', in Julia M Puaschunder (ed), *Intergenerational Responsibility in the 21st Century* (Vernon Press 2018); Antonio Fruttaldo, 'Climate-Induced Migration and International Law: Assessing the Discursive Legal Construction of Climate Refugees' (2017) 21(2) *Anglistica AION* 77.

the rights of non-human entities – such as genetically enhanced humans, cyborgs, or uploaded brains – be regarded as human rights?[74]

Notably, discussions on the evolution of the human rights regime often seem to adopt an additive approach, focusing on developing a new generation of rights rather than framing the present juncture as an interregnum between eras.[75] It is not, however, uncommon to assert that human rights have historically developed through a series of controversies.[76] Puaschunder has argued that an additional controversy – centred on the impact of digitalisation on human lives – has led to the emergence of a new generation of human rights. She refers to this emerging framework as 'human rights online'. She claims that, currently, three pressing areas of concern have been identified that demand concrete human rights attention in the online sphere: First, the focus may shift from protecting individuals against governmental surveillance to regulating the interference of private entities that exploit big data insights and infringe on privacy. Second, with freedom of expression increasingly being challenged by the need to control hate speech on contemporary online platforms, human rights could play a vital role in safeguarding stability, decency, and human dignity while maintaining an overall climate of online freedom of speech. Third, the heightened anonymity of virtual spaces presents challenges for credibility and accuracy of online content, as well as the democratisation of online platforms.[77]

In a similar vein, Choi-Fitzpatrick's perspective on the evolution of human rights suggests a sense of disjuncture. He argues that significant changes occurring across multiple sectors – particularly in tectonic geopolitics, climate and energy, and science and technology – may intersect or combine in ways that

---

74 Mathias Risse, 'The Fourth Generation of Human Rights: Epistemic Rights in Digital Lifeworlds' (2021) 8(2) *Moral Philosophy and Politics* 351, 354. See Mathias Risse, *Political Theory of the Digital Age* (Cambridge University Press 2023). For different typologies of the fourth generation of human rights, see Serhii M Perepolkin, Danylo S Perepolkin and Milena V Averianova, 'Typology of the Fourth Generation of Human Rights' (2021) 1(1) *Journal of International Legal Communication* 91; Lijue Song and Changshan Ma, 'Identifying the Fourth Generation of Human Rights in the Digital Era' (2022) 7(1) *International Journal of Legal Discourse* 83.

75 Choi-Fitzpatrick (n 1), 109. For an overview of implications of AI-driven systems on the first and second generation of human rights, see Noémi Nagy, '"Humanity's New Frontier": Human Rights Implications of Artificial Intelligence and New Technologies' (2024) 64(2) *Hungarian Journal of Legal Studies* 236.

76 For the distinguished five controversies related to the influence of religion and ancient secular traditions, European traits, socialist ideologies, imperialism, and globalisation on human rights, see Ishay (n 9).

77 Puaschunder (n 20).

fundamentally disrupt the status quo within human rights thinking. According to him, human rights scholars are already attuned to much of this disruption. However, what is required, at a minimum, is the capacity to imagine these intersections and create new avenues for rights protection. The human rights agenda should shift its focus to anticipating opportunities rather than merely responding to threats.[78] The required imagination and focus must also extend to questions of the rights of future generations and intergenerational human rights.

3. FUTURE GENERATIONS AND HUMAN RIGHTS IN THE VIRTUAL WORLD

3.1 Defining Future Generations and Their Rights

The legal framework surrounding the rights of future generations is inherently complex primarily due to the difficulty of defining, in legal terms, what constitutes future generations and what their rights encompass. There is no universally accepted legal definition or shared understanding of the concept or scope of future generations' rights.[79] Additionally, the term 'future generations' overlaps with several related concepts, including unborn generations, intergenerationality and transgenerationality. A closely related notion is that of sustainable development.[80]

From a legal perspective, a key challenge arises from the fact that future individuals lack a clearly identifiable identity and the recognised status of legal subjects. Legal frameworks typically centre on living individuals, and legal systems have traditionally been oriented toward the present. One unresolved question is how the timeframe for defining a generation as 'future' should be determined. According to Gosseries, *non-overlapping generations* refer to individuals who do not exist simultaneously. In contrast, under the concept of *overlapping generations*, future rights holders may be able to defend their rights themselves if the actions of present-day decision-makers lead to rights violations in the future.[81]

---

[78] Choi-Fitzpatrick (n 1), 109, 111–12, 117.

[79] See Mutanen (n 4); Joerg C Tremmel, *A Theory of Intergenerational Justice* (Routledge 2009), 43–46.

[80] See Marcus Düwell, 'Human Dignity and Future Generations' in Marcus Düwell and others (eds), *The Cambridge Handbook of Human Dignity* (Cambridge University Press 2014), 551; Marcus Düwell, Gerhard Bos and Naomi van Steenbergen, *Towards the Ethics of a Green Future. The Theory and Practice of Human Rights for Future People* (Routledge 2018).

[81] Gosseries (n 4).

Another challenge lies in determining how to effectively secure the rights of future generations in practice and what obligations, institutions and measures this would require. Moreover, future generations do not form a homogeneous group. These considerations are also closely linked to the complex question of which present entity could represent future generations in defining their rights.[82]

Conceptions of the rights of future generations are fundamentally tied to the broader understanding of rights and the notion of intergenerational justice. Traditional conceptions of rights and justice focus on the distribution of rights and obligations among existing individuals at a specific moment in time. Consequently, applying these frameworks to issues concerning future generations is inherently complex. Nevertheless, defining rights and justice remains a classic question in legal philosophy, which cannot be explored in depth here. It is sufficient to reference Griffith's concept of the *problem of cross-temporal normative relations* in the context of intergenerational rights. According to this view, the chosen ontology of time constrains the types of explanations that can be provided for obligations directed towards the future.[83] This problem also serves as a foundational starting point for examining the rights of future generations within the human rights framework.

3.2 Understanding Intergenerational Human Rights

Human rights law does not limit itself to present generations. Neither the UN Universal Declaration of Human Rights nor any other human rights instrument contains a temporal limitation or limits rights to the present time. The foundations for international law to address the rights of future generations are established in international instruments in an array of subject areas.[84] In this framework, human rights extend to all members of the human family, including both present and future generations. For example, the recent UN Pact for the Future is intended to protect the needs and interests of present and future generations.[85] In addition to international human rights documents,

82 Elizabeth Dirth, 'European Approaches to Institutions for Future Generations' in Jan Linehan and Peter Lawrence (eds), *Giving Future Generations a Voice: Normative Frameworks, Institutions and Practice* (Edward Elgar Publishing 2021), 193–95.

83 Aaron M Griffith, 'Intergenerational Rights and the Problem of Cross-Temporal Relations' (2018) 83 Erkenntnis 693.

84 Maastricht Principles on the Human Rights of Future Generations 2023 ('Maastricht Principles').

85 UN Res 79/1 (n 33), Section IV on youth and future generations, paras 58–63; Annex II: Declaration on Future Generations.

the terminology of future generations has been incorporated into EU law. For example, the preamble of the EU Charter of Fundamental Rights states that the fundamental rights of the Union also entail responsibilities and duties towards future generations.[86]

In EU law, as well as in international law, issues concerning future generations are often related to sustainable development and other environmental considerations.[87] Articles 3, 21, and 37 of the EU Charter of Fundamental Rights refer to sustainable development,[88] and several other sources of EU law highlight the principles of sustainable development or the concept of common heritage.[89] International environmental treaties and declarations almost invariably establish sustainable development goals, which are also linked to safeguarding the status and rights of future generations.[90] Although such references to intergenerational responsibility are often not legally binding, they may still have legal significance.

Due to the prominence of environmental legal issues, the rights of future generations and intergenerational justice have increasingly become integral to legal discussions and the broader human rights discourse. The degradation of ecological sustainability leads to human rights violations, including infringements on the rights to life, health, food, water, housing, and development, all of which have significant long-term consequences. A fundamental principle concerning the rights of future generations is that decisions made today regarding the living environment and natural resources must not unduly restrict the lives of unborn generations.[91] This connection between future generations

---

86 Charter of Fundamental Rights of the European Union [2012] OJ C326/391. For an overview of EU rules on future generations and their rights, see Katalin Sulyok, *Protecting the Interests of Future Generations by the European Union: an overview of the existing powers and legal bases in EU law* (Jesuit European Social Center 2024).

87 Mutanen (n 4), 1080, 1090–91.

88 Charter of Fundamental Rights of the European Union (n 86).

89 See Treaty on European Union [2016] OJ C202/13, Article 3(3).

90 See UNGA, 'Rio Declaration on Environment and Development' (12 August 1992) UN Doc A/CONF.151/26 (Vol. I), Principle 3; Convention on Access to Information, Public Participation in Decision-Making and Access to Justice in Environmental Matters [1998] UNTS 2161 447, preamble. See also, e.g., UNCRC, 'General Comment No. 26 on children's rights and the environment, with special focus on climate change' (22 August 2023) UN Doc CRC/C/GC/26, stating that '[G]overnments must protect the rights of children today as well as children in future generations.'

91 See, e.g., Gerhard Bos and Marcus Düwell (eds), *Human Rights and Sustainability: Moral Responsibilities for the Future* (Routledge 2016); Gareth T Davies, 'Climate Change and Reversed Intergenerational Equity. The Problem

and human rights has also become evident in climate litigation, where the legality and adequacy of state environmental protection measures have been challenged on human rights grounds, particularly from the perspective of individuals living in the future.[92]

The effects of the climate emergency and climate actions have primarily been examined through the lens of the traditional human rights system and its obligations.[93] However, safeguarding biodiversity, the right to a healthy environment, and the associated broad participatory rights are gaining increasing prominence in the international human rights discourse. A key indication of this shift is the United Nations General Assembly's resolution *The human right to a clean, healthy and sustainable environment* in July 2022. This non-binding resolution emphasises the interconnectedness of sustainable development, environmental protection, and poverty eradication in the realisation of human rights for both present and future generations. It also underscores the adverse effects of the sustainability crisis on the rights enjoyed by different generations.[94]

While the rights of future generations and intergenerational justice are fundamentally linked to questions concerning the use of natural resources, human rights research on future generations has increasingly expanded to include other areas as well.[95]

---

of Costs Now, for Benefits Later' (2020) 10(3) *Climate Law* 266; Düwell, Bos and van Steenbergen (n 80).

92 See, e.g., *Duarte Agostinho and Others v Portugal and 32 Others* App no 39371/20 (ECHR, 9 April 2024). Compare to *Verein KlimaSeniorinnen Schweiz and Others v Switzerland* App no 53600/20 (ECHR, 9 April 2024). For analysis of climate litigation, see Annalisa Savaresi and Joana Setzer, 'Rights-based Litigation in the Climate Emergency: Mapping the Landscape and New Knowledge Frontiers' (2022) 13(1) *Journal of Human Rights and the Environment* 7.

93 See UNHRC, 'Report of the Special Rapporteur on the issue of human rights obligations relating to the enjoyment of a safe, clean, healthy and sustainable environment (1 February 2016) UN Doc A/HRC/31/52; UNHRC, 'Report of the Special Rapporteur on the issue of human rights obligations relating to the enjoyment of a safe, clean, healthy and sustainable environment' (24 January 2018) UN Doc A/HRC/37/59.

94 UNGA Res 76/300 (1 August 2022) UN Doc A/RES/76/300. For construction of the human right to a healthy environment, see John H Knox, 'Constructing the Human Right to a Healthy Environment' (2020) 16 *Annual Review of Law and Social Science* 79.

95 Mutanen (n 4).

Such research has emerged, for example, from intergenerational perspectives on human dignity and justice,[96] children's rights,[97] as well as the anthropocentrism and human-centred nature of the human rights system.[98] Overall, it has been reported that the rights of future generations have long been neglected in both the analysis and the application of human rights.[99]

In line with human rights documents, a common perspective in intergenerational human rights research is that human rights are understood to extend to both present and future human generations. However, cataloguing intergenerational human rights and the mechanisms for their realisation has not become a dominant trend within human rights discourse. Taking a critical approach, Riley argues that existing human rights law mechanisms are insufficient for regulating issues of intergenerational justice, which requires its own international constitutive norms and a reduction of the regulatory freedom of states.[100]

In this vein, significant progress has been made with the *Maastricht Principles on the Human Rights of Future Generations*, adopted in 2023 and developed by legal and human rights scholars, practitioners, and representatives from civil society organisations and social movements. These principles illustrate how the realisation of the rights of future generations necessitates specific attention to the unique rights of particular groups and communities, such as children and youth, women, and indigenous peoples.[101] They also provide an example of a general set of human rights standards with legal relevance

---

96 See, e.g., Düwell (n 80); Marcus Düwell, 'Human Rights and Intergenerational Ethics' in Stephen M Gardiner (ed), *The Oxford Handbook of Intergenerational Ethics* (Oxford University Press 2021); Alex Gosseries, *What is Intergenerational Justice* (Polity Press 2023); Gerry Liston, 'Enhancing the Efficacy of Climate Change Litigation: How to Resolve the "fair share question" in the Context of International Human Rights Law' (2020) 9(2) *Cambridge International Law Journal* 241; Joerg C Tremmel, *Handbook of Intergenerational Justice* (Edward Elgar Publishing 2006).

97 See, e.g., Aoife Daly, 'Climate Competence: Youth Climate Activism and Its Impact on International Human Rights Law' (2022) 22(2) *Human Rights Law Review*.

98 See, e.g., Marie-Catherine Petersmann, 'Life Beyond the Law – From the "Living Constitution" to the "Constitution of the Living"' (2023) 82(4) *Zeitschrift für ausländisches öffentliches Recht und Völkerrecht* 769.

99 'Maastricht Principles' (n 84).

100 Stephen Riley, 'Architectures of Intergenerational Justice: Human Dignity, International Law, and Duties to Future Generations' (2016) 15(2) *Journal of Human Rights* 272.

101 'Maastricht Principles' (n 84).

and may play a transformative role in recognising the human rights of future generations.

While the discourse on intergenerational human rights does not frame them as distinct from the existing human rights regime, the perspective of future generations introduces new emphases to human rights discussions. A key shift in this regard is that the rights of future generations add a dimension of foresight to human rights considerations.[102] Much of the academic debate in the human rights field, including future-oriented scholarship, remains focused on near-term challenges. However, Choi-Fitzpatrick has adopted an exceptionally long-term temporal perspective, seeking to elevate the temporal and causal vantage point from which the human rights project is viewed and to draw attention to an uncertain future. Accordingly, it may be that human rights continue exactly as we know them but eventually apply only to a limited portion of the world's inhabitants. Alternatively, human rights might apply universally, but the current actors tasked with maintaining the field, such as governments, may be rendered powerless to do so.[103]

In addition, intergenerational perspectives bring a collective dimension to the human rights discourse, as the rights of future generations are primarily framed as the rights of groups.[104] The discussion of future generations' rights has been closely linked to the rights of children and youth, who are regarded as a crucial bridge between present and future generations.[105]

At the same time, the concept of rights holders in human discourse is expanding, influenced by the temporal perspective of future generations' rights and the recognition of rights extending beyond humans, such as those of elements of nature.[106] This challenges the anthropocentric foundations of both the human rights system and the legal system more broadly. The discussion of the fundamental rights of other species raises complex questions, particularly

---

102 César Rodríguez-Garavito, 'Climatizing Human Rights: Economic and Social Rights for the Anthropocene' in Malcom Langford and Katharine G Young (eds), *The Oxford Handbook of Economic and Social Rights* (Oxford University Press 2022).

103 Choi-Fitzpatrick (n 1), 105, 115–16, 119. See also William MacAskill, *What We Owe the Future* (Basic Books 2022).

104 Rodríguez-Garavito (n 102).

105 See Daly (n 97); Aoife Daly, 'Intergenerational Rights Are Children's Rights: Upholding the Right to a Healthy Environment through the UNCRC' (2023) 41(3) *Netherlands Quarterly of Human Rights* 132.

106 David R Boyd, *The Rights of Nature: A Legal Revolution that Could Save the World* (ECW Press 2017); Erin O'Donnell and Julia Talbot-Jones, 'Creating Legal Rights for Rivers: Lessons from Australia, New Zealand, and India' (2018) 23(1) *Ecologyand Society*; Rodríguez-Garavito (n 102).

concerning legal subjectivity and the representation of rights holders. More broadly, securing the rights of future generations can be seen as a pathway to protecting interests that are even more challenging to safeguard than those of future human generations.[107]

3.3 Role of Intergenerational Rights in Digitalisation Debates

Currently, human rights research in the field of digitalisation addresses only selected aspects of the interaction between intergenerationalism, human rights and digitalisation. For instance, Halsband has examined the normative issues related to intergenerational justice arising from the use of AI. Regarding obligations toward future persons, she highlights various fields, such as environmental protection policies, climate mitigation policies, pension schemes, and public debt, where AI can function as a decision-support mechanism. Conversely, in areas such as policymaking, the use of AI may have detrimental effects on future people.[108] In addition, some scholarly attention has been given to recognising children's rights in relation to digital technologies, particularly concerning challenges related to their ability to have a voice in digital environments.[109]

Overall, it is evident that contemporary academic and practical efforts to examine the impact of digitalisation on society and law have yet to fully address the role of intergenerational human rights in digitalisation. This state of the art reflects that the rights of future generations remain expressly unregulated in the digital context, with the notable exception of the UN Pact for the Future, which provides intergenerational guidelines relevant to the digital world. This gap in rules and legal thinking is particularly noteworthy given that existing studies often assume that the continuous advancement of digitalisation will be accessible to future generations.[110] Furthermore, the development of digitali-

---

107 See Petersmann (n 98). See also Elena Cima, 'The Right to a Healthy Environment: Reconceptualizing Human Rights in the Face of Climate Change' (2022) 31(1) *Review of European, Comparative & International Environmental Law* 38.

108 Aurélie Halsband, 'Sustainable AI and Intergenerational Justice' (2022) 14(7) *Sustainability* 3922.

109 Amanda Third, Sonia Livingstone and Gerison Lansdown, 'Recognizing Children's Rights in Relation to Digital Technologies: Challenges of Voice and Evidence, Principle and Practice' in Ben Wagner, Matthias C Ketterman and Kilian Vieth (eds), *Research Handbook on Human Rights and Digital Technology: Global Politics, Law and International Relations* (Edward Elgar Publishing 2019).

110 Julia M Puaschunder, 'The Future of Artificial Intelligence in International Healthcare: An Index' in Herta Nagl-Docekal and Waldemar Zacharasiewicz

sation and virtual reality presents potential opportunities for the expansion of human rights, both for the current generation and those to come, warranting further academic inquiry.

The issue of intergenerational human rights in the virtual world concerns the long-term effects of virtual reality on the fundamental rights of future generations. The complexity of intergenerational human rights does not become any simpler when examined in a virtual context; rather, the same foundational challenges persist. These include questions such as who, in the present, can make decisions on safeguarding future rights and who can represent future generations in the digital world.

Moreover, significant intergenerational aspects include sustainability, leadership, and equality in digital environments. Questions of sustainability encompass environmental responsibility, resource management, and the long-term impacts of technological advancements. Digital leadership involves the use of digitalisation to shape digital worlds and create virtual spaces fostering human rights across generations. Ensuring equal access to the virtual world and fair opportunities to navigate online environments is of critical importance. The active use of digitalisation and the creation of internet content and virtual realities should not remain the exclusive domain of the young and technologically proficient.

Overall, there is a pressing need to integrate the complex interplay between digitalisation, human rights, and future generations into academic and policy discussions. Moreover, it is imperative to place the protection and promotion of the human rights of future generations at the forefront of the legal regulation of digital technology. As digitalisation and virtual spaces become increasingly embedded in society and law, it is essential to continuously monitor and address emerging intergenerational concerns through both political and academic discourse.

4. CONCLUSION: NAVIGATING THE CONTINUUM BETWEEN REAL AND VIRTUAL HUMAN RIGHTS

This chapter has highlighted how artificial intelligence, big data analytics, virtual environments, and other technological advancements are reshaping the human rights' landscape. The interplay between digitalisation and human rights presents complex challenges, including privacy violations, freedom of expression concerns, and issues related to misinformation, sustainability and inequality. Simultaneously, digitalisation offers significant

(eds), *Artificial Intelligence and Human Enhancement: Affirmative and Critical Approaches in the Humanities* (De Gruyter 2022).

benefits – enhancing everyday life, improving public sector efficiency, and even strengthening human rights protection. The key challenge is to maximise these benefits while mitigating emerging risks as digitalisation evolves.

Balancing the positive and negative implications of digitalisation necessitates rethinking both traditional human rights and the more recent concepts of 'digital human rights' or 'human rights online'. Existing definitions of digital human rights often focus on their availability, while neglecting the crucial aspects of securing and promoting them. Furthermore, the rights of future generations remain largely unaddressed, both within the digital realm and the broader human rights framework.

This research identifies a critical gap in understanding how human rights frameworks can adapt to the present and future realities of the digital age. To address this, the concept of *virtual human rights* emerges as a response to the specific challenges posed by AI, digitalisation and virtual environments. Just as human rights have historically evolved in response to societal transformations, the changes in human life brought about by virtual environments should be reflected in the human rights regime. Given the rapid development of the virtual world, human rights considerations will likely become increasingly relevant in the context of virtual realities. This study argues that this evolution will create a continuum between real and virtual human rights, as illustrated in Figure 11.1.

The concept of virtual human rights extends the existing human rights framework to better address novel contexts. It acknowledges the interconnectedness of human generations (past, present, and future), human rights (real and virtual), and different realities (physical, augmented, and fully virtual). Understanding this continuum is crucial for determining how human rights may take shape and exert influence in both real and virtual worlds.

Ultimately, virtual human rights must be seen as an extension of, rather than a departure from, real-world human rights. While challenges remain, the evolving nature of human rights suggests that this framework can adapt to the new realities of the digital age, ensuring the protection and promotion of fundamental rights in both physical and virtual spheres.

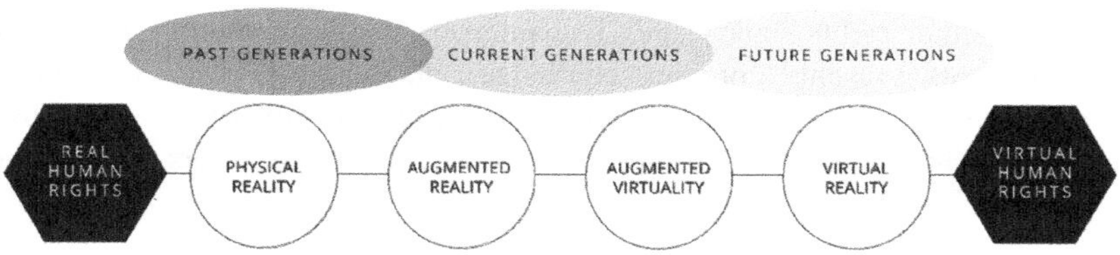

Figure 11.1 *Continuum of realities, future generations and human rights*

Currently, virtual human rights can be better understood as an issue of intergenerational rights, more oriented towards the future than existing frameworks. Virtual human rights extend beyond 'digital human rights' or 'human rights online'. While digital human rights primarily focus on access and protection within online spaces, virtual human rights emphasise the integration of human rights into the very fabric of virtual environments. For instance, cryptocurrencies can be seen as a form of virtual equity, representing digital assets whose value stems from decentralised networks rather than traditional financial institutions. Similarly, virtual human rights encompass mechanisms designed to uphold human rights standards within virtual worlds while ensuring their alignment with existing real-world human rights protection.

The realisation of human rights in the virtual world is essential for advancing both the quality of virtual experiences and broader human rights objectives. Human rights should not only serve to counteract digitalisation's negative effects but also to promote well-functioning and ethically responsible technological development. Ensuring that digital technologies evolve responsibly alongside human rights considerations is essential in shaping a just and equitable virtual world. In this effort, AI and other technologies could be leveraged to enhance human rights protections, potentially through automated mechanisms that monitor and enforce human rights compliance in virtual spaces.

Despite the conceptual promise of virtual human rights, integrating them into virtual worlds presents challenges. The relationship between technology and human rights is complex and non-linear. Furthermore, virtual human rights differ from real human rights in that they are specifically tailored for virtual realities and may have little or no direct connection to physical reality. However, at present, physical and virtual realities remain deeply interconnected, allowing human rights principles to remain relevant in both spheres. Looking ahead, human rights may even serve as a safeguard against potential risks posed by AI and virtual environments.

One of the greatest challenges is defining human rights in the context of the virtual world and determining whether their scope should be expanded. This involves considering who can hold these rights and whether their application should extend beyond human actors. While some may question the relevance of *human* rights in entirely virtual realms devoid of human presence, it is crucial to remain open to various future scenarios and their implications for the human rights framework.

12. Explorative futures of the metaverse: relations, contradictions, and future folds

Toni Ahlqvist, Mikkel Knudsen and Amos Taylor

INTRODUCTION[1]

As a metaphor, the metaverse is simultaneously intriguing and mind-boggling: it integrates transcendental aspirations of building and mastering an alternative world with the promise of a technological haven that could liberate us from the burdens of material reality. The promissory expectations linked with the metaverse go something along these lines, but, in actual existing reality, a fully operating metaverse is still more of a promise than something actually within sight. However, given the accelerating rates of technological development, we might quite soon find ourselves knocking at the gates of, more or less, operative alternative realities.

Therefore, it is about the right time to dive into more prospective waters and ask the following questions: What kinds of multiple forms will these alternative realities take and what novel lifeforms will they enable? What kinds of new social positions, practices, identities, and subjects will emerge? What are the new collective structures that will come about? What possibilities and activities will the metaverse open for organisations, companies and nation states? What will this new reality mean for the individual human psyche? What will it mean for the evolution of human culture? And what are the linkages between this new reality and the material basis of our actually existing reality? Who will be the metaverse elite; that is, the people inhabiting this space, and who will be 'the others' of the metaverse; that is, outsiders and

[1] The authors would like to thank the Research Council of Finland (project number 353056) and Business Finland (project number 6819/31/2023) for financial support of this research.

technological pariahs without access or opportunities? What will our collective price be for building this ultimate techno haven?

In this chapter, we approach these ideas from the perspective of the discipline of futures studies, borrowing from the discipline of philosophy. We open up explorative and experimental perspectives to the metaverse and view it through three theoretical lenses: (1) relational; (2) contradictions or dialectics; and (3) future folds. By proposing these views, we argue that it is problematic to perceive a sociotechnical context as complex as the metaverse with only a singular theoretical lens. The metaverse is both plural and simultaneous; it is an idea, a framework, a space and an infrastructure. Through these perspectives, we also offer some partial answers to some of the questions posed above.

The primary contribution of the chapter rests on the exploration of future folds. This is a conceptual novelty, adapted from the ideas of Gilles Deleuze, that we find apt not only for diving into the multiple aspects of the metaverse but also as a conceptual framework in other circumstances where we are faced with a fundamental a priori uncertainty about future developments, and where these developments are likely to consist of stratified layers of activities and continuously developing networks and assemblages inducing both material and immaterial consequences. Within the field of futures studies, so often dealing with emergence and uncertainty, this could have broad applications.

In the following section, we initially discuss the metaverse through relational and dialectical lenses. We will then unravel various dialectical aspects related to this discussion. In a following section, we open up a novel perspective on future folds based on a combination of Deleuzian philosophy, strategic foresight and conceptual and natural history. The folds are simultaneously existing and parallel bent strata of the metaverse that continuously metamorphose and evolve. In the concluding section, we will wrap up the key themes and discuss the possible repercussions of this exploration by asking the question: What does it mean to move towards metaversal futures?

THE METAVERSE – RELATIONS AND CONTRADICTIONS

In the chapter we discuss explorative and hypothetical connections between virtual environments and actual environments, virtual entities/avatars and human entities, and past, current and future generations. We also speculate upon the natures of the metaverse. We suggest that there could be different kinds of parallel dynamics and dimensions that we call future folds, or parallel future folds.

Boundaries, Closures, Rights

If, as this book infers, we aim to prescribe *real rights in virtual worlds*, a series of questions arise. *Who* (or *what*) should be assigned rights, and who (or what) should be left rightless? Before we even get to the point of discussing the nature of assigned rights or the (virtual and material) worlds in which such rights should function, the boundary problem of constituting the demos arises.[2]

In essence, our future folds face two key boundary problems. First, what are the boundaries of the metaverse? When can something be said to be *inside* the metaverse vis-à-vis being *outside* the metaverse? Second, of those entities involved in the metaverse, who should have rights or the right to set rights? Without jumping too far ahead in the narrative of this chapter, we might note that even current multi-player online games are likely to provide an arena for interaction between three different groups – humans with strong offline democratic rights, humans with limited offline democratic rights (citizens of autocracies, youths under the age of 18, etc.), and non-human entities with practically no current rights. However, as we shall see, it is not a given that this particular rights order will be sustained forever. For example, based on the principles of democratic theory, it is not obviously true that democratic inclusion is the privilege of human beings, or that artificial intelligence technologies per se should be excluded from having rights.[3]

There are interesting parallels between the imagination of rights in the metaverse and the imagination of rights for future generations, which has moved from a niche idea among political philosophers to something explored by several governments around the world.[4] In democratic theory, the question of future generations has become a paradigmatic case of the boundary

---

[2] For insights on the boundary problem from democratic theory, see, e.g., Robert A Dahl, *Democracy and its Critics* (Yale University Press 1989); Gustaf Arrhenius, 'The Democratic Boundary Problem Reconsidered' (2018) 1 *Ethics, Politics & Society: A Journal in Moral and Political Philosophy* 89; Ludvig Beckman, 'Deciding the Demos: Three Conceptions of Democratic Legitimacy (2019) 22(4) *Critical Review of International Social and Political Philosophy* 412.

[3] Ludvig Beckman and Jonas Hultin Rosenberg, 'The Democratic Inclusion of Artificial Intelligence? Exploring the Patiency, Agency and Relational Conditions for Demos Membership' (2022) 35(2) *Philosophy & Technology*.

[4] See e.g. Maija Airos and others, 'Ennakointi ja tulevat sukupolvet lainvalmistelun prosesseissa, instituutioissa ja käytännöissä' (Foresight and future generations in legislative processes, institutions and practices) (Publications of the Government's analysis, assessment and research activities 2022:66).

problem,[5] and the philosophical conundrum essentially boils down to how one relates to – assigns rights to, decides preferences on behalf of, etc. – someone we can never meet and who may never come to live as a human in the material flesh-and-blood sense. We believe that the question of rights in the metaverse provides a similar, and similarly interesting, boundary case for future democratic theorising, and that conceptually the two cases have something to offer each other that future scholars should seek to exploit.

If we here engage in imagining a metaverse, what kind of task are we facing? We are definitely facing a future-oriented task with some known factors, some knowable factors and some not so known, but factors that can be speculated upon. And obviously, there are always the notorious 'unknown unknowns', things and events that are beyond knowing.

Relational Contradictions in the Metaverse

An important feature of the metaverse, as we outline it, is its dialectical basis.[6] Here we are interested in this basis: the contradiction between material and immaterial, actual and virtual. We argue that this dialectical basis is key to understanding the metaverse, also from the perspective of future generations and their rights. Nonetheless, it is critical to understand that this basic contradiction also has its generative aspects, as is well argued by Castán Broto.[7] Her notion of a 'generative contradiction' is a useful lens for analysing the basic dynamics of the contradictions. She sees contradiction as a generative force that builds the drive for change that is, then, mediated via 'utopian aspirations and concrete action'.[8] The idea of generative contradiction is a co-constitution, where opposing tendencies are fundamental to one another's existence.[9] Conceptually, generative contradiction emphasises action and concrete instances of reality that open up new possibilities and risks. The basic premise is to understand the conditions in which the contradiction rests rather than the actual contradiction as such.

---

5 Mikkel Knudsen, Toni Ahlqvist and Amos Taylor, 'Defining "future generations": Epistemic Considerations on Conceptualizing a Future-oriented Domain in Policy and Law-making' (2023) 28 *Journal of Futures Studies* 3.

6 See Toni Ahlqvist, 'An Outline of Future-oriented Dialectics: Conceptualising Dialectical Positions, Trajectories and Processes in the Context of Futures Research' (2022) 143 *Futures* 103037.

7 Vanesa Castán Broto, 'Contradiction, Intervention, and Urban Low Carbon Transitions' (2015) 33 *Environment and Planning D: Society and Space* 460.

8 Ibid., 461.

9 Ibid., 462.

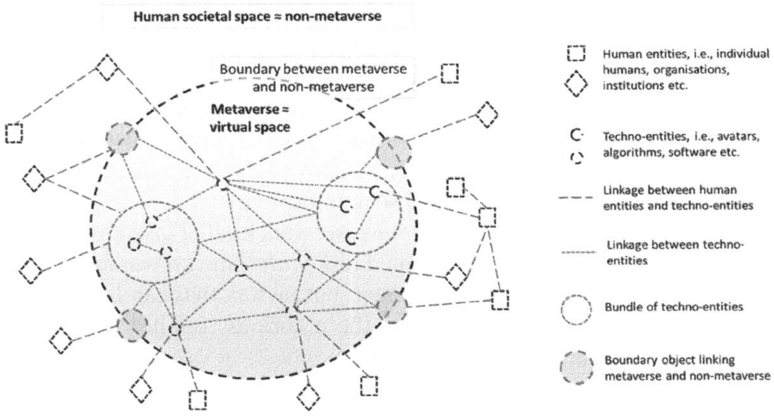

Figure 12.1 *Metaverse as a relational spatial domain*

One key aspect of our take on the metaverse is that the future folds are characterised by various contradictions that are spatially and topologically relational.[10] This means that we are thinking the folds via various contradictions that have spatial and topological dimensions (Figure 12.1 above). The metaverse could be conceptualised as a spatial domain with specific technological, social and spatial boundaries. In one sense, these boundaries are sharp and easily experienced: this becomes clear when one logs in and out of the metaverse. In another sense, the boundaries between the metaverse and the non-metaverse form a zone that is not univocally mapped or marked: it is an ongoing, continuous interaction between human entities and techno-entities that may be activated through various sociotechnical settings and technological devices: computers, virtual reality solutions, mobile phones, watches, glasses, rings, sensors, bodily attachments, haptic solutions, etc.

Human entities may interact with each other and with techno-entities inside the metaverse but also with significant others in the non-metaverse or the material world. Various entities, such as human entities, human-driven avatars, techno-entities and bundles of avatars and techno-entities, linked by various spatial and topological relations, span the metaverse. These entities could also criss-cross to material reality through different solutions, gateways, and boundary objects, connecting material and immaterial domains.

[10] See Toni Ahlqvist, 'Engineering Spatial Fixes: Relational Spatial Practices, Strategic-topological Approach and the Construction of a Finnish Science-technology District' (2013) 95 Geografiska annaler: Series B, Human Geography 89.

Table 12.1 Seven relational contradictions of the metaverse

Contradiction	Manifestation of the basic contradiction	Generative potential	Generative risks
1. Materiality / Immateriality	Basic contradiction The metaverse is drawn between the relational materiality of information technology (computers, mobile phones, servers, calculation centres, etc.) and the relational immateriality of events and instances in the metaverse. Tension also exists between immaterial activities in the metaverse vs. material activities in the non-metaverse (e.g., environmental impact of enabling technologies – energy, minerals etc.).	A multiplicity of generative potentials could emerge.	A multiplicity of generative risks could emerge. Overuse of natural resources. Bias of using natural resources to drive the metaverse.
2. Localisable spatial context / Virtual realities	A spatial context that can be localised; embedded setting of the actors and stakeholders. Seemingly boundless virtual realities unravelled by the metaverse.	Possibilities for localised enclaves of the metaverse. Could be utilised as a platform for local community and local services.	Corporate fold of the metaverse could infiltrate the localised enclaves. There could be generational digital gaps in the use of local services.

Contradiction	Manifestation of the basic contradiction	Generative potential	Generative risks
3. Human bodies / Virtual avatars	Relations at the level of individual human subjects. Relations between human bodies in the physical environment and avatars in the virtual environment.	Potential for amending your identity using a virtual avatar. Unravelling new horizons: avatars could basically be anything imaginable. Escapism as a positive disengagement.	Negative bodily and mental impacts of the interaction between two realities. Escapism as a negative disengagement.
4. Human bodily cognition / Technological calculative cognition	Human cognition bounded by brains, body and imagination. Technological calculative cognition bounded by data sources.	New possibilities for amending human cognition using technical means. New human-metaverse interfaces.	Long-term cognitive impacts are difficult to estimate.
5. Metaverse insiders / Metaverse outsiders	A societal contradiction between people who have access to the metaverse and people who do not have access.	Various citizen activities could reduce the emerging digital gap.	Extending the digital gap: a metaverse with 'full capacity' has a high potential to become an exclusive elite platform. Formation of various metaverse levels: elite metaverse(s), 'riffraff' metaverse, those completely outside the system.

Contradiction	Manifestation of the basic contradiction	Generative potential	Generative risks
6. Humans and human-driven entities / Techno-entities	The generational rights of humans may be complemented by the various kinds of 'rights' of techno-entities in the metaverse (software avatars, algorithms…). The rights and activities could have interesting repercussions when contemplating inside and outside the metaverse.	Interaction between human societal sphere and the metaverse could catalyse surprising generative outcomes.	Interactions could be complex to follow: intuitive and counterintuitive outcomes.
7. Techno-entities / other techno-entities	Generative contradiction among techno-entities of the metaverse. Self-generating dynamics between various techno-entities (including various forms of AI, algorithms, software etc.).	Potential to generate novel dynamics that could have applicability in the 'actual reality'. Intuitive and counterintuitive outcomes.	After a certain time, the outcomes of the contradiction will probably be impossible to contain. The outcomes could even be hard to track or understand.

Source: Authors.

In Table 12.1 we outline seven contradictions based on these spatially and topologically envisioned relations. We argue that the first contradiction, that of materiality–immateriality, is a primary contradiction that can be located at the basis of the other six contradictions mapped in Table 12.1. An important aspect of this contradiction is the two levels: (1) the relations between events and trajectories in actual reality (non-metaverse) and virtual reality (metaverse); and (2) the tension between immaterial activities in the metaverse versus material activities in the non-metaverse. This tension could boost various kinds of consequences in the future. Many of the contradictions are actually in existence already in the context of sociotechnical infrastructure and the use of technological instruments. However, in the metaverse, the aspects of these contradictions could develop in novel directions and have unforeseeable consequences.

THE METAVERSE THROUGH THE LENS OF FUTURE FOLDS

We contemplate the metaverse as an outcome of a basic contradiction: that of materiality and immateriality (see below). In this vein, the metaverse can be depicted using Deleuzian thinking as a machinic phylum,[11] an assemblage constructed out of the relational dynamics of the folds. Deleuze and Guattari[12] define machinic phylum as 'a constellation of singularities, prolongable by certain operations, which converge, and make the operations converge, upon one or several assignable traits of expression'.[13] They also emphasise it as 'matter in movement, in flux, in variation, matter as a conveyor of singularities and traits of expression'.[14]

These definitions aptly depict the materiality–immateriality tension of the metaverse, especially when thinking of the metaverse simultaneously as a 'new reality'; that is, a novel operational environment, and as a material infrastructure operated through material structures, linkages and flows. Therefore, we argue that the metaverse is characterised not just by relations and relational contradictions, but also by future folds; that is, stratified layers of activities and of continuously developing networks and assemblages that induce various material and immaterial consequences.

Three Interpretations of the Future Fold

Here we outline three interpretations of the *fold* that all contribute to and fit the notion we depict here. The first is a Deleuzian interpretation based on the philosophy of Gilles Deleuze.[15] This multifaceted theory contains complex, yet highly useful ideas on which to build the theoretical notion of a *future fold*. The second interpretation is one presented in the journal *Foresight* by Charles Ogilvy[16] based on Thom.[17] The third interpretation, which also holds

---

[11] Gilles Deleuze and Felix Guattari, *A Thousand Plateaus: Capitalism and Schizophrenia* (Minnesota University Press 1987).

[12] Ibid.

[13] Ibid., 406.

[14] Ibid., 409.

[15] Gilles Deleuze and Jonathan Strauss, 'The Fold' (1991) 80 *Yale French Studies* 227; Gilles Deleuze, *The Fold. Leibniz and the Baroque* (The Athlone Press 1993).

[16] Charles Ogilvy, 'Facing the Fold: From the Eclipse of Utopia to the Restoration of Hope' (2011) 13 *Foresight* 7.

[17] Rene Thom, *Structural Stability and Morphogenesis* (Addison-Wesley 1989).

some useful practical aspects for our chapter, comes from the fields of physical geography and geology.

The first interpretation is inspired by Gilles Deleuze's treatise, *The Fold*.[18] Here Deleuze reads the social landscape through the metaphor of the fold and bases his arguments primarily on the philosophy of Leibniz. In his book, Deleuze gives the notion multiple meanings and settings but does not explicitly ponder its future-oriented temporalities. In Deleuze's thinking, *the fold* is a metaphor and concept to depict different kinds of stratified, intertwined, and entangled characteristics of material and immaterial societal processes. The notion is unravelled as a complex concept that simultaneously refers to detailed and tangible material things, but also to more metaphorical layers and twists of various abstract immaterial dimensions. Here, we want to utilise the notion of *the fold* to depict simultaneous, parallel entanglements of the metaverse and explore how the notion could open up novel perspectives for this domain. Therefore, we have to tease out a more instrumental version of the notion of the fold in order to use it as an interpretive tool.

In his book, Deleuze depicts the fold in a cyclical manner, as an entangled and intertwined form of activity domains:

> [a] fold is always folded within a fold, like a cavern in a cavern. … the curves of conical forms, sometimes ending in a circle or an ellipse, sometimes stretching into a hyperbola or a parabola. The model … is the 'origami,' … the art of folding paper.[19]

Folding also has its opposite, unfolding. Deleuze[20] defines that folding and unfolding refer to the processes of 'enveloping-developing' and 'involution-evolution'. For Deleuze, the fold is also a domain of power, an activity: 'The fold is Power… Force itself is an act, an act of the fold.'[21]

Deleuze offers some directions for the notion of the fold, but it remains at a rather metaphorical level. The interpretation provided by O'Sullivan[22] adds interesting elements to the Deleuzian notion that resonate with trajectories discussed in this chapter. For example, O'Sullivan[23] argues that 'new technologies' play a part in the formation of folds that he defines as 'a new image of thought' and '… a reconfiguration of space and time (a new folding) and

---

18 Deleuze (n 15).

19 Ibid., 6.

20 Ibid., 8.

21 Ibid., 18.

22 Simon O'Sullivan, 'From Possible Worlds to Future Folds (Following Deleuze): Richter's Abstracts, Situationist Cities, and the Baroque in Art' (2005) 36 *Journal of the British Society for Phenomenology* 311.

23 Ibid., 324.

an opening up of the closed monad of our subjectivities to other non-human worlds'. These depictions of the fold as a 'new image of thought' and as a 'reconfiguration of space and time' are also very useful for the purposes of this chapter. O'Sullivan constructs interesting linkages between the folds and technologies. For example, he talks about 'robotic monads' traversing in 'different spatial and temporal rhythms', and about folding 'silicon assemblages' with 'carbon ones' and 'all sorts of genetic foldings', emerging from the field of molecular biology, 'producing all sorts of strange beings'.[24] In the Deleuzian vein, O'Sullivan[25] envisions various future folds: first, a research-driven fold combining molecular biology, genetic code and the silicon-carbon fold; second, a machine fold constructed out of information technology and cybernetics; and, third, a fold of 'language within language', a sort of novel expression that could refer to a sort of software code or language-based AI.

The second root for the future fold in this chapter is the notion of the fold used by Ogilvy.[26] Coming from a different, and explicitly future-oriented, theoretical direction compared to that provided by Deleuze, he likens the fold to 'facing a landscape'.[27] With the landscape metaphor, Ogilvy seems to be referring to a kind of wide-ranging 'vantage point' or a lens through which the observer can grasp the landscape in its variety: 'facing both positive and negative scenarios at once', 'both optimism and pessimism' and delving into 'the uncertainty and complexity of an unpredictable future'.[28] For this purpose, he suggests that scenario analysis could work as a methodology for 'facing the fold'. Ogilvy argues that facing calls for an 'acute sense of freedom' that relieves the observer of the 'intellectual dishonesty involved in holding either branch of the fold as a single-point forecast'.[29] He proposes that the process empties 'the naivete of callow optimism': 'You have looked at the dark side; you have seen the very real risk; and still you are able to move ahead constructively.'[30] Consequently, what is at stake here is the exploration of an entire spectrum of future alternatives, confronting the positives and negatives. One can 'choose the high road, but you are always well aware of the off-ramps to the low road'.[31] Approaching the fold as a vantage point through which to understand the spectrum of the emergence is an excellent notion from our perspective.

---

24 Ibid.
25 Ibid.
26 Ogilvy (n 16).
27 Ibid., 11.
28 Ibid., 13.
29 Ibid..
30 Ibid., 14.
31 Ibid..

The third interpretation of the fold likens it to a natural formation: in physical geography and geology, a fold is constructed of bent rock strata that form various shapes, curves and rhythms.[32] However, there is also another iteration that utilises this kind of natural metaphor, which is highly important for our thinking: the idea of temporal sedimentation in the conceptual historiography of Koselleck.[33] In the essay *Sediments of Time*, Koselleck used the following definition of the 'sediments or layers of time':

> [it] refers to geological formations that differ in age and depth and that changed and set themselves apart from each other at differing speeds over the course of the so-called history of the earth. … By transposing this metaphor back into human, political, or social history as well as into structural history, we can analytically separate different temporal levels upon which people move and events unfold, thus ask about the longer-term preconditions for such events.[34]

Here, we perceive the concept of a future fold as an extension of this idea of sediments of time.[35] Using this notion, Sandford[36] talks about the 'thickness' of time with a focus on the 'thick present': 'a thick present has duration, and, within a thick present, ideas of the past, present and future are entangled, appearing alongside each other'. The central distinction is that Sandford addresses the sedimented entanglement of temporal states (past, present, future) with an eye to how it appears in the (thick) *present*, while we use the concept of the future fold specifically to address entangled *future* states. In the context of futures research, this geological dimension – containing multiple overlapping, parallel folded layers – brings in the important dimension of simultaneity and complexity.

Folds, Layers, Future Images

Future folds, as we outline them here methodologically, are parallel and entangled dimensions of an entity under scrutiny. Consequently, they are not the same as the perhaps most common methodological concept in futures studies: scenarios. Future folds are not scenarios because they are not alternative directions of futures. On the contrary, folds are parallel interacting complex layers

---

32 For an excellent review, see Seyed Tohid Nabavi and Haakon Fossen, 'Fold Geometry and Folding – a Review' (2021) 222 Earth-Science Reviews 103812.

33 Reinhard Koselleck, *Sediments of Time. On Possible Histories* (Stanford University Press 2018).

34 Ibid., 3.

35 Ibid.

36 Richard Sandford, 'Reparative Futures in a Thick, Virtuous Present' (2023) 154 *Futures* 103278.

of a context; layers that mutate continuously but can still be logically identified and characterised.

To carve up our own definition of a future fold in the context of futures research, we suggest the following depiction:

Future fold is a layered pattern in a context [in this case metaverse] that can be identified and stratified so that it forms a plausible future interpretation of this context. In that context, there could be many, or even a multiplicity, of such patterns that simultaneously affect the context. A future fold can be logically separated from other parallel folds that simultaneously exist in the context and define the context.

Again, stressing simultaneity – the multiverse of metaverses, if you will – these archetypal future folds or versions of them are likely to exist in parallel with each other. However, each future of the highlighted future folds cannot only be logically separated from each other, but is also likely to produce distinguishable internal logics steering the discussion on rights. That is, the imagining of rights in the metaverse is the imagining of separate rights logics for each imagined future fold.

Exploring Future Folds in the Metaverse

In this section, we outline the key features of the future folds we perceive as the probable, possible and radical aspects in the metaverse.

Corporate folds

The future fold best describing an extrapolation of current circumstances is a corporate fold, created and dominated by big tech businesses and, primarily, *for* the (financial) benefit of private corporate actors. These folds represent the assetisation of the metaverse, where speculation and monetisation of emerging features are common. Corporate folds will probably be the most pervasive strata of the metaverse. It is the Meta metaverse writ large.

Access is determined by a financial logic: If entities pay, they can go anywhere they like. Spaces exist if there are markets for them; for example, corporate-minded settings, such as financial agoras, developer milieus, idea incubator spaces, and other variations of the office hotel gone online, or consumer-minded settings providing options for shopping, live concerts, role-playing and entertainment. The defining separation between the active and passive multitude rests on the financial ability to partake – the corporate fold of the metaverse provides both a spotlight and a motor for global economic inequality.

The radical novelty of the fold is the rise of new non-human actors with increasing economic power. Like algorithmic trading crowding out humans in the 2010s stock market,[37] AI- and algorithm-driven corporate actors crowd out human-dominated corporations. For example, while the early breakthroughs of the corporate metaverse were based on corporations owned by humans providing other humans with intimate access to almost-material concerts with other humans such as Taylor Swift, the entertainment world has shifted. In the corporate fold, the analogy is an AI independently setting up an all-AI corporation generating AI superstars watched by humans and non-human technological entities in sync. In *The Grapes of Wrath*, Steinbeck's characters famously described the bank as if it had become a sentient being – it makes decisions that all men inside the bank disagree with; men made it, but they cannot control it. For the financial moguls of the corporate fold, there is now a slight difference – men still cannot control it, but they have only made the thing that made it.

What is the prime concern of the boundary problem in this universe? The attempt to set and enforce strict boundaries that limit metaverse actors to influence *inside* the metaverse with as little offline implications as possible.

Public folds

The state-driven metaverse for the provision of public services and with a high degree of state regulation can be imagined as both positive and negative. It is open to state citizens and regulated according to the borders in the physical world. The hypothesis is that it will remain a more or less regulated fold; regulated according to state structures and institutions, following a division of labour in specific ministries. The public folds replicate the spatial peculiarities of the physical world in the digital world, for good and for bad. For example, there are only limited possibilities for freely flowing innovative exploration, while autocratic regimes have extended their capabilities of surveying their citizens into a new and highly intrusive domain. Therefore, the potential for emerging novelties is conditioned by the opportunities enabled by the state structures.

For a while, civic and democratic spaces have been hoped for, where democratic actions would join in a virtual space, for issues to be debated and where decisions could be instantaneous. A critical lens on how virtual environments have been developed, and many of these spaces have been built upon mirror versions of real-world governance, imposing these hierarchies rather than the possibility of making new online democratic formulations. This has been called 'implicit feudalism' by Schneider in his exploration of governable spaces,

---

37 Ludwig B. Chincarini, *The Crisis of Crowding: Quant Copycats, Ugly Models, and the New Crash Normal* (John Wiley & Sons, Inc 2012).

where the consequences have ramifications beyond the online metaverse,[38] as 'feudal defaults train us to give up on our communities' democratic potential', toward autocratic tech CEOs and authoritarian tendencies among politicians. The question on the public governance side is: are we perpetuating real-world structures and their colonial or antiquated systems?

Securitised folds

The securitised folds manifest a world of increasing tensions with a multitude of geopolitical blocs. Troll armies, hacker invasions, and hybrid operations are part of the fabric. As cybersecurity, or 'cyber' as the British government has branded it, has taken on wider implications by situating the security threats related to the metaverse as a core paradigm and thriving lucrative industry, the prospect for future generations is that of surveillance, firewalls, credentials and threats of punishment (as currently seen in China through elaborate surveillance systems, or for Iranian women expressing their views on social media). These types of hyper vigilant metaverses in the future would prescribe narrow pathways for social interaction and promote sterilised environments under strict guidelines. Augé referred to such liminal places as airports and shopping malls as non-spaces, culturally stripped-down spaces where control was exerted.[39] The origins of the hacker counter-culture were based on the ideas of exploration and liberation and the subversion of dominant systems.[40] The securitised reaction to subversion is not a negotiation with hacker expression or discourse, but rather an institutional response devoid of humanity. Such control systems are autonomous, faceless and unrelenting. At the same time, rule-based systems are essential; self-governing systems define their own rules and guiding principles, and as with many online environments, should promote safe interactions and protection for all as a fundamental right. However, as monitoring cases with Facebook and other social media platforms show, this is often inadequate to protect against online predators, and this is psychologically difficult for humans to monitor (as they are often exposed to harmful content themselves). However, the emphasis of control systems is rather geared towards protecting copyright issues. Therefore, securitisation is a facet of ownership.

---

[38] Nathan Schneider, *Governable Spaces: Democratic Design for Online Life* (University of California Press 2024).

[39] Marc Augé, *Non-Places: An Introduction to an Anthropology of Supermodernity* (Verso 1995).

[40] See, e.g., Sadie Plant, *The Most Radical Gesture: The Situationist International in a Postmodern Age* (Routledge 1992).

Rogue and chaotic folds

As an antidote to future folds dominated by the singular logics of the corporate or public sector kind, rogue and chaotic future folds involve a multiverse of metaverses with loosely structured constellations of spaces driven by individuals, small groups, hackers, etc. This is populated with a spirit of a continuously evolving 'virtual wild west' in which counter-cultural currents and anarchic mindsets thrive. There is little organised control, but as a side effect, this chaotic fold has reframed group identification both on- and offline. In polarised societies, the majority has become a collection of independent minorities, with less adherence to traditional community boundaries (e.g., spatial), and with decreasing between-group interaction.

Emerging and rapid folds, and those that cannot be known

The metaverse is inhabited in parallel by constantly emerging folds that may abruptly burst into existence just to disappear almost as rapidly. There is a continuous and discontinuous evolutive process that results in a multiplicity of mutations, alterations and variations. Some of these outcomes will eventually be integrated into the more robust 'driving folds'; for example, of corporate origin. The majority of these variations will endure only briefly and then explode into nothingness, just to burst out as new signals and codes. Then there are vibrations so prompt and perturbations of such a high velocity that these cannot be read or decoded. Some cannot even be known by human entities – these events of differential orbitals could become the future directions of techno-entities.

Taleb suggests the concept of black swan events, and the metaverse itself could become a sudden disruptive event, or if such system-wide changes occur it would be a frequent breaking of what would be considered stable.[41] Experiments in the metaverse could have surprising spillover effects, and these could be connected to real-world impacts, or even outer world impacts (beyond ours via nature, AI, outer-space etc). Ilmola and Rovenskaya propose that ontological uncertainties, those unknown unknown issues, are the most important to consider, and are often missing from most foresight work.[42] Ritchey refers to this extreme as 'genuine uncertainty' and as being different from risk: '[r]isk is defined as a type of uncertainty based on a well-grounded (quantitative) probability', whereas on the other hand, 'genuine uncertainty' embodies processes and outcomes which cannot be ascribed to well-grounded probabili-

---

41 Nassim Nicholas Taleb, *The Black Swan. The Impact of the Highly Improbable* (Penguin Books 2008).

42 Leena Ilmola and Elena Rovenskaya, 'Three Experiments: The Exploration of Unknown Unknowns in Foresight' (2016) 106 *Technological Forecasting & Social Change* 85.

ties.[43] At what point does the metaverse portray the qualities of such genuine uncertainties?

The possibilities of the metaverse based on these principles, these gaps, can be speculated on and inferred by their absence. Virmajoki suggests that there are limits to the conceivability of futures, and we must conceive futures based beyond our understanding of the development of knowledge and the sciences.[44] The metaverse can be ascribed as a tool, based on future sociotechnological imaginaries yet to be formed, where its fundamental logic is alien to us. Or through accidental or future acts or combinations of events and breakthroughs.

CONCLUDING REMARKS – TOWARDS METAVERSAL FUTURES?

In this chapter, we unravelled various explorative viewpoints of the metaverse. We explored the metaverse via three kinds of intertwined theoretical lenses: relations, contradictions and future folds. Our base premise was that the metaverse is a plurality: an idea, a space, an infrastructure. It is a sociotechnical imaginary heavily invested in by various actors, primarily operating in the sphere of technology, mainly representing a 'Silicon Valley world order'.

Relations and relational contradictions unravel inherent tensions in any sociotechnical domain – the primary contradiction being the one between materiality and immateriality. Even the simple mapping presented in the chapter leads to various contradictions that outline this primary tension not only in the metaverse, but also in other kinds of domains where humans interact with technologies, or, using a term introduced in this chapter, techno-entities. Furthermore, the theory of future folds developed in this chapter has analytical potential for understanding the complementary and contradictory impacts of parallel sociotechnical strata. The five folds we present suggest kinds of archetypal, and simultaneously evolving, expressions of an area that is fairly uncertain.

In addition to the theoretical and methodological perspectives, we also pondered the intriguing, but inherently wicked and restless question of the demos, or future generations, inhabiting this potential future dimension. The critical questions are: what kinds of lifeforms will emerge in the metaverse? What will their relations to the lifeforms in the actual material reality be? What opportunities do we have of even partially imagining and grasping the future possibilities of future generations in this speculative environment? Our chapter

43 Tom Ritchey, *Wicked Problems – Social Messes: Decision Support Modelling with Morphological Analysis* (Springer-Verlag 2011).

44 Veli Virmajoki, 'Limits of Conceivability in the Study of the Future. Lessons from Philosophy of Science' (2022) 142 *Futures* 102993.

may not have contributed any definitive solutions or answers to these tricky conundrums, but at least we have proposed new ways of approaching and critically engaging with these kinds of questions.

A grand question that emerges is spelled out in the section title above: What could the futures of the metaverse be, 'the metaversal futures', and are we heading in these kinds of potential directions? We suggested that – despite the future potentials – we will need novel frameworks to critically ponder and discuss the emerging sociotechnical frameworks. We argue, perhaps even a little boldly, that the approaches discussed in this chapter – through relations, contradictions and folds – have the potential to operate as interpretive, hermeneutic tools in various kinds of futures, metaversal or otherwise. These tools provide a window of opportunity for contemplating simultaneities and parallels in various sociotechnical settings; that is, through relations, contradictions and folds, that have effect simultaneously and in a continuous fashion.

Finally, we also argue that these tools provide valuable complementary instruments for mapping alternative futures; for example, with scenario analysis focused on depicting alternative future images via narratives and numbers. The tools proposed in the chapter remind the analyst that it is not just about opening up future alternatives, but also about critically engaging with parallel developments – interacting, mutating, continuously renewing existing contradictions as well as catalysing novel ones – that may already be here in the present, and could therefore have potential for transforming futures in unexpected ways.

Index

Printed and bound by CPI Group (UK) Ltd, Croydon, CR0 4YY

17/06/2026

14902647-0002